REPORTING WAR AND CONFLICT

Reporting War and Conflict brings together history, theory and practice to explore the issues and obstacles involved in the reporting of contemporary war and conflict. The book examines the radical changes taking place in the working practices and day-to-day routines of war journalists, arguing that managing risk has become central to modern war correspondence. How individual reporters and news organisations organise their coverage of war and conflict is increasingly shaped by a variety of personal, professional and institutional risks.

The book provides an historical and theoretical context to risk culture and the work of war correspondents, paying particular attention to the changing nature of technology, organisational structures and the role of witnessing. The conflicts in Iraq, Afghanistan and Syria are examined to highlight how risk and the calculations of risk vary according to the type of conflict. The focus is on the relationship between propaganda, censorship, the sourcing of information and the challenges of reporting war in the digital world. The authors then move on to discuss the arguments around risk in relation to gender and war reporting and the coverage of death on the battlefield.

Reporting War and Conflict is a guide to the contemporary changes in warfare and the media environment that have influenced war reporting. It offers students and researchers in journalism and media studies an invaluable overview of the life of a modern war correspondent.

Janet Harris is an award-winning documentary producer/director, having worked for many years at the BBC and as a freelancer with experience of working in Iraq in war and post-war. She holds a PhD on the media coverage of the British military in post-war Iraq and teaches the practice and theory of documentary production at Cardiff University, UK.

Kevin Williams was until recently Professor of Media and Communication History at Swansea University, UK. He has written widely on the history and theory of the media, including several books on war reporting, such as co-authoring *The Fog of War: The Media on the Battlefield* (1986) and *War and Peace News* (1985). His most recent book was *International Journalism* (2011).

REPORTING WAR AND CONFLICT

Janet Harris and Kevin Williams

Routledge
Taylor & Francis Group

LONDON AND NEW YORK

First published 2019
by Routledge
2 Park Square, Milton Park, Abingdon, Oxon OX14 4RN

and by Routledge
52 Vanderbilt Avenue, New York, NY 10017

Routledge is an imprint of the Taylor & Francis Group, an informa business

British Library Cataloguing in Publication Data
A catalogue record for this book is available from the British Library

Library of Congress Cataloging in Publication Data
Names: Williams, Kevin, 1955- author. | Harris, Janet. author.
Title: Reporting war and conflict / Kevin Williams and Janet Harris.
Description: London ; New York : Routledge, 2018. | Includes bibliographical
references and index.
Identifiers: LCCN 2018020886| ISBN 9780415743679 (hardback : alk. paper) |
ISBN 9780415743785 (pbk. : alk. paper) | ISBN 9781315750286 (ebook)
Subjects: LCSH: War--Press coverage. | Journalism--Political aspects. |
Journalists--Crimes against.
Classification: LCC PN4784.W37 W55 2018 | DDC 070.4/333--dc23
LC record available at https://lccn.loc.gov/2018020886

ISBN: 978-0-415-74367-9 (hbk)
ISBN: 978-0-415-74378-5 (pbk)
ISBN: 978-1-315-75028-6 (ebk)

Typeset in Bembo
by Taylor & Francis Books

"Safe journalism is not good journalism"
(unnamed veteran war correspondent)

CONTENTS

ACKNOWLEDGEMENTS

This book is an amalgamation of theory and practice, bringing together the experience of working as a war correspondent in some of the most dangerous areas of the world with an understanding of the history of war correspondence. The focus is on an attempt to unravel and interrogate the work and working environment of war correspondents. Conversations between the authors over the years about the personal and historical experiences of reporting war repeatedly turned to the question of the types of risk that war correspondents face – or believe they face – in their daily work. Clausewitz in 1832 wrote that "war is the realm of uncertainty", and his description of warfare equally if not more so applies to war reporting. In putting flesh on the bones of the risks and fears that shape war correspondents' work, a number of people should be thanked. The authors first met on the Erasmus Mundus MA in Journalism, Media and Globalisation programme, which brought together students on a scheme organised by several European universities, Aarhus, Amsterdam, City-London, Hamburg and Swansea, where a second-year specialism in War and Conflict is taught. We would like to thank all of the partner institutions in this programme as well as the students who passed through the Swansea specialism, many of whom had worked as freelance reporters covering war and conflict, for stimulating, thoughtful and sometimes heated conversation about war reporting. Particular thanks are due to Hans-Henrik Holm at the Danish School of Journalism, whose energy, commitment and intellectual drive was responsible for the establishment and successful running of the MA. Thanks to members of the course teams in Aarhus, Amsterdam, Hamburg and London.

Janet Harris would like to thank the numerous Iraqis, soldiers and camera crews that she worked with in Iraq and from whom she learned about the problems of reporting conflict. Kevin Williams would like to thank Clare Hudson for her continuing support and intellectual insights and Aaliyah

Williams for being there. Many thanks to the patient people at Routledge. Perhaps the greatest thanks and appreciation is reserved for Kitty Imbert who over a long period of time had to face news of a variety of often unusual set-backs that held up the delivery of the manuscript. Thank you for your patience and understanding Kitty.

PREFACE

This book is about the work of war correspondents.[1] The focus is primarily on Western war reporters and the Western news organisations that employ them. Hence it is firmly located in the 'Anglo-American' ethnocentrism that pervades the study of the mass media, journalism and mass communication. The authors are aware of this limitation and are presently engaged in a study of non-Western war and foreign reporters to make a contribution to the redress of what they see as an imbalance in the study of international journalism. While recognising that there is significant diversity in the ways in which war reporters do their job, the focus on Anglo-American war reporting represents the pre-eminence of its practices and values in the international news system. The history of war reporting reflects the domination of British and American news organisations in the coverage of war and conflict and the evolution of practices and procedures through the actions and activities of white, Western men and latterly women. This imbalance in the global media and information order was powerfully articulated in the MacBride Report in the early 1980s, and while globalisation and new media technology have had a profound impact on the structure and agency of the order, they have not fundamentally changed the imbalance.

The pervasiveness of the Anglo-American way of war reporting has extended its reach since the MacBride Report documented the expansion of Anglo-American values and practices across the world, which it articulated through the process of media and cultural imperialism. In today's global media order many of those who report on war and conflict for Western news organisations are from Africa, Asia and Latin America. No longer is reporting the world dominated by British, American, Canadian and Australian reporters. The increasing use of foreign nationals to cover the world is a feature of most Western media systems. People from a variety of cultural backgrounds act as staff correspondents as well as delivering the support than enables staff reporters to do their job. The infrastructure of contemporary war reporting is provided by an array of stringers, freelancers, translators, drivers, security staff and fixers drawn from all corners of the world. The arrival of this array of personnel coincides with the ever increasing 'precarious' nature of employment in the profession. Full-time practitioners are being replaced by freelance reporters, and through the advent of new technology, a variety of non-professional information gatherers and providers are crucial to generating news from war zones. However, the system is still rooted in Anglo-American structures, practices and values. These are challenged by new news organisations such as Al-Jazeera, BuzzFeed and Vice News. Practitioners from non-Western backgrounds, including European correspondents who have always offered an alternative to Anglo-American journalism (see Broersma, 2007), are wrestling with new ways of articulating news values. The challenge to the Anglo-American way of war reporting comes from an assortment of political, economic, technological, organisational and ethical changes that characterise the 21st century. These are transforming not only the environment in which war correspondents have to work but also their approach to the job and how it is done and their conception of the role of war correspondent. For many observers, practitioners and scholars, these changes are intimately tied to the new attention being paid to the personal safety of war reporters (see Palmer, 2018).

Lindsay Palmer, in a book published at the time of the submission of this manuscript, makes the case that the professional practice of war correspondence is witnessing the rise of a new phenomenon which she labels "safety culture". She describes this as "a highly discursive, performative process through which the entire profession began to think, plan, and *talk* more about safety in the field" (Palmer, 2018: 17). Our discussion mirrors Palmer's approach but locates the rise of safety culture in the broader context of risk and the emergence of the risk society. She emphasises changes in the profession following the 9/11 attacks, which had a profound impact of Anglo-American society. While 9/11 might have changed careers and lives, as Palmer acknowledges, it meant different things in different parts of the world, which reflected the different ways journalists have responded to the event. Many of the 'new' trends identified by scholars and practitioners in the working environment of war reporters precede the events of 9/11. Some can even be traced back to the early days of the profession. However, for journalists everywhere, and perhaps more so in the non-Western world, reporting war, always a risky profession, has become even more risky. What distinguishes the post-9/11 world is that more journalists are dying bringing news of war and conflict to their audiences. Chris Paterson (2014), in his sober and compelling analysis, highlights how war correspondents today are 'targets' for combatants in wars and conflict. The extent to which the profession is more dangerous is debateable. Estimates of the number of correspondents who lost their lives covering war in the 19th century are few and far between, but anecdotally danger and risk-taking have been part and parcel of war reporting since the days of its so-called pioneer William Howard Russell. In fact these characteristics have been essential to differentiating the subculture of war journalism from the rest of the profession. However, in the contemporary environment, risk and risk-taking are becoming central to the identity and practice of war reporting.

Formal mechanisms of risk assessment were introduced for war reporters in the wake of the Bosnian wars in the 1990s. This does not mean that risk assessment was not part of the work of correspondents prior to this; rather, the emergence of safety courses and training programmes was an acknowledgement that "risk taking is an essential part of the journalistic endeavour" (Loyn, 2013: 4). Since Bosnia, managing risk has become pivotal in the work of the war correspondent. Editors and owners, managers and controllers, security consultants and experts as well as the correspondents struggle to control the risk in reporting war and conflict. The attempt to take control of the process has led many journalists to complain that safety is beginning to undermine their ability and capacity to do their job well. They believe managing risk has taken over. The ways in which risk plays a role in defining war reporting is the main consideration of this book. We are interested in whether the growing emphasis on risk is changing war correspondence. The focus on risk is not confined to threats to personal safety but embraces a range of personal and professional risks which are part of the balancing act required of the war correspondent as they assess the actions and decisions they take in war zones. Risk is not static but evolves as journalism, technology and society changes – and most tellingly as the nature of war develops.

Note

1 The term 'war correspondent' has historical antecedents, but as the nature of journalism becomes more fluid, it is applied here to all journalists who report on war.

INTRODUCTION

Reporting war is a risky business. Threats to personal safety and individual well-being are central to any understanding of the experience of the journalist on the battlefield. War correspondents emphasise these threats in their accounts of covering war, often incorporating the word 'danger' in the title of their books.[1] This is reinforced by cultural representation of their work. Films with titles such as *Under Fire* (1982) or *The Year of Living Dangerously* (1982) draw attention to the hazards that the correspondent faces in going to war, a theme repeated in novels, television drama and documentaries (see Korte, 2009). Being in the middle of a war zone is dangerous; as the BBC's veteran foreign correspondent John Simpson put it, "I'm not in favour of journalists being killed, of course, but whoever said reporting was supposed to be a safe profession?" (quoted in Pollard, 2009: 32). Coping with fear, suffering, danger and death is how many reporters evaluate their performance on the battlefield. The job is about being "in harm's way" (Bell, 2012a).

In recent years war reporting has become more hazardous. Journalist unions and organisations have documented the increasing number of reporters killed in action. The International Federation of Journalists (IFJ) in 2005 was blunt in its assessment of the present dangers.

> Five years into the 21st Century a dark and sinister cloud hangs over journalism around the world. More editors, reporters and media staff are killed, targeted, kidnapped and subject to violence than ever before. Independent media are under intolerable pressure.
>
> This pressure comes directly from ruthless terrorists, with no respect for civilisation and human rights, who have targeted and murdered journalists in all continents.
>
> *(IFJ and Statewatch, 2005: 2)*

The IFJ's assessment is echoed by leading war correspondents such as Martin Bell, who refers to journalists operating in a "new and more dangerous world, in which journalists are no longer peripheral observers but influential players in the theatre of war; they are exposed to dangers of a kind not encountered by any of the great war reporters" (Bell, 2008: 222). The kidnapping and murder of *Wall Street Journal* reporter Daniel Pearl in 2002 ushered in a new era, at least for Western journalists, of war reporting. Journalists are now firmly in the firing line and the informal code of conduct that allowed them to operate in war zones with some degree of protection and consent from the warring parties has lapsed. There is talk of a "war on journalism" in which front-line correspondents are now considered as legitimate targets by combatants (Knightley, 2001, 2003b; Paterson, 2014). The intensification of personal threat led to a growth of declarations on the safety of media personnel in conflicts (see Balguy-Gallois, 2004) and the proliferation of training courses and manuals for those embarking on the reporting of wars (see Maniati, 2013). In the age of the war in Syria and ISIS, the work of the war correspondent has never been riskier.

The danger of working in war zones is compounded by the problems of dealing with the trauma of war often encountered on getting home, the legacy of a hazardous profession. Coming to terms with the "graphic memories of human cruelty and depravity" is not simply a matter of individual struggle; it is also about the "callousness and cruelty of news organisations" (Hedges, in Feinstein, 2006, ix). Anthony Feinstein (2006) draws attention to the lack of interest that the profession has traditionally shown in the psychological problems of returning war reporters. Until recently, "not only had most of the news organisations neglected to provide for the psychological welfare of their war reporters, but trauma researchers had ignored them too" (Feinstein, 2006: 4). One Australian journalist bitterly recounts the time when "emotionally damaged journalists were stuck in the corner of the newsroom, and management waited for them to drink themselves to death" (quoted in Anderson and Trembath, 2011, loc. 295). Feinstein (2006: 11) points out that the plight of war reporters has been accentuated by the way in which news organisations have sanitised the content of war reports. By "pandering to their viewers' sensitivities, they also inadvertently cleanse the image of the working lives of war journalists, obscuring the many risks and dangers they confront" (Feinstein, 2006: 11). It has only been with the rising death toll of journalists at war that news organisations have discovered their duty of care to their employees.

The risks and fears of what Chris Ayers, in his book *War Reporting for Cowards*, describes as a "fucked-up profession" (2005: 19) have been accentuated by a transformation in the nature of war and warfare. Since 9/11 the so-called 'global war on terror' has provided a new set of parameters and circumstances within which the war correspondent has had to do his or her job. The attacks on New York and Washington led George Bush to declare the global war on terror. On 20 September in a speech to the US Congress that was televised to the nation, he avowed that "our war on terror begins with al Qaeda, but it does not end there. It will not end until every terrorist group of global reach has been found, stopped and defeated."[2] The declaration led, amongst other things, to the bombing of Afghanistan, the intervention in Iraq against Saddam Hussein and a variety of covert operations in several countries around the world to destroy particular terrorist targets. Subsequent acts of political violence committed in Madrid, London, Bali and Beslan reinforced the global nature of terrorism. On taking office in 2009, the Obama administration distanced itself from the 'war on terror' rhetoric, but it continued to take the war to terrorists wherever they were deemed to operate. Drone strikes increased during the Obama presidency, with the administration approving more than seven times as many strikes as George Bush. The rules of engagement have also been extended, which has increased the likelihood of civilian casualties (*The New York Times*, 2012).

It is argued that the framing of global politics through the discourse of the "war on terror" or the "new terrorism" has escalated a climate of fear and uncertainty (see Mythen and Walklate, 2006; Nohrstedt and Ottosen, 2008). "Fear of 9/11-like events makes it possible for governments to pass emergency legislation and creates a public environment where permanent fear has become the predominant state of mind" (Nohrstedt and Ottosen, 2008: 2). The processes involved in creating such a situation "not only articulate a reduced notion of safety" but they also have "negative consequences for ethnic minority groups" in many countries in the West as well as other parts of the world (Mythen and Walklate, 2006: 123). The war on terror is depicted as an all-consuming battle between good and evil waged between the West and an assortment of shadowy 'terror networks' and unstable 'rogue states'. Indiscriminate violence and brutality from drone strikes to public beheadings characterise the new warfare, and in the midst of this struggle the practice of journalism has become more risk inclined and journalists more risk aware.

Many scholars adhere to the view that the practice of journalism has been transformed since 9/11. The global war on terror is profoundly different from what has gone before, and as a result the way in which war is reported has changed. Barbie Zelizer and Stuart Allan (2002: 1) assert that the "familiar notions of what it means to be a journalist, how best to practice journalism and what different publics can reasonably expect of journalists in the name of democracy" have been "shaken to their foundation". Not only is the work of the war correspondent or the journalist who reports on war more dangerous, but it is also more difficult in other ways. A series of changes in the media landscape has presented new and more challenging problems for the reporter in the field. News organisations are downsizing, newsgathering is more commercial and competitive technology is making it possible to provide more immediate pictures and reports from the battlefield, and sources including the military and the terrorists are becoming more sophisticated at using correspondents to get their messages across. The Internet has increased the speed of communication, reducing the time to check the facts of a story. It has allowed other actors, particularly those involved in conflict, not only to record their own accounts of events in the war zone but also to challenge correspondents' reports. The reporter in the field is subject to commentary on his or her reporting from home offices as well as from domestic and global audiences. Technology has brought the correspondent in the field into closer contact with editors, increasing the pressure on reporters to work in particular ways. The growth of blogging has afforded a space for correspondents to tell their own personal stories of war outside editorial control and professional conventions. It has also led to correspondents having to react and respond to their audience to defend their accounts of events. These and other changes have led to speculation about the 'end of war journalism' or the 'death of the war correspondent'. Whether you accept this prognosis or not, it is clear that changes in the nature of warfare and the media environment present new challenges to the reporting of war and its representative in the field, the war correspondent.

Professional, political and personal uncertainties pervade the literature of contemporary war correspondents. There has always been a strong demand for the reminiscences of war correspondents. In addition to writing about their own personal experiences of the battlefront, they have deliberated the nature of war reporting, both in mainstream and specialist publications. David Welch (2007) draws attention to a growth in recent times of the number of memoirs published by war correspondents. The tone of these memoirs, autobiographies and recollections differs from the commentaries of their predecessors on their experiences at war. Hand-wringing and angst now sit more firmly alongside the recall of heroic moments and exploits. Correspondents have always written about their near-death experiences, the plight of the victims or survivors of war and the loss of fallen comrades. What singles contemporary descriptions out is the insecurity and uncertainty that frames the discussion.

War reporters are – and always have been – risk-takers; it sets them apart from many other professions and occupations. Most accounts of risk circulating in contemporary Western culture represent risk as "negative, something to be avoided" (Lupton and Tulloch, 2002: 113). The sociologist Ulrich Beck (1992, 2006), who introduced the concept of the 'risk society', argues that risk avoidance is the goal of most individuals, professions and occupations. He believes avoidance is a rational response in a society in which there are ever more perceived risks. Those who take risks either are not fully informed *or* misunderstand what is happening *or* are acting irresponsibly. Their conduct is deemed to be "foolhardy, careless, irresponsible" (Lupton and Tulloch, 2002: 114). There are, however, some occupations such as war correspondence that freely and habitually embrace risk.

War correspondents are often described – and often describe themselves – as addicted to danger. They are 'war junkies'. Risking life and limb to travel to the most dangerous places in the world is usually attributed to individual characteristics. War reporters take risks because of the thrills and excitement involved. It is the adrenalin rush to which they become hooked. BBC's Jeremy Bowen (2006: 3) sums up the view of many of his colleagues when he writes of war reporting as "compelling, addictive and fun". Risk-taking is also seen as a characteristic of machismo. Covering wars is an opportunity to affirm one's manliness. The portrayal of war correspondents in novels, films and popular culture in general regularly focuses on their heroic qualities and endeavours (see Korte, 2009). War reporting is also represented as the highest form of journalism. According to Kate Adie (1998: 14), journalists "frequently deal in trivial and fashionable sensation", and it is only "every so often we find ourselves witnessing events which are truly important" such as war and conflict. Bowen (2006: 3) like many of his colleagues believes that war reporting "helped me build a career, made me a better journalist and most of all felt worthwhile". Other reporters emphasise the glamour: according one of America's most famous reporters, Walter Cronkite, "nothing in the field of journalism is as glamorous as being a war correspondent" (quoted in Nicholson, 2012: xviii). The allure of fame and the attraction of becoming a household name propel some correspondents to take risks. A whole host of personal and individual attributes are put forward to account for the risk-taking nature of war journalists. Studies on risk and everyday life conclude that "voluntary risk taking is often pursued for the sake of facing and conquering fear, displaying courage, seeking excitement and thrills, achieving self-actualisation and a sense of personal agency" (Tulloch and Lupton, 2003: 11). However, in some professions risk-taking is about more than personal considerations; it is an integral component of the occupational culture.

Not all practitioners of war reporting sign up to the notion that their work validates risky behaviour. Adie (2015) refutes the risk-taking aspect of the job as a "myth" perpetuated in films and on television and associated with "a few daft individuals who do not live long". Susan Carruthers (2000: 20), in her excellent overview of the media at war, warns of how war reporters have promoted stereotypes of their work and mythologised their profession. However, risk-taking would appear to be deeply embedded in the occupational culture of war correspondence. Undertaking hazardous actions is a matter of cultural choice (Douglas, 1992: 103). Individuals do not regularly take risks for their own sake – usually they are accepted as a part of activity that has to be undertaken because of need, obligation or desire (Ale, 2009: 3). In the case of war reporters, they embrace risk and danger because it is an intrinsic part of their occupational culture. How they manage the risks and dangers is influenced by a set of arrangements, tales, practices, values, understandings, requirements and traditions which have come to characterise their occupation. The internalisation of these occupational values is not straightforward. Different types of correspondents and different generations have alighted on different traditions, myths and customs to delineate their role, performance and identity. As a subculture of journalism, war reporting is manifest in its daily routines and rituals as well as the frustrations and limitations expressed by its practitioners. The performance of war correspondents in the field is shaped by their sense of what their occupation, organisation and society expect of them, and what they deem necessary to report on conflict – which is not always consistently or correctly interpreted.

The ample literature produced by war reporters of their trials and tribulations provides a number of justifications for putting themselves at risk. One overriding justification is the notion of 'being there'. The war correspondent "goes into the field with the army, expecting to send his reports from ... 'the front'" (Bullard, 1914: 3). He or she is the labourer at the chalkface of war and conflict, providing an eyewitness account of what happens on the battlefield. War correspondents have to establish their credentials by showing they are there on the battlefield: "a piece to camera with bullets whistling around your ears is always desirable, because it establishes you in the middle of the story" (Bowen, 2006: 157). Simply being there has ceased to satisfy as the justification for reporting from the battlefield. There has to be a reason to be there, and post-1945 war journalists have emphasised the need to 'bear witness' or provide 'personal testimony'. Janine di Giovanni (2006: 61) is described as going to "suicidal lengths" to bear witness to human rights abuses around the world and to bring back the stories of the "small voices". Freelance war photographer Theodore Liasi (2013) discovered that the "one single common denominator shared" by the war reporters he came across in the field "was their sense of trying to bring back home the plight of and injustices suffered by their fellow human beings, seemingly forgotten or ignored". Veteran war correspondent Marie Colvin, days before her death in Syria, justified being there to "expose what was happening" in circumstances she described as the "worst we've seen" (quoted in Pollard, 2012). Two years previously, in a commemoration of reporters who had died on assignment, Colvin had made an impassioned plea for the need to "go to places torn by chaos, destruction, and death … and trying to bear witness". She acknowledged war reporting involves "taking risks, not just for yourself but often for the people who work closely with you" and the need "to report these horrors of war with accuracy and without prejudice", concluding that "someone has to go there and see what is happening. You can't get that information without going to places where people are being shot at, and others are shooting at you. We do have that faith because we believe we do make a difference" (quoted in Greenslade, 2010).

Bearing witness sits alongside a number of other factors that shape the occupational culture, including being first with the story, exposing the military and political authorities to scrutiny and producing the first 'rough draft of history'. Individual reporters negotiate these professional demands in different ways – shaped by personal, organisational and cultural considerations. How they manage risk is located within the context of unspoken assumptions, established moral beliefs and taken-for-granted practices that constitute the culture of war reporting. In their accounts of their experiences, war correspondents rarely focus on the occupational needs, obligations and desires of their profession. They tend to emphasise the agency of the reporter to overcome the obstacles placed before him or her in getting to stories in the war zone and to subvert restrictions placed on the reporting process. Negotiating the dangers of the battlefield is at the heart of the narrative of their recollections, and attention is drawn to various threats to personal safety and their ability to overcome them. Managing personal risk in the context of a climate of intimidation and violence is clearly an overwhelming consideration; returning home safely to family, friends and colleagues is the priority of anyone caught up in such dangerous circumstances as a war zone. The emphasis on the rugged individualism of the reporter in the personal testimonies of the correspondents belies the organisational imperatives that drive their work. Correspondents calculate risks to their personal safety in relation to their professional obligations and commitments. Personal reputations, the ethos of the news organisation, the relationship with sources of information and an understanding of audience expectations are some of the considerations that shape their calculations of risk.

These organisational pressures are manifest in the correspondent's relationship with the news desk. This is a crucial occupational consideration that shapes everyday working life. There are few accounts of war news from the perspective of the news desks or those who work in the home offices, and when the role of the news desk is mentioned, it is the correspondents' view that mostly prevails. The interventionist predisposition of the home office is acknowledged, but more often than not it is the ability of the correspondent to resist that is highlighted. The back cover of Ed Harriman's book *Hack* (1987) states that he survived "the minefield of journalism" with "only a few stories chopped, a few others consigned to the waste bin". An unnamed BBC correspondent, dishing out advice to reporters going to war, is quoted as saying, "don't be bullied by news desks back home wanting things that are impossible" (quoted in Liasi, 2013: loc. 469). Correspondents – depending on whose work you read – are continually at war with their news desks or in the process of continuous bargaining over what they should do. Tension has been exacerbated in recent years with the development of new technology which allows the home office more control over the movements of their men and women in the field. It is increasingly difficult to go off-message and follow one's own leads or angles. The disposition of the news desk is an important calculation in making a risk assessment of a story. Failure to respond to what the home office wants can curtail the capacity of the correspondent to file or lead to a drying up of assignments or, in the world of freelance work, can result in the termination of a commission.

Growing uncertainty pervades the relationship between war correspondents and their sources of information. War reporters, like most of their colleagues in news journalism, rely on sources of information to tell them what has happened. Correspondents do not witness most of what takes place on the battlefield. They often are not able to get to where the action is. Some have chosen not to go or have been prevented by the combatants. Some believe that being close to the action is no place to make an honest and accurate assessment of what is taking place. Editors have expressed the opinion that news sources are especially important in war zones as they contribute to the trustworthiness of the news: "we need news sources to give credibility to news" (quoted in Ibrahim *et al.*, 2011: 8). The dependence on news sources has to be seen in the context of the increasingly problematic nature of sourcing news from contemporary war zones. Sourcing war news is more challenging as a result of the growth of new media technology, the increasing sophistication of combatants in using the media and the heightened complexities of the 'hostile environments' in which war reporters now have to work.

The availability of social media and mobile phones is facilitating an exponential growth in the number of accounts of events in war zones. The major global networks routinely broadcast mobile phone video footage posted by bloggers, activists and citizen journalists from all sides of the conflict. The sheer volume of this material is making it more difficult for correspondents and editors to establish the veracity of what they are told or shown. In war zones which are not accessible to correspondents, such as in Syria, the ability to check the validity of the torrent of online information is heavily diminished. Reliance on online sources "creates the real risk of the same partial, misleading, and motivated narrative in mass media as in social media" (Lynch et al., 2014: 6). For journalists on the ground, more information is today available, and a larger number of sources are within reach. The highly factionalised nature of contemporary asymmetrical conflict means that war correspondents are increasingly dependent on their locally hired fixers to negotiate access to sources of information and assess their veracity. The consequences of misjudging war zone sources can be high, particularly in the more intimidating parts of the world, and hence managing the relationship with their fixers is an increasingly important part of the work of war correspondents. Many correspondents have resolved the dilemma of maintaining personal security and gaining access to sources by becoming embedded with the military. Over 600 reporters were embedded with US military units during the invasion of Iraq in 2003 (Paul and Kim, 2004: xiii). Embedding potentially impairs the critical judgement of the war correspondent; as Bell (2008: 226) comments, at its worst embedded reporting "is deeply and dangerously misleading". However, it is another example of the growing complexities of managing relationships with sources of information and the increased risks involved.

The management of risk at a number of levels is ever more central to shaping the working environment of war correspondents. Aidan White, General Secretary of the IFJ, refers to the emergence of a "culture of risk awareness" amongst journalists (IFJ, 2003: iv). This book seeks to discuss the everyday working lives of war correspondents from the perspective of the risk consciousness that increasingly shapes their working experience. Risk has always been part of reporting war, but in the 21st century it has become more deeply embedded in the occupational culture of the war reporter. Drawing on risk theory and the personal experiences of war reporters, including those of one of the authors, this book explores how risk and risk management have come to permeate the occupational culture and how calculations of risk are increasingly central to determining the coverage of war and conflict. Stuart Allan (2002: 209) defines risk as "the chance or possibility of danger (harm, loss, injury and so forth) or other adverse consequences actually happening". As we shall see, the notion of what constitutes risk is subject to considerable debate in the scholarly literature. However, discussing how risk is incorporated into the everyday working lives of war reporters, this book conceptualises the notion more broadly than simply threats to personal safety; it also examines the professional, organisational and occupational risks confronting correspondents. These risks are becoming more important in shaping the working practices of war correspondents and consequently their coverage of war and conflict. At a time when journalists are becoming more concerned about the risk to their personal safety in war zones, changes in the political economy and technology of reporting are accentuating the risks correspondents face in their everyday work routines.

It is also argued that the everyday working lives of correspondents is located in the context of the "culture of fear" which is associated with the rise of the risk society (Glassner, 2009). The war on terror, climate change, global warming, financial meltdowns, pandemics and mass migration are some of the global transformations which are seen as contributing to a permanent state of fear amongst publics around the world. Fear breeds more violence, trauma and social disintegration and helps to create more authoritarian politics with enhanced police powers, increased invasions of privacy and growth of surveillance (see Glassner, 2009). This poses a challenge to journalism. It is often argued that the media and journalism amplify risk and promote panic, alarm and fear amongst the public. Journalists are blamed for exaggerating risk, "whipping up hysteria" and distorting reality (Kitzinger, 1999: 55).

Less attention is paid to how the culture of fear shapes the practice and performance of journalism and, in particular, that of war correspondents. A sense of uncertainty, fear and anxiety increasingly pervades the work environment of war correspondents; it is a major component in shaping what Pierre Bourdieu (1984) would describe as the "habitus" of war journalism.

This book examines how risk is an integral part of war reporting. It is divided into three sections. The *first section* provides some history, theory and context to the development of the specialism of the war correspondent. The way in which risk is integral to war reporting is examined in relation to the history of war reporting, with particular attention to the changing nature of technology, organisational structures and the role and identity of the war reporter. The section consists of four chapters. The first chapter, "Risk and war journalism", outlines the notion of risk and the risk society and applies risk theory to the ways in which news organisations, individual reporters and society understand and assess the risks and dangers of reporting war and conflict. Risk-taking is emphasised as intrinsic to the profession of war correspondence and how it has changed with the transformations in warfare. The second chapter, "Bearing witness: morality, risk and war reporting", discusses one of the main ways in which contemporary war correspondents justify or explain taking the risks they do to get a story. A number of reasons are given by correspondents to justify risk-taking, but bearing witness is increasingly used. The evolution of the notion of bearing witness is explored, what is meant by 'bearing witness' today is reflected on, and the particular problems such a justification present for the risks taken by war reporters are examined. Chapter 3, "Organisational and occupational risks and war reporting", considers the evolution of the organisational context and occupational culture of war reporting and how it encourages the taking of risk. It examines how institutional, commercial, social and personal considerations lead correspondents to understand risk-taking. The changing political economy of war reporting is identified as an important factor in making the practice of war reporting riskier, and the increased professionalism and power of sources of information in determining how correspondents work on the battlefield is evaluated. The extent to which these factors have impacted on 'doing the job' is seen as an essential aspect of war reporting. Chapter 4, "Technology and risk management: telegraph, telex and Twitter", deliberates the extent to which technology has shaped correspondents' calculations of risk and risk-taking in their practice and performance. Technology has had both adverse and advantageous consequences for war reporters, but many of these consequences have contributed to making the job more uncertain and risk oriented.

The *second section* deals with the reporting of particular types of conflicts, drawing on the perspective of being on the ground as a reporter – the traditional nation state wars, the asymmetrical wars that have come to characterise the post-Second World War society and the hybrid wars that represent the new world order and especially the post-9/11 international environment. Drawing on the experience of reporting of Iraq, Afghanistan and to a lesser extent Syria, the section examines how risk and the calculations of risk vary according to the type of conflict. It contains three chapters focusing on the reporting of different types of conflict. Chapter 5, "The media on the battlefield: risk and embedding", evaluates the traditional form of conflict between nation states, which presents a threat to the survival of each society. The nature of war has changed significantly in the post-war period, but the clash of force between nation states remains a preoccupation of world politics. Chapter 6, "Asymmetrical risk", focuses on post-2003 Iraq, a war or, rather, insurgency which typifies the wars that have become increasingly prevalent in the post-1945 period – struggles inside nation states. Many of these have taken place inside the so-called Third World or Global South and are associated with decolonisation. However, the end of the Cold War led to the re-emergence of intra-national struggles in Europe with the collapse of the Soviet Union. Chapter 7, "Risk and reporting new forms of war and conflict", concentrates on the wars that have come to shape the contemporary world post 9/11. These conflicts represent the further development of asymmetrical warfare and pose a new and altogether different challenge to the war reporter. For many correspondents they have led to a rethinking of the role of the contemporary war correspondent in the reporting of war.

The *third section* looks at the arguments around risk in relation to specific aspects or components or themes in war reporting. These include the impact of war reporting on shaping the response of policymakers and how the news media are used by government, the military and non-governmental organisations (NGOs) to shape public understanding of conflict, how the victims and casualties of war are reported, the issue of gender and war reporting, the relationship between propaganda, censorship and reporting, and the question of the nature of war correspondence in the digital world. Chapter 8, "Risk and the reporting of death, dying and the casualties of war", considers how the impact of war on people is reported and represented, including the construction of victims and the nature of death and dying. In the digital world, combatants and participants can bypass the media and the reporter to present their own picture of war by posting it online. The consequences of this development for war reporting are examined. Has this changed the image and understanding the public has of war – has it made war more 'real'? How this has impacted on the way in which reporters behave on the battlefield is discussed. Chapter 9, "Gender, risk and war reporting", examines the part gender plays in shaping the way in which war is covered. The evolution of female war correspondents is described, and the extent to which they report wars differently from their male counterparts is assessed. Comparisons are made of women correspondents from different societies as well as their assessment of the risk-taking side of the profession. How men and women respond to the psychological trauma of covering wars is also contrasted.

Notes

1 For example, Hanigen, Frank, ed. *Nothing but Danger: Thrilling Adventures of Ten Newspaper Correspondents in the Spanish War*, London: Harrap, 1940; Nicholson, Michael, *A Measure of Danger: Memoirs of a British War Correspondent*, London: Harper Collins, 1991; Darrow, Siobhan, *Flirting with Danger: Confessions of a Reluctant War Reporter*, London: Virago, 2000.
2 Address to a Joint Session of Congress and the American People, 20 September, 2001.

1

RISK AND WAR JOURNALISM

The opening chapter[1] discusses the practice of war reporting in the context of 'risk society'. It provides a brief discussion of the concept of the risk society and the different ways in which it has been interpreted in relation to war and conflict. The conceptualisation of the role of the media in the construction of risk in modern society is discussed. Two particular aspects have been taken up in the scholarly literature: the role of the media in the amplification of risk *and* the risk assessment made by media practitioners in the execution of their work. How risk is calculated and negotiated in everyday life is the particular focus of the chapter. The extent to which risk perception is a matter of personal and social factors is considered, and their relevance to professional and work practice is evaluated. Unlike most other professions, journalism embraces risk-taking in its daily working routines. A particular framework has determined the attitudes of war correspondents to risk and risk-taking and why risky behaviour is encouraged or embraced by the profession. War correspondents make calculations of risk at a number of levels – personal, professional, organisational and social – which are central to understanding the daily practices and routines of war reporting. These calculations have consequences for how war and conflict is covered and the kind of knowledge of warfare we receive.

The risk society

Risk is a concept that has been deployed across the social sciences to underpin much contemporary research. There are, however, substantial differences in how risk is defined and used between and within different disciplines, and as Karen Henwood and her colleagues (2008: 421) point out, "[m]ultiplicity, variability and incongruity in the meanings of risk" are "encountered throughout the research process". Deploying risk as a concept to understand the work of journalists, let alone war correspondents, is fraught with problems. Like many concepts that have been used successfully in analysis of the media – such as 'moral panics', 'public sphere' and 'hegemony' – it has become sufficiently elastic to embrace a variety of circumstances in a number of ways. There is insufficient space in this book to discuss and unravel the different conceptualisations of risk, but it is important to stress at the outset that "what is perceived as risk and how that risk is perceived will vary according to the context in which, and from which, it is regarded" (Henwood *et al.*, 2008: 422). However, the starting point for most discussions of risk is the notion of the 'risk society', which is associated with the German sociologist Ulrich Beck (1992).

Beck deploys this notion to explain how modern societies react to the industrial, technological, medical, environmental, social, chemical and nuclear hazards and dangers that confront them. These are perceived to be growing at an alarming rate as a result of the process of modernisation. Beck argues that modernisation is eradicating the structures of industrial society and creating, in its place, a risk society. He differentiates between the hazards of previous ages and the risks of contemporary societies, arguing that "the historically unprecedented possibility, brought about by our own decisions, of the destruction of all life on this planet ... distinguishes our epoch" (Beck, 1991: 22–3). The natural hazards of the past such as earthquakes, plagues and volcanoes are distinct from the human-made risks of contemporary society. Risk society is "where we switch the focus of our anxieties from what nature can do to us to what we have done to nature" (Beck, 1998: 10, citing Giddens). Nothing could be done about the hazards of the past as they were seen as acts of God, nature or the supernatural. Contemporary risk is the product of human agency in a society in which something can be or is expected to be done to protect individual citizens. Beck argues that risk is a consequence of the increased capacity of modern societies to offer security from the potential risks of everyday life.

Risk permeates the lived experience of most people in Western societies. Nearly every aspect of our lives, work, relationships, food consumption, health, travel, leisure and security are subject to risk concerns. A number of scholars in political science and international relations have speculated on how the rise of the risk society has influenced the conduct of war (see Coker, 2009; Heng, 2006b; Rasmussen, 2006). This has generated a rich discussion from which a number of points of relevance for the work of war correspondents can be drawn. First, the risk society has implications for the ways in which war is understood. Beck (2000) asserts that the end of the bipolar world of the Cold War has led to the disappearance of specific enemies and the emergence of generalised dangers and risks. The notion of a distinct 'threat' from an opponent with particular intentions and specific capabilities has been replaced by a world of potential non-specific risks which need to be managed (Heng, 2006a). Set-piece conflicts between nation states are being replaced by the projection of military force in the context of a world of shadowy networks and rogue states. Uncertainty increasingly characterises this form of war. The global risk society is characterised by a "bewildering array of risks", and calculating how these risks might "become identifiable threats" preoccupies military thinking (Heng, 2006b: 11). Confronted with uncertainty, the military and government have come to interpret security by the prediction, anticipation and management of potential risk. Discouraging or preventing action shored up the notion of deterrence that dictated superpower strategy during the Cold War. However, in the age of the risk society, the proliferation of an array of 'unknowns' means that military strategy is less concerned with the fixed certainties of the threats and dangers of yesterday and more concerned with the fluid uncertainties that characterise modern life.

There are numerous problems attached to the prediction of unspecified threats and risks. Christopher Coker (2009: 2) draws attention to the costs and human failings involved. Events such as the Iraqi invasion of Kuwait in 1990 and the 9/11 attacks were predicted, but the problem was the "failure to act" on the predictions. The costs involved in taking pre-emptive action are deemed significant in a world which is dominated by speculation about possible scenarios. The news media and journalism play a crucial role in the speculation about potential dangers, threats and risks. In the 24-hour news culture much of what appears in the news media is a mixture of facts, information, misinformation, disinformation and speculation. Much of the research into the impact of rolling news has focused on the consequences for policymakers going about their business (see Livingston, 1997; Robinson, 2005). Some scholars have focused on the generation of a product labelled "global news" (see Clausen, 2003; Cottle, 2006). There has been less evaluation of the nature of news in a 24-hour news culture (Cushion and Lewis, 2010). What is evident from the work that has been conducted is that the promise of more airtime to overcome the brevity of conventional news culture and investigate and explain more fully the context to the events of the day has not been realised. The emphasis on the breaking news story has resulted in the opposite: "disposable news reaches its apotheosis in the repetitive rush of the 24-hour news cycle" (Cushion and Lewis, 2010: 6). Speculation plays a considerable role in filling airtime surrounding the updating of breaking news events. The visual component of 24-hour news provides evidence of the news media at the heart of unfolding events while speculation props up the words that accompany the pictures. Journalism in this news culture can be described as a licence to speculate, a capacity that is enhanced by new technology which, through personal blogs, allows correspondents to present their views and feelings about dangers and threats.

Second, the risk society at war envisages that warfare should be prosecuted safely. The notion that warfare can be conducted according to a set of rules and regulations has a long history which includes The Hague Conventions of 1899 and 1907, the first multilateral treaties governing the conduct of warfare. Subsequent treaties have added to these conventions, although for most of the 20th century many, if not most, of the rules specified under the conventions have been violated. However, the advent of new technology in the late 20th century led to the discourse of the 'clean war'. Martin Shaw (2005) describes the new Western way of war in terms of the unwillingness to accept deaths of Western combatants and the desire to avoid civilian casualties. There is a growing public and political expectation that civilian casualties and collateral damage should be at an acceptable level. The military, as one NATO commander stated on the eve of Operation Desert Storm, are told "to avoid our own casualties and fatalities … [and] collateral damage to the extent possible and … bring it to a quick end" (quoted in Osinga and Roorda, 2016: 56). High-tech warfare is supposedly "bloodless and antiseptic" (Kellner, 2000: 221). Laser-guided smart bombs provided the image of high-tech precision bombing during the first Gulf war. The notion that targets and buildings could be taken out with limited loss of life was promoted by the US military. Videos were released to indicate that "US bombs always hit their targets, did not cause collateral damage and only took out nasty military targets" (Kellner, 2000: 220). Civilian loss of life, when exposed, such as with the death of a large number of ordinary men, women and children in the Amiriya bunker in 1991, was explained away as the Iraqis using civilians to protect military targets. Human failings were responsible; not the smart military technology. Despite the rhetoric of clean war and the promotional images of smart bombs, it was found after the war that less than 10 per cent of the bombs dropped during the war were 'smart' and that more than two-thirds missed their targets (Kellner, 2000: 221). However, the first Gulf war was an important stage in the history of war propaganda as it marked "a deliberate attempt by the authorities to alter public perception of the nature of war itself, particularly the fact that civilians die in war" (Knightley, 1991: 5).

The notion of a clean war has put the safety of civilians and combatants at the centre of military planning in a risk society. Reassuring Western publics is nevertheless fraught with problems. A number of high-profile attacks in cities such as London, Madrid and Paris since 9/11 have accentuated the widespread sense of anxiety which has been labelled as a "culture of fear" (for example, Altheide, 2013; Furedi, 1997; Glassner, 2009). The post-Cold War world is perceived to be more dangerous. The result is that citizens in Western democracies believe they are more at risk than ever before despite their security in statistical terms being higher than at any other time in the last century. Fear is fuelled by the stream of news of the daily atrocities which are reported from many parts of the Global South, a more prominent feature of the everyday lives of people in this part of the world. Governments drawing attention to the state of threat at any given time enhances fear and uncertainty.

The news media play a crucial role in reporting the casualties of war, and their capacity to report scenes from the battlefield has been accentuated by the technological changes of the last few decades. War correspondents can report live and direct from the battlefield and hold to account official interpretations of the impact of military action in a more direct way than ever before. Increased capacity has not been accompanied by increased commitment to report warfare. News organisations have been pulled in different directions in responding to their enhanced capacity to report from the battlefield. On one hand, they have become more cautious in showing casualty images and pictures, particularly of soldiers from their own countries. In 1993 grim images of US servicemen killed in Somalia were aired on

US TV screens, but a decade later, pictures of the bodies of US service personnel slain in an ambush in the Iraq War were not broadcast because they were 'too shocking' to be shown to the US public. The debate about showing images of dead combatants, particularly if their families had not been informed, has accompanied the rise of television and new media. This discussion has to be seen in the context of the growth of official efforts to manage images of death, destruction and warfare since the early 1990s. Military and political unease has been enhanced by the ability of ordinary people "to access the soldiers' own images and stories directly through war blogs, mass emails and popular video-sharing sites", which "throws in to sharp relief the way in which mainstream media and government cover the realities of war" (Anden-Papadopoulos, 2009: 921). On the other hand, news organisations – print and broadcast – in the digital world are increasingly dependent on visual images. Demand for such images has been accelerated by increased competition in the global news market, the need to fill more time and space in the round-the-clock news culture and the growth of alternative news-gatherers and disseminators such as citizen journalists. The pressure on correspondents to produce more compelling images has been accompanied by the increased emphasis they place on their role as the "witness who arouses conscience" (Seib, 2002: 121). Human rights have become ever more central to global politics, and correspondents have increasingly identified their job in terms of documenting violations of individuals' civil liberties and of the collective rights of peoples and marginal groups, including providing personal testimony in the international legal processes against abusers. War reporting has moved from acting as eyewitnessing conflict to bearing a moral and ethical responsibility to record the suffering of the victims of war (see Mellor, 2012a, 2012b). This has led to journalists becoming more involved in conflict and taking more risks to get the story.

Third, information in the age of the risk society is central to military strategy. Martin Bell (2008: 229) describes how military commanders on the ground during the Gulf War in 1991 placed the media presentation of their operations as one of the highest priorities. They knew, as Bell emphasises, that the failure to win the war of words and images could lead to military defeat. This is in part a legacy of the Vietnam War, which for many soldiers across the world was lost not on the battlefields in south-east Asia but in the living rooms of the American people. Graphic pictures of the fighting and the deliberate misrepresentation of the war by the American news media were held responsible for the country's first military defeat on the battlefield (see Williams, 1992). The truth of such claims is a matter of dispute, but the failure to manage the media and control the flow of information about the war shaped military, public and media perceptions of the reporting. More significant has been the need to respond to the changing nature of war and warfare and the rise of the risk society. David Miller (2004a) highlights the development of the Pentagon's total spectrum dominance outlined in their Joint Vision 2020 statement. This states that "US forces are able to conduct prompt, sustained and synchronised operations with the combination of forces tailored to specific situations and with access to and freedom to operate in all domains – space, sea, land, air and information" (quoted in Miller, 2004a: 3). Total spectrum dominance is, as Miller describes, more than another form of spin and propaganda; rather, it places news management and information control at the heart of military operations, integrating them into the command and control systems of the modern armed forces.

The 2003 assault on Iraq witnessed the 'weaponisation of information'. A variety of mechanisms were developed to build up 'friendly' information and to denigrate 'unfriendly' information. Supporting friendly information provision was manifest in the information centres established across the region and worldwide. A PR campaign was launched to gather public support at home and abroad for the use of military force. Perhaps the highest profile of the efforts to promote the official perspective was the embedding of journalists with military units on the ground. Putting journalists into uniforms and locating them on the front line with the armed forces was not "innovative" as some claim (Paul and Kim, 2004: 3). However, the extent and degree to which this took place in Iraq represented a significant departure from previous conflicts. Reporters from a variety of countries were embedded with US and Coalition army units, travelling with them, seeing what they saw and standing side by side with them under fire (see Paul and Kim, 2004). The unprecedented access is seen by some as facilitating the reporting of the Iraq War: journalists were given "remarkable access", the military gained "much more favourable coverage" and the public "saw a type of picture that they had never, never had an opportunity to see before" (Brookings, cited in Paul and Kim, 2004, 110). The embedded media system may have been a "win-win-win" plan (Brookings, in Paul and Kim, 2004: 110), but it accentuated the risks to war correspondents in a number of ways. First, it located more reporters simultaneously on the battlefield than in previous conflicts. Second, it forced journalists who wanted to be unencumbered by restrictions to act unilaterally to report the war independently. Denied a number of facilities, including transmission and transport, unilateral reporters put themselves at risk to get to the story and get their stories back. Several celebrated correspondents, such as ITN's Terry Lloyd, were killed. But it was perhaps the targeting of outlets that carried alternative accounts of the war, the unfriendly reports, that has most enhanced the risk.

The second component of information dominance is the "ability to deny, degrade, destroy and/or effectively blind" enemy capabilities (Winters and Giffin, quoted in Miller, 2004a: 11). No distinction is made between the information actions of adversaries and independent outlets or media. The intention is to ensure that any obstacle to attaining total information dominance is removed. This has led to accusations of targeting journalists, with the US attacks on Al Jazeera's offices in Kabul (2001) and Baghdad (2003) and the Palestine Hotel (2003), where most international reporters based in Baghdad stayed, the most high-profile examples of such a policy. In 2005 the Committee to Protect Journalists reported that US military fire was the second most common cause of the death of journalists in Iraq (cited in Paterson, 2014: 5). The Israeli Defence Force has been blamed for the deaths of several journalists in recent years as part of its clampdown on the press.

The International Press Institute stated that the shooting of an Italian photo-journalist "seemed to be part of a concerted strategy by the Israeli Army to control the press" (quoted in Paterson, 2014: 103). This is in addition to the deaths of journalists at the hands of terrorist groups in the Middle East and the Arab world. It is not only that journalists are deliberately targeted and killed. They are also increasingly threatened, coerced, hassled and intimidated on a regular basis with a level of violence previously unknown (see Cottle *et al.*, 2016). On today's battle-field the neutrality of the war correspondent is no longer accepted by the warring parties. They are part of the conflict and considered as legitimate targets. The BBC's Kate Adie has talked about the "compete erosion of any kind of acknowl-edgement that reporters should be able to report as they witness" (quoted in Paterson, 2014: 8).

The advent of new information technology has further imperilled the lives of war correspondents. The contributions of the mobile phone, the Internet, satellite dishes and so on to facilitating modern war reporting have been well documented. Less attention has been paid to the dangers such technology has brought into the lives of correspondents. Surveillance is an essential component of the new infor-mation strategies of Western states. Digital surveillance takes many forms. Satellite phones can be monitored, and the location of the caller can be identified (see Sambrook, 2016: 30). The deaths of the celebrated war correspondent Marie Colvin and the photographer Remi Ochlik are attributed to government forces being able to locate and target the reporters from the use of a satellite phone. New technology has also allowed warring parties to communicate directly to their fol-lowers and the public. This means that journalists are becoming less useful as con-duits of information and propaganda, further undermining their neutrality on the battlefield. Alan Rusbridger, former editor of *The Guardian*, emphasises that "there is no such thing as confidential communication" and draws attention to the inability of correspondents to maintain the confidentiality of their sources because of the threat of surveillance (quoted in Ponsford, 2014), an additional risk to their ability to do their job.

The risk society has had a profound impact on the conduct of war, which it can be argued has had a destabilising effect on war reporting. It has propelled the war correspondent to the centre of the battlefield, no longer an observer of events but an actor in the struggle between warring parties. Changes in professional attitudes and organisational needs have played their part in the transformation of the role and practice of war reporting. The notion of bearing witness and the competitive demands of the 24-hour news culture are two factors behind the transformation. However, the shift in information policy and the advent of new technology are just as significant. Government and non-government combatants place more emphasis on the role of information in the prosecution of war, and hence the role of war correspondents has been accorded more attention. Technology has enhanced the capacity of the correspondent to report from the battlefield, which has increased the attention of the warring parties on what they report. The pres-sures on correspondents to report war in particular ways has never been more acute. War reporting is at the heart of modern conflict and, hence, is a more risk-disposed assignment than it has traditionally been. The extent to which risk is a defining feature of contemporary war reporting and the nature of these risks has to be understood in the context of the contribution of the media and journalism to the risk society.

Media and the risk society

The media play no part in Beck's conceptualisation of the risk society, although according to Simon Cottle (1998: 9),

> it is clear from the statements … scattered across Beck's writings that ideas of the "risk society" are theoretically predisposed to privilege the mass media as a key site in the social construction, social contestation and, further, the social criticism of, or social challenge to, risks and the deficiencies of institutionalized responses to these.

Scholars have attempted to fill the gap left by Beck in a number of ways. This has taken the form of risk communication, concentrating on how the media have framed the risks of everyday life. The objectivity, rationality and accuracy of media coverage have been interrogated, and problems have been raised about how audiences make sense of what they consume in the news media. The news media have frequently been criticised for 'selective amplification' or the 'hyping' of risk; for example, in the areas of health (Murdock et al., 2003) and disasters (Vasterman, 2005; Vasterman et al., 2005). Jenny Kitzinger and Jackie Reilly (1997: 319) demonstrate how "rather than simply mirroring a 'risk society', media attention to risk is highly selected". Why certain risks and risky behaviours are amplified by the media has been the subject of scholarly research, and a variety of factors have been identified. Some scholars (see below) have related selective amplification to the ways in which news is produced and to how journalists work, but relatively little attention has been paid to how risk has shaped the work and working environment of reporters.

Professionals working in risky environments, such as the fire and police services and the medical profession, have developed methods to protect themselves against the risks they encounter in their everyday work. Journalism was, until recently, an exception. Journalists have been sent to cover wars, disasters, demonstrations and danger without any preparation of how to negotiate the risks involved. The haphazard preparations made for going to war are highlighted in Evelyn Waugh's novel *Scoop*. The leading character, William Boot, in his casual approach to preparing for his assignment, captures the essence of the experience of many, if not most, war correspondents in the 20th century. Feinstein (2006) notes that it was only at the beginning of the 20th century that news organisations started to send their employees on safety courses. Protecting themselves against the dangers of the battlefield and modern warfare was stressed. Several studies have examined how safety has been maintained in the face of the various dangers of war, and Feinstein and other scholars have examined the effects of negotiating risk on war correspondents. Feinstein has concentrated on how reporters deal with trauma in the field and, more recently, in newsrooms, in social media teams and on picture desks, where graphic and disturbing imagery is seen as having increased with the advent of user-generated content (Feinstein et al., 2014). Post-traumatic stress disorder has figured prominently in this type of research, and this focus is reinforced by the personal accounts of many contemporary war reporters which deal with the risks of war reporting to personal mental health and safety.

Over recent years, war correspondents have justified the dangers they face and the threats to their individual safety and mental well-being by stressing the importance of 'being there' to bear witness to the world about what is happening in the zones of conflict (see Chapter 2). Marie Colvin explained why she continued to risk her life in the most dangerous of situations, stating that the Assad regime was "killing" its people "with impunity" and that she "should stay and write what [she] can to expose what is happening here" (quoted in Pollard, 2012). The Assad regime's effort to ban foreign journalists from entering the country to witness these atrocities further compelled Colvin to report the story. She believed in the need to bear witness whatever the cost, something that she shared with many of the leading war reporters since William Howard Russell's days. The reasons for witnessing may have changed since the Crimean War, but the commitment to witnessing has remained constant. It is the price of witnessing that has risen with the increasing death toll of correspondents. This raises the question of whether the price today is too high. Many news organisations have recently stopped sending their correspondents into high-risk war zones such as Syria, and they have attempted to discourage freelance journalists from taking up the slack by no longer accepting their work if it is from places they do not send their own reporters (see Armoudian, 2017).

Embracing the moral dimension of bearing witness is often portrayed as a matter of personal choice or preference. Some journalists have taken their commitment to the process of witnessing as far as giving evidence at trials of those prosecuted for war crimes and atrocities. Ed Vulliamy of *The Guardian* testified at the International Criminal Tribunal for the former Yugoslavia, stating that it was "a chance for some kind of reckoning for the only people I really cared about – the victims" (1999: 605). He believed that bearing witness might sometimes result in the reporter having to abandon his or her 'neutrality'. This position is seen by some other war reporters as presenting a risk to their professionalism as it impairs their objectivity and impartiality and raises questions about how they deal with their sources. Several journalists and news organisations got together to defend the right of journalists not to testify. They argued that by becoming legal witnesses they ceased to be observers and turned into participants in the story, thus making it more dangerous for their fellow reporters to cover the abuses of war (Spellman, 2005). Personal preference or disposition is often seen as shaping the extent to which correspondents take on the risk of testifying against those alleged to have committed atrocities. However, it is possible to argue that such decisions can only be understood in the context of the broader occupational culture. War reporting today is often driven by a particular set of professional understandings that have emerged from a growing sense of dissatisfaction with the conventional approach to covering conflict. It is not just that contemporary reporters are targeted by combatants; their changing motivations in covering war have put them in the firing line. To understand how risk is inculcated into war correspondents' work, we need to look at literature on risk and everyday life.

Risk and everyday life

Beck associates modernity with individualisation; people, he argues, consider themselves as the "centre of the conduct of life, taking on multiple and mutable subjectivities, and crises are seen as individual problems rather than socially based" (Tulloch and Lupton, 2003: 4). Beck (1992: 135) describes this as "reflexive" modernity. He argues that "more and more areas of life are released or disembedded from the hold of tradition" (Elliott, 2002: 298), and the "traditional certainties" can "no longer be taken for granted" (Beck, 1998: 10). The disappearance of traditional social roles connected with gender, class and work "forces people into making decisions about their own lives and future courses of action" (Elliott, 2002: 298). Central to this decision-making process is the assessment of risk.

John Tulloch and Deborah Lupton (2003) examine how people define, experience and think about risk as part of their everyday lives. They argue, as Beck does, that people produce their own "risk biographies" to adjust to life in a risk society and concentrate on identifying the risks people see as confronting them on a daily basis and how the risks are dealt with. Problems they have examined include sickness, family and marital breakdowns, and unemployment. Tulloch and Lupton criticise Beck for the emphasis he places on the individual, deeming him to give insufficient consideration to the social and cultural aspects of risk-taking. They explore the extent to which factors such as gender, social class, ethnicity, sexual orientation, occupation, geographical location and nationality influence people's perceptions and experience of risk. They state that the "ways in which risk is dealt with and experienced in everyday life, are inevitably developed via membership of cultures and subcultures as well as through personal experience" (Tulloch and Lupton, 2003: 1). Groups and subgroups operate with a set of shared values and assumptions which have developed over time. Studies have highlighted the particular social group characteristics that lead to risky behaviour despite conflicting knowledge (see Bloor, 1995).[2]Tulloch and Lupton note that understandings of risk are often "non-reflexive in that they are taken-for-granted" and acknowledge that risk knowledge is "historical and local" (2003: 6, 1). They state, "what might be perceived to be 'risky' in one era at a certain locale may no longer be viewed so in a later era, or in a different place" (Tulloch and Lupton, 2003: 1). Therefore, what is considered risky is "constantly contested" and "subject to disputes and debates over their nature, their control and whom is to blame for their creation" (Tulloch and Lupton, 2003: 1). Scott Lash (2000) refers to this as "risk cultures".

Work on risk and culture is most closely associated with the anthropologist Mary Douglas. According to Fardon (2013: 2), Douglas argues that "different institutional arrangements encourage different perceptions of the urgency of risks, the need to resolve them, and the resolution to do so". Her understanding of the arrangements that shape the nature of institutions focused on two dimensions, which she labelled "group" and "grid" (see Fardon, 2013). According to Zinn (2004: 10),

> While the grid dimension describes the degree to which an individual's life is circumscribed by externally imposed descriptions, the group dimension represents the extent to which people are driven by or restricted in thought and action by their commitment to a social unit larger that [sic] the individual.

The central assumptions of Douglas' approach to risk are that there is a relationship between "social organization and the responses to risk and that culture are [sic] adequately represented by the dimensions of the grid/group scheme" (Zinn, 2004: 9). As an approach to cultural and risk analysis, the grid/group framework has been subject to scrutiny, but Douglas' work draws attention to the role of competing social and individual dispositions and identities in shaping perceptions of what are risk and risky behaviour.

Understanding the risk society entails the acceptance of a certain general disposition to taking risk. Avoiding unnecessary risks has always been seen as an essential component of human behaviour. Today's increasingly risk-averse society entails "that an activity should not be embarked on if there are risks" (Ale, 2009: 111). Lupton and Tulloch (2002: 113) emphasise that "most of the accounts of risk circulating in contemporary Western expert and popular cultures portray it as negative, something to be avoided". Despite society's focus on risk aversion, there are still people who take risks. There are a number of reasons put forward to explain why certain groups or individuals take risks. There are few activities which are totally without risk, and even the most risk-averse people have to calculate "how safe is safe enough" (Ale, 2009: 110). Some degree of risk-taking is regarded as part of the activities we undertake – it is a component of what we have to or want to do (Ale, 2009: 3). Calculations take into account different aspects and qualities of an activity, and risk is not the sole factor that influences deliberations (Ale, 2009: 105). Douglas (1992: 103) highlights that undertaking risky activities is not simply about calculating the risks but also a matter of preference and cultural choice. Avoiding risk can "conflict with one of our other basic needs, or with the needs of others", and "we need a way to decide, to choose" between them (Ale, 2009: 9). Other justifications for risky behaviour include social esteem and self-fulfilment. Risk aversion can be understood as a "*prima facie* obligation [which] is always in force, but which can be overridden by other obligations" or considerations (Espinoza and Peterson, 2012: 9).

Taking risk is also deemed irrational. It "must be accepted that human beings are often not rational" (Anand, 1993: 19). According to Lupton (1999: 111), risk-taking is "portrayed by experts as inaccurate or irrational", but it "often makes sense in the context of an individual's life situation, including the cultural frameworks". Risks are not taken just for their own sake but are accepted as a part of activity that responds to a variety of other requirements, wants, obligations or desires (Ale, 2009: 3). Risk-taking activity can be part of rational calculation. "Risks are a side effect of benefits that we want to obtain. These benefits are to some extent balanced by the costs incurred by the risk" (Ale, 2009: 112). Bernadus Ale (2009: 101) points out that risky behaviour has to be seen in the context of "our judgement as to whether the risk is worth taking, given how much the activity means to us", and as a result "people can differ substantially over the acceptability of [the] risk". Risk perception varies and calculations about risk are inherently complex as "the harms and benefits need not be of the same kind and may not even affect the same people" (Espinoza and Peterson, 2012: 10).

The conclusion that can be drawn is that there is an 'acceptable' level of risk for a given action, which depends on personal values and priorities. An individual chooses "the act that is best with respect to beliefs and desires that [he or she] holds", particularly with respect to personal, emotions-based preferences (Anand, 1993: 1). The consideration includes not only subjectively expected benefits (or value) of an action but also factors such as moral perception of the action, investments (in terms of money, time, education or preparation) needed and opportunity costs (Anand, 1993: 4). "There are ethical and personal subjective variations at stake" when making the decision whether to take the risk or not "even more than with the perception of risk, which also involves subjective valuations" (Ale, 2009: 112). In short, individuals take risks because they value some actions above simple risk-avoiding behaviour.

The moral or ethical primacy of other values can be seen as overriding the consideration of safety. Taking risk occurs when the subjective cost associated with action is lower than the subjective moral or ethical benefit resulting from it. For example, the risk of injury, death or loss of money or status is less important than outcomes such as saving someone's life. This has been found to be a significant factor in justifying risky choices made by firefighters (Nelkin and Brown, 1984: 97). The emphasis is not on "high-level" moral principles that could make some actions *always* more morally desirable so that any risk is justified. Rather, it is the expression of "a general ethical statement about some moral value" which has no claim to generalisation (Espinoza and Peterson, 2012: 8). As such, these principles are applicable on a case-by-case evaluation of every potentially risky situation. The moral assessment of risk-taking is unlikely to yield unambiguous results, as drawing a line between morally "permissible and impermissible risks" is impossible because it is "an area in which there is no precision and exactness to be found" (Espinoza and Peterson, 2012: 9).

Another concept that is deployed to assess risk-taking in practice is "edgework" (Lyng, 1990, 2005). It is applied to the pleasure and emotional buzz some people can experience when voluntarily taking risks. Coined by Stephen Lyng, the concept of edgework explores why people take risks as part of leisure activities that "involve a clearly observable threat to one's physical or mental well-being or one's sense of an ordered existence" (1990: 857). Edgework is understood as exposing oneself to an extreme, potentially lethal risk. The main value ascribed to risk-taking in this context is that it "takes place around cultural boundaries; such as those between life and death, consciousness or unconsciousness, sanity or insanity" (Lupton, 1999: 151). Edgework combines heightened emotional intensity with the ability to control one's fear. Heightened feelings are brought together with "an emphasis on skilled performance" and ability "not to give into fear" (Lupton, 1999: 152). Based on Lyng's approach, the practical considerations of edgework have been researched. Despite, or because of, being dangerous, "such situations make possible the display of daring, resourcefulness, skill and sustained endeavour, where people are only too aware of the risks involved in what they are doing but use them to create an edge which routine circumstances lack" (Giddens, 1991: 132). Edgework may undermine the basic security of the individual, but it provides compensation through the positive feelings it evokes. "There is the belief among those who engage in edgework that 'mental toughness' [which it requires] is an innate ability, possessed by only a select and elite few" (Lupton, 1999: 152). Lupton argues that such activities create a strong feeling of community and closely bind together people who engage in them. Edgework is not only about physical elation but in certain quarters of everyday life, such as in the routine of war reporting, it is seen as "vital to self-realisation and improvement", an opportunity for personal growth and a professional "test of fire" (Lupton, 1999: 152 ff.).

The literature on risk-taking and everyday life identifies a number of explanations for risk-taking. It can be accounted for by irrationality, and in some cases people take risks without knowing why they do so. This offers little as a way forward as an explanation for professional practice; yet it cannot be ignored. The stipulation that for many people moral values take precedence over risk aversion provides a more fruitful way of understanding why certain individuals take risks. The literature on edgework justifies risk-taking in a number of ways, one of which is the calculation of the practical goals that can be achieved from taking a risk, such as a better job or a higher salary – calculations of professional advancement. Other scholars suggest that risk-taking must be seen in the context of the emotions it provides, such as the adrenaline rush or thrill-seeking or the increased feeling of control over one's own body or life. These arguments suggest that risk-taking can in certain circumstances be regarded as a rationally justifiable choice. Lupton (1999: 152) refers to the "fellowship of danger" that binds people together. Journalists and, in particular, war reporters are an example of a professional group that willingly and freely exposes itself to taking risks. This is not simply a matter of individual choice; it is engrained into the professional ideology of journalism, encouraged by the cultural characteristics of news organisations and expected by audiences. Assessment of risk in the professional practice of individual media practitioners depends on a number of different considerations.

Risk and journalism

Getting risk wrong is the theme of much scholarly research into risk and journalism. Inaccurate or incomplete reports tend to present risks as being more certain than they actually are. Journalists are criticised for the selective reporting of risk, the failure to explain risk, not giving enough attention to particular risks and the amplification of other risks. For some, there is the question of whether journalists should report risk at all; not to do so might avoid unnecessary panic. More specifically, studies have found that journalists are too dependent on 'official sources' in their coverage of risk and that they focus on short-term remedies rather than long-run solutions, which encourages risky behaviour. Whatever the perspective, journalism is identified as playing an important role in the construction of risk and the risk society. Calculation of risk is also an essential component of the occupational culture and organisational structure of journalism. Given the importance attributed to the media in the construction of risk and the attention paid by scholars to how professional groups calculate and frame risk, it is surprising that there has been limited examination of the how journalists manage risk in their everyday work. The research that has been done has tended to concentrate on the aspects of the news production process which lead journalists to be selective in their reporting of risk and that shape reporting to construct particular understandings and interpretations of risk and risky behaviour (see Kitzinger, 1999; Kitzinger and Reilly, 1997). Jenny Kitzinger and Jackie Reilly (1997) cite journalists' training, newsworthiness, the organisation of news beats and source competition as contributory factors explaining why certain risks are "highlighted" and others "overlooked". They are critical of how standard news production studies have "failed to account for the reporting of 'risk'". Few news production studies have attempted to explore how risk plays a part in the decision-making process of journalism. There is little consideration of how the practice of journalism is both facilitated and inhibited by the orientation of the media and journalism to the risk society.

It is important to stress that any assessment of risk and journalism practice must be anchored in the notion of contestation. News production is a matter of contestation between the various actors involved in the gathering, processing and dissemination of news. What is newsworthy, or which stories have news value, is often a process of negotiation. Alexander Cockburn (1988) talks about the "terms of the trade" of the profession as reporters try to sell their stories to the news desk or bargain with sources to obtain information. Such negotiations are determined by a number of factors from the personal values of those involved to the institutional requirements of the organisation they work for to the expectations of the society in which they work. Consensus and conflict are apparent; while there is agreement that certain stories should be done, there are other stories that are subject to differences of opinion. How stories should be covered is open to more discussion and disagreement. Disputes and competition in the processing of a story take place within an environment characterised by an unequal distribution of power and authority and subject to intervention from forces external to the production process. This is the occupational culture and organisational environment in which journalists make risk calculations.

There are a number of ways in which journalists incorporate calculations of risk into their work practices. First, sourcing news entails making judgements about the truthfulness and motives of those who are telling you their stories. Misjudgement can result in consequences for professional and personal standing as well as the reputation of the news organisation that publishes the account. Not only will sources become more sceptical of approaching you with their stories but news organisations may perceive you as a liability. Second, the failure to produce stories represents an editorial risk. Editors and news desks expect their men and women in the field to generate a constant flow of news stories. This satisfies institutional requirements such as the costs incurred in deploying reporters and the need to fill the page, screen and airwaves. Letting down the home office and editors can lead to various penalties from the loss of an assignment through the spiking of stories to the non-cooperation of the desk. Pamela Shoemaker and Stephen Reese (1991), in their study of the news production process, identify a number of levels at which negotiation over the content of news take place. These can be seen as having corresponding levels of risk. What is perceived as risk will vary according to these levels and risk-taking behaviour will be assessed according to calculations made at each level.

The different levels identified by Shoemaker and Reese (1991) are individual, organisational, social and cultural. They are subject to different scholarly interpretation, but from the perspective of risk-taking, they can be described as follows. At the individual level, journalists' work is shaped by a series of psychological factors – personal, political and professional. Their disposition to their work and how they do it is a product of their attitudes and understanding. Journalism is also shaped by the organisational routines and structures in which practitioners function. These routines and structures constrain and facilitate action, and individual decisions have to be made within the organisational environment. The growth of freelance reporting in the last couple of decades has not minimised organisational influences. In fact, the need to sell stories to major news outlets has made freelance reporters more conscious of the organisational environment in which they operate. The occupational culture of reporters is characterised by both conflict and co-operation which determine their everyday experiences. Relationships with other social institutions involve another type of negotiation that journalists go through in their daily work. Stories do not grow on trees; they cannot be picked and packaged. Most journalists rely on external sources for information about what is happening. Much of the 'legwork' in gathering news and information is not done by reporters but by their sources. This environment has been transformed in the wake of new technology, and government and non-government organisations are more professional and effective in their public relations and propaganda techniques. Finally, there are cultural expectations of the journalist. Shoemaker and Reese focus on the ideological parameters within which journalists have to work in any society. However, society has expectations of how journalists should perform their roles. Barbara Korte (2009: 13) draws attention to the need to deliver a performance for an audience, something particularly visible in the world of contemporary television. The role playing that audiences demand is manifest in the cultural representations of the profession, fictional and non-fictional. Although roles are not fixed, but subject to contestation, they "configure and foreground certain aspects" of journalists and their behaviour. Risk-taking therefore has to be seen in the context of a variety of factors including group dynamics, trust in colleagues and sources, professional status and standing, the editorial process, audience expectations as well as the working environment of a particular story. These are all elements that constitute the risk biographies of journalists.

Risk and the war correspondent

There are then a number of reasons why journalists are risk inclined. Notions such as cultural choice, professional advancement and thrill-seeking are all reasons why journalists take risks. These factors are particularly applicable to war zone journalism. It is claimed that "to some, war reporting is exciting; it's an adventure. To others, war reporting is a noble cause ... still other journalists like war reporting because it can provide a quick path to professional success" (Sullivan, 2006: 12). These seemingly different motivations share the same theoretical precept – they assume that a value, whether it be the thrill, ethical or moral concern or career aspiration, takes precedence over basic risk aversion. However, it can be argued that the manner in which these motivations are woven together distinguishes the risk culture of war correspondence.

A number of characteristics have been identified which distinguish war reporters as a group. Despite the claim that there is convergence in the practices and orientations of journalism, the profession is, unlike most others, practiced in a variety of ways. There are shared values that give some coherence to journalism, but distinct occupational subcultures exist within the profession making it "difficult to generalise about the practices, experiences and self-images of news workers within them" (Harries and Wahl-Jorgensen, 2007: 621). What distinguishes war reporting as a 'beat' is a matter of scholarly deliberation. Several characteristics have been put forward. War correspondents are seen as exercising a greater degree of autonomy. There is a perception within the profession that they have more independence and freedom from their news desks. They are spared the editorial restrictions that constrain other correspondents. Before the advent of the new media, this was regarded as a product of geographical distance between the editor back home and the reporter in the field. Editors did not have the information about the circumstances on the ground to make decisions about who to talk to, logistics, hazards and storyline. In the confusion of war, more emphasis is placed on the man or woman on the spot, who can assess the lie of the land. As a result, war reporters are often labelled as 'mavericks' or 'individualists' who plough their own furrow. Their degree of autonomy is seen as singling them out as the 'elite' of the journalism profession. Mark Pedelty (1995), in his anthropological study of the press corps who covered the brutal war in El Salvador in the 1980s, distinguishes the status of correspondents primarily on the basis of their autonomy to follow their own leads and deploy their own strategies to obtain stories.

War reporting is also differentiated on commercial grounds. War is a 'big story', and the commercial gains to be made by media outlets from its prosecution have been emphasised. For editors and owners, war not only sells copy, increases circulation and boosts profits, but also provides a regular supply of the product, helping to manage costs. This gives war correspondents some degree of primacy in the newsgathering process. Wars, as David Welch (2007: xiv) puts it, offer reporters "unique opportunities to impose themselves on a news story". The specialism is regarded as the high point of career aspiration in journalism. War correspondents have regularly acquired a degree of stardom, highlighting the extent to which the specialism is deeply anchored in our culture. They are envied by colleagues and celebrated by society. War reporting is also seen as the apogee of eyewitnessing, viewed traditionally as one of the defining qualities of journalism. The function of witnessing in wartime demands different abilities and aptitudes to those required in other forms of journalism. The proximity of the war correspondent to his or her primary sources is unlike that of other correspondents, and interaction with sources often takes place under a more pressurised set of circumstances. War correspondents display a high degree of camaraderie, manifest in familiar flak-jacketed reporters turning up in large numbers when conflict breaks out. Behind this assessment is the assumption that war reporters are more closely connected to one another by the dangerous nature of their job. War reporters also have a more nuanced relationship with objectivity. Patriotism and professionalism rub up against each other more violently in the reporting of war and conflict. The fear of being accused 'unpatriotic' has exercised considerable sway over war reporters. Other characteristics could be added, and the extent to which they identify the 'exceptionalism' of war reporters or whether they indicate a greater intensity or simply an extension of the work of the everyday reporter are moot points. While war correspondents are not a homogeneous group, there is a degree of commonality in the experiences, values, attitudes and approaches of the people who report wars that differentiates them from other types of journalists.

The exceptionalism of war correspondents is seen as making them more risk oriented than other reporters. Their daily dance with death, as the more sensational accounts of the work would put it, is crucial in shaping the culture of risk that surrounds what they do. However, what makes them prone to risk-taking is not simply a matter of how they deal with "moments in hell" (Harding Davis, 1910). The means by which war correspondents cope with death and destruction and manage trauma and stress has been documented in recent years. Less emphasis has been placed on the other aspects of their working environment that make risk-taking an intrinsic component of their job. Individual correspondents negotiate these pressures in different ways. Brian Creech (2017) stresses that the "exposure to risk is unevenly distributed" between correspondents, with freelance and local journalists facing a greater variety of risks. How they manage risk at the personal level has to be seen in the context of their interpretation of audience expectations, organisational demands, market conditions, professional beliefs, the aims and hopes of sources, the actions of fellow correspondents and so on. Managing the hazards and dangers of operating on the ground has to be set against calculations about other risks, such as letting down sources, failing to satisfy the news desk and negotiating relationships with colleagues. In recent years, moral, commercial, organisational and technological changes have accentuated the risk-taking environment in which war reporters work, and these are the subject of the next three chapters.

Notes

1   This chapter draws on the work of and conversations with Dominic Sipinski, an Erasmus Mundus master's degree student who wrote his dissertation on risk and freelance war correspondents in 2014.
2   Mick Bloor demonstrated this with the example of female and male prostitutes whose lack of power in their relationships with their clients caused them, in spite of knowledge to the contrary, to participate in unsafe sex practices.

2

BEARING WITNESS

Morality, risk and war reporting

To understand why war correspondents take risks, it is important to identify the explanations provided by the profession. Risk-taking has been justified on several grounds. Some correspondents draw attention to the competitive element of the job, and being 'first with the news' is the pinnacle of this aspect of their work. For others, there is an obligation to posterity. Their job is to provide the 'first rough draft of history'. Scrutinising the powers that be, holding the military and government and combatants to account for their actions, is part of the watchdog role of journalism. Imparting the truth of the battlefield by 'being there' and offering an eyewitness account of what has happened is also emphasised. In recent years the notion of 'bearing witness' to conflict has become more prevalent in how war correspondents make sense of the role of journalism in wartime. Conflict initially was defined exclusively in relation to the battlefield. Reporting war was a matter of tactics, strategy and the exploits of those involved, the military. The soldiers at the front became the staple component of coverage. As war reporting developed, the impact of war on a broader range of actors was taken into account. Those caught up in conflict, the civil population, increasingly became the subject of war correspondence. As the boundary between the home front and the battlefield has become more blurred, the civilian victims of conflict are more central to the story. Bearing witness to the broader suffering of war is today the main reason given by many journalists for taking risk.

This chapter examines the evolution of the notion of bearing witness and its implication for risk-taking. Being an eyewitness on the battlefield has guided war reporting since the days of William Howard Russell. Correspondents have put themselves in personal danger in order to 'tell it like it is'. The commitment to objectivity and independent observation that grew with the development of news journalism in the 20th century reinforced this notion. Technological developments such as the telegraph, telex, camera and radio enhanced the capacity for and commitment to eyewitnessing. Bearing witness takes this commitment further by articulating a moral dimension to war reporting. Richard Sambrook (2010: 6) draws attention to how much international reporting has come to be informed by a "narrative of conscience, a focus on victims and the humanitarian consequences of big events". This commitment provides greater legitimacy for journalism's presence on the battlefield and has been incorporated into the expectations that editors and audiences have of war correspondents. By serving as a witness to death, destruction, killing and suffering, war reporting provides the profession with a "more noble purpose" as well as justifying intrusion into the anguish and distress of others (Tait, 2011: 1221). The capacity to bear witness has been further enhanced in the digital age. Transport and telecommunications advances have not only transformed the ability of war correspondents to bear witness to extraordinary events around the world but media technology such as the mobile phone has increased the number of people able to witness. Previously marginalised individuals now have the capacity to narrate their own experiences of war, and news organisations have integrated their accounts into the reporting of global events (see Anden-Papadopoulos and Panatti, 2013). This is a challenge to traditional correspondents. Some journalists place more emphasis on their role as witnesses, being willing to provide personal testimony at the criminal trials of alleged perpetrators of war atrocities (see Tumber, 2008). This is part of a reassessment of the role of war reporters in the form of the "journalism of attachment", a journalism which "cares as well as knows" (Bell, 1998: 16). The strengthening of the commitment to bear witness has led war correspondents to embrace a greater level of risk as a result of the need to be closer to those caught up in warfare.

Eyewitnessing

Eyewitnessing is a central tenet of news journalism. It is "the oldest and perhaps most valuable tool in the journalist's arsenal" and "a foundation of war reporting" (Carr, 2014). The concept has undergone considerable changes over time. Barbie Zelizer distinguishes a number of stages in the evolution of eyewitnessing, highlighting how in each period the method throws up "issues within journalism about the most effective way to craft credible and authoritative narratives for happenings in the real world" (2007: 425). War and conflict have provided an important backdrop to journalism's need for eyewitnessing as well as highlighting the problems associated with it as a means of newsgathering. Zelizer emphasises the problems of 'being there' but perhaps pays less attention to *why* correspondents are there. Changes in the motivations of reporters for being at war are noticeable in the contemporary world. Witnessing in today's world of risk and uncertainty is more complicated. Kelly Oliver (2004) draws the distinction between two kinds of witnessing: *eyewitnessing*, which refers to descriptions of battlefield deaths; and *bearing witness*, which is concerned with the evaluation of these deaths. Increasingly war correspondents are preoccupied with the moral, ethical and political evaluation of what they have witnessed.

The shift to bearing witness has been gradual. The earliest articulation of journalists' witnessing during wartime is attributable to the London *Times*' most celebrated editor, John Delane. In response to an enquiry from Russell in 1854 about whether he should comment on what he had seen or hold his tongue, Delane stated: "Continue, as you have done, to tell the truth, and as much of it as you can, and leave such comment as may be dangerous to us, who are out of danger" (quoted in Knightley, 2003a: 11). The job of the correspondent in the field to tell what he or she sees became the yardstick by which the war correspondents of the 19th century plied their trade. Being present on the battlefield as a means of truth telling was motivation for the early war reporters. Russell, in his reports of various military encounters during the Crimean War, would often tell his reader that he was unable to verify what had happened because he had not been present (see, for example, The Times, 1854). F. Lauriston Bullard (1914: viii), in his account of the lives of the most celebrated war correspondents of the 19th century, summed up the commonly held view amongst these reporters that "it is of vast importance to humanity that the truth shall be told about war". Tales of their work concentrated on the struggles to be present at the fighting and to get the story back (see Bullard, 1914; Mathews, 1957). Moreover, as Bullard notes, witnessing events was not necessarily seen by these reporters as an act of indifference. For some of them, "publicity is the greatest agency for the promotion of the cause of peace" (Bullard, 1914: viii). The cause of peace was not their only motivation. Many British reporters in the late 19th century regarded the act of witnessing as part of extolling the glories of the empire. Russell articulated the notion of speaking up on behalf of the ordinary soldier. While his criticism of the treatment of the rank-and-file soldier was modest by contemporary standards, Russell's reporting drew attention to the role of the reporter in speaking for those involved in conflict. Russell's rival, Edwin Godkin of the *Daily News*, cast the war correspondent as the eyes and ears of the public. He believed that the presence of the reporter on the battlefield of the Crimea "brought home to the War Office the fact that the public had something to say about the conduct of wars and that they are not the concern exclusively of sovereigns and statesmen" (quoted in Knightley, 2003a: 16).

The American Civil War generated copy – not typical of the coverage of 19th-century warfare – that focused on the plight of those involved, on the "futile, bloody side of war" (Knightley, 2003a: 32). War correspondents started to write atrocity stories in the late 19th century. These reports initially tended to be part of the story of war rather than any attempt on the correspondents' behalf to strike an 'anti-war' posture or to speak on behalf of the victims of the excesses of warfare. During the American Civil War, these stories were a feature of the propaganda efforts of a partisan press to depict the enemy as barbarous and brutal (Wilkinson-Latham, 1979: 79). The advent of photography promised to show the true horrors of war. Roger Fenton and James Robertson, possibly the first war photographers, went to the Crimea to photograph the conflict, but their dispositions led them to take group pictures of military personnel and panoramic views of the battlefield (Gervais, 2010). Their representation of war was devoid of suffering. Felice Beato, an Italian who became a British citizen, produced more vivid pictures of death and destruction during the Indian Mutiny (1857–58) and second China war (1860) (Wilkinson-Latham, 1979: 75). However, it was Matthew Brady's pictures of the American Civil War battlefield that challenged the romantic image of warfare. *The New York Times* (1862) described Brady's photographs as doing "something to bring home to us the terrible reality and earnestness of war". His pictures of the dead on the battlefield were displayed in an exhibition *The Dead of Antietam*, which drew considerable press attention. These pictures were not and could not be reproduced in the newspapers – they were more likely to be incorporated into the newspapers as sketches and drawings (Gervais, 2010: 374). The images of war in the public domain for most of the 19th century were the business of war artists and illustrators; they dominated the visual culture of war, which with some exceptions glorified and/or sanitised war rather than exposing its horrors. The risks of representing war as it actually was proved too great in Victorian society, which romanticised warfare and its combatants and contextualised conflict as part of the imperial venture.

Correspondents in the late 19th century slowly began to reflect on their role as eyewitnesses. Russell had expressed the view during the Crimean War that the "horrors of war cannot be described" (quoted in Zelizer, 2007: 415). This was not simply a matter of unpalatable accounts but of the practical problems of looking for facts about events that the war correspondent had not witnessed. Russell's concern about the suffering of those swept up by war was reinforced by his experience of the Indian Mutiny. This led him to privately express his unease about colonialism and the attitudes of the British towards the Indian people. In print, however, he did not pursue his personal disquiet, though he was one of the few journalists to write about the mass executions of Indians in the aftermath of the mutiny. The risk to his reputation was a major consideration. Still, the work of war correspondents was slowly infused by a humane and moral dimension. This to some extent reflected growing efforts to establish a universal code of practice for warfare. In 1863 the International Red Cross was set up by Swiss citizen Henri Dunant in response to what he had witnessed in the wake of the Battle of Solferino in 1859. More than 30,000 helpless, wounded soldiers from both sides were left on the battlefield with no one to care for them. In 1864 Dunant published the Geneva Convention, which subsequently spawned a variety of other conventions and protocols on the conduct of war. In 1899 under the First Hague Convention, the protection of journalists – or "persons who follow the armed forces without directly belonging thereto" as the Convention referred to them – was mentioned. These practical efforts to provide some form of legal protection and relief for those involved in war and conflict were part and parcel of a growing discourse of humanitarianism that correspondents and statesmen found it difficult to ignore. The press, aided by the development of the telegraph, brought the plight of casualties in a variety of conflicts to public attention. The conscription of ordinary men into the army fuelled public interest in the conduct of war, and the ability of *The Times* to bring down a government over its treatment of British soldiers in the

Crimea underlined for officials and generals that public opinion at times of war had to be taken into account (see Quataert, 2014).

The most celebrated case of the coverage of the horrors of war at this time was the reporting of the atrocities committed in the 1870s by Turkish forces against the Christian population of what is today modern Bulgaria. Over 15,000 men, women and children lost their lives, and more than 50 villages were razed to the ground (Bullard, 1914: 142). The London *Daily News* commissioned the celebrated war correspondent Januarius MacGahan to cover the war, and he produced a series of stories drawn from the eyewitness accounts of survivors. MacGahan's accounts "startled humanitarianism in England into a flame" (Bullard, 1914: 142), led to a change in British government policy and "caused worldwide indignation against the Turks" (Knightley, 2003a: 55). His reports were also used by Russia to declare war on the Turks. A colleague described MacGahan as "stirred by the suffering he had witnessed" (quoted in Bullard, 1914: 144). His reporting provided some impetus to the humanitarian side of war reporting, although it did not accord with the output of most of his fellow war correspondents; they tended to follow the flag and glorify atavistic war (Stearn, 1992: 139). Their reproduction of atrocity stories must be seen in the context of the official propaganda efforts and the political nature of the press in this period.

Eyewitness accounts during the 19th century were determined by the political disposition of the newspapers. Independent judgement of what happened had to be balanced against the political needs of the politicians, parties and factions who owned and, by and large, controlled the press. Correspondents were caught up in the 'war of words' that surrounded conflicts and crises. By the late 19th century, governments were increasingly sophisticated in using the press to shape public opinion at home and abroad – and atrocities served as part of the propaganda efforts of the warring parties. This was emphasised in the second Anglo-Boer war (Kent, 2013). Outrages committed by the Boers were highlighted by the British government and taken up by its supporters in the press. Many of these stories were untrue. J. A. Hobson (1901: 223), in his anti-war polemic of the period, describes newspaper accounts of incidents of Boer brutality as being characterised by "vague words … from anonymous mouths, unverified and impossible of contradiction". Eyewitness accounts in such circumstances were seen as politically tainted. Doubts about the credibility of on-the-scene reporting had been raised since the American Civil War, when exaggeration and fabrication shaped eyewitness stories (see Risley, 2012; Andrews, 1955). For reporters whose countries were not at war, independent judgement was easier to exercise. For those who were citizens of combatant nations, it was much more difficult, and fake sketches and fabricated stories were a feature of war reporting in the late 19th century. The practical problems of accessing events in the 'fog of war' and verifying the claims of sources reinforced scepticism about the ability of correspondents to eyewitness what happens on the battlefield.

The ability of war correspondents to provide independent eyewitnessing was transformed in the 1830s by the culmination of a number of changes to the profession (Broersma, 2007; Hoyer and Pottker, 2005). These changes allowed the individual reporter in the field to acquire greater autonomy. On-the-spot reporting had been facilitated in the 1830s by development of skills such as shorthand, which enabled the reporter to more efficiently reproduce an eyewitness account (Smith, 1977: 162–3). Technological innovations such as the electric telegraph made it possible for correspondents to provide eyewitness accounts of wars and crises further afield and get them back to home offices more quickly. The demand for newspapers to have their own men and women at the scene of a major story was further heightened in a more competitive newspaper market. The casual, ad hoc arrangements for gathering news were replaced by the employment of regular full-time correspondents (Elliott, 1977). War correspondents had high profiles; war was a 'big story' which enabled newspapers to put on circulation. The status and notoriety of these correspondents were boosted by the introduction of the byline (see Campbell, 2006). There had been a noisy debate[1] from the 1830s about the non-attribution of newspaper reports. Signed articles had appeared in the French and US press in the 1830s, but these were the exception. Most contributions to the press were anonymous. The byline was taken up in France following a law in 1850 that forced reporters to sign political articles (Reich and Boudana, 2014: 417). During the American Civil War, correspondents were compelled to add their names to their articles. General Joseph Hooker imposed the byline on war reporters in 1863 "as a means of attributing responsibility and blame for the publication of material he found inaccurate or dangerous to the Army of the Potomac" (quoted in Schudson, 1978: 64). Naming reporters was intended to secure "better and more careful – that is to say more responsible – work" (quoted in Campbell, 2006: 124). In the process it enhanced the reputation and exposed the identity of war journalists. Regular usage of bylines featured earlier in French newspapers than in American and British ones (see Reich and Boudana, 2014), but crucially the byline provided reporters with a greater public profile. This helped to increase their autonomy in the newsgathering process, enabling them to take more initiative and empowering them in their relationships with news editors and organisations.

The emergence of named correspondents constructed a new kind of risk. Eye-witnessing became a matter of personal calculation and competitive advantage for war correspondents. Sustaining and exploiting a reputation became an element in correspondent's decisions about the risks worth taking in the pursuit of the story. Winston Churchill gained an international reputation for his reporting of the second Boer war for *The Morning Post*. This was based on his fortuitous escape after being captured and his 'colourful' description of what happened. His eyewitness accounts of his war were embellished and in some cases fabricated. Thomas Pakenham (1979: 365–6) has shown how Churchill's report of the relief of Mafeking was made up; he was miles away riding across the Veldt at the time. Embellishment and fabrication enabled Churchill – other correspondents did the same with greater or lesser success – to build his reputation, and in this he was colluded with by his newspaper and the British public. The latter wanted tales of heroism and derring-do, and the exploits of individual correspondents could draw in the readers; the former wanted to satisfy this demand. Taking risks with the truth was more easily done when the war was going well for your side and the attitudes of your fellow correspondents were the same.

'I' witnessing

Bearing witness to conflict and warfare has been interpreted by war correspondents in two distinct ways. They are there to act as the ears and eyes – and sometimes the conscience – of the audience, their readers, listeners and viewers, to provide them with a full and truthful account of what is happening. They are also there to act for those who suffer trauma or injustice, the victims of war to whom they give voice. Today many reporters would concur with the BBC's Fergal Keane (2005: 365) when he states that his practice of journalism is motivated by the "concept of international justice" and that the "weak need protecting". Other practitioners would see this as contradicting the fundamental principles of the profession. The claim to 'bear witness' is a challenge to the practices of objectivity, the basic tenet of journalism. However, 'being there' is essential to the ability of the reporter to tell the objective truth about events. Many war correspondents understand the notion of witnessing as being "to repeat what I hear, to observe the circumstances, note the detail, and confirm what is going on with accuracy, honesty and precision" (Adie, 1998: 46). Presence is the authority on which objectivity is practiced.

The commitment to 'being there' is accompanied by personal need. Jon Steele, in his book *War Junkie*, places considerable emphasis on the correspondent's role in speaking on behalf of the innocent. "Telling their stories gave me a reason to stay alive", he says (Steele, quoted in Tumber, 2006: 443). Correspondents justify the risks to their lives and the lives of those who work closely with them in terms of their capacity to "make a difference in exposing the horrors of war and especially the atrocities that befall civilians" (Colvin, 2012). However, the moral compulsion to speak on behalf of the innocent victims who suffer the outrageous misfortunes and suffering of warfare adds to the risks taken by correspondents. The passion – some correspondents refer to what they do as a 'calling' – involved in the modern process of bearing witness, exemplified by Marie Colvin, Anthony Shadid and Remi Ochlik amongst others in Syria, encourages reporters to get closer to the action to share combatants' and victims' experiences of warfare.

Personal involvement in hostilities was experienced acutely during the 1920s and 1930s. The Great War had left an indelible mark on war journalism. Failure to fully report the devastation and death brought the profession into disrepute. People no longer fully trusted what they read in their newspapers. They no longer believed what journalists wrote. War reporters such as Sir Phillip Gibbs, knighted for his services to journalism, had to apologise for their reporting (Gibbs, 1923). More significantly, a new generation of war reporters was born who were motivated by a commitment to report what they witnessed and to challenge any effort to censor or control where they could go and what they could write and report. These men and women took risks not only in going to war zones but also in speaking out about what they saw and how they were treated. They believed that taking these risks was necessary if the profession was to regain the public's trust and re-establish its authority.

Balancing the integrity of the profession and the personal commitment of the reporter was a problem during the interwar years. Taking sides, in the sense of making judgements about who was telling you what, and informing your readers of this was risky. John Reed was an example of the new breed of war correspondent. Politically sympathetic to the new force of communism, Reed is most celebrated for travelling to Russia to record the Soviet revolution. His short working career as a journalist – he died in Russia at the age 34 – shook the profession. Reed took sides with the ordinary man and woman and their struggles. His form of journalism broke new ground by championing the underdog and providing powerful descriptions of war, political protest and revolutionary action. He went to Mexico in 1911 to cover the conflict ignited by Pancho Villa's revolution. He completely identified with the peasantry and lived and breathed their struggle. A contemporary described his journalism as follows:

> his reports overflow with life and movement: simple, savage men, capricious cruelty, warm comradeship, splashes of colour, bits of song, fragments of social and political dreams, personal peril, gay humour, reckless daring. ... Reed's mingling of personal adventure with camera-eye close-ups lighted by a poet's vision made superb reporting.
>
> *(Wolfe, 1965: 38)*

Reed learned much of his trade from Lincoln Steffens, who edited *McClure's Magazine*, which specialised in muckraking journalism, seeking to expose social ills in order to bring about change. Commitment to political and/or social causes was adopted by reporters such as Reed, John Spivak and Agnes Smedley. They placed themselves at the heart of the events they were reporting and expressed themselves in textual terms in the first person.

In the wake of the 'Red Scare' in post-war America, the political nature of such reporting made it more difficult to practice. However, the technique of personal testimony permeated war correspondence of this period. Personal experience was highly valued. Noel Monks, writing for the *Daily Express*, referred to the "days in foreign reporting when personal experiences were copy" (quoted in Deacon, 2008: 46). He described such reports as 'I' stories, and they were a notable feature of the reporting of the most significant conflict of the period, the Spanish Civil War (1936–39). The most celebrated exponents of this kind of reporting were Martha Gellhorn and her then husband, Ernest Hemingway. They valued their independence and individuality and identified with parties to conflict. Kate McLoughlin (2007: 8–9) notes several features that tended to demarcate this kind of journalism. The articles were long, they featured irregularly, and they did not adhere to tight deadlines, which consequently meant there was an interval between the events described and the publication of the article. Reporters had a looser relationship with their editors and the publications they filed for – many of them were seasoned special correspondents who worked on a freelance basis or staff correspondents with considerable internal status within the news organisation (Deacon, 2008: 49). They often travelled alone, relying on the communities they passed through, and prided themselves on including their insights into what they themselves felt and the feelings of the people caught up in the events they reported.

The emphasis on personal experiences and observations was sometimes motivated by narrow ideological considerations. For some reporters, it was a matter of their political affiliation – Claud Cockburn, who wrote under the pseudonym Frank Pitcairn for the *Daily Worker*, is an example of a reporter whose partisanship influenced what he reported during the Spanish Civil War. He abused personal testimony to misrepresent events in favour of the republican side – or rather the communist element of the republican cause (see Deacon, 2008; Preston, 2008). His equivalent on the nationalist side was Cecil Gerahty of the *Daily Mail*, an ardent Francoist (Deacon, 2008: 60–1). For other reporters, personal testimony was a response to editors' demand for more human interest copy in an age of acute newspaper competition. For most correspondents, personal testimony was the basis on which to demonstrate the integrity of their reporting (Deacon, 2008: 46). First-hand news was deemed the only way to establish the veracity of the stories and facts reported. Described as 'reportage', this kind of journalism thrived between the wars. Often associated with French journalistic culture, it brought together literature and reporting, providing a personal account of war which demanded the reporters attain close proximity to events and the people involved. Reportage was facilitated by technological developments, in particular the advent of the lightweight camera, the Leica. It is not surprising that there was a need for closeness, most famously summed up by war photographer Robert Capa, who said, "if your pictures aren't good enough, you are not close enough". The essence of good reportage was that you had to be more involved and intimate with your subjects. This meant reporters being in the line of fire and taking greater risks.

The arrival of radio placed more emphasis on personal testimony in reporting conflict. The amount of original radio reporting of war was limited (see Krause, 2011), but sound broadcasting in the 1930s had an impact on the practice of war journalism. The ability to reproduce the sounds and action of war more vividly and directly fuelled demand for personal testimony of warfare. H. V. Kaltenborn was the first American radio reporter to broadcast live from the battlefield, hidden in a haystack between the warring parties in the Spanish Civil War (Finkelstein, 2010: 115). His experience highlights the danger of performing 'I' witness journalism. Correspondents' attempts to get closer to the fighting in order to capture the true face of war increased the threat to personal safety – it also added, as many found out, to the professional risk of doing the job.

Perceptions of their political or personal stance towards the conflict being covered led to criticism of war reporters' performance. During the interwar years, many reporters were expelled from Spain, Italy, Germany and several countries in Eastern Europe (see Desmond, 1984: part 1). The capacity to do the job was more problematic; access was more difficult, and during the Spanish Civil War, few correspondents had the opportunity to report from both sides. The dangers of being used by the warring party to which you were accredited became more acute – sometimes the credibility of reporters was undermined as they passed on dubious information from the sources to which they were close. Attacks on individual reporters and news organisations because of their coverage of Spain had been apparent before the civil war broke out – for example, the Havas agency in Madrid was riddled with bullets in 1934 (Desmond, 1984: 36). A number of correspondents were arrested and expelled on espionage charges, and during the war, several reporters – including Arthur Koestler, who worked for the *News Chronicle* – were nearly executed for 'spying' (see Deacon, 2008; Desmond, 1984; Preston, 2008). Reportage brought correspondents into conflict with their news desks. Herbert Matthews and Lionel Farnsworth, who reported for *The New York Times* from Madrid and Barcelona respectively, regularly found their accounts cut and changed (Prieto, 2007: 4). Their coverage of the war was the subject of protests from religious and political organisations. Matthews, in particular, was the recipient of a sustained campaign. While he was trying to personalise his journalism, some of his readers perceived him to be pushing an increasingly one-sided picture of the situation. Vituperative criticism from the Catholic Church eventually posed a threat to his career; he increasingly struggled to "capture headlines on the front few pages with the frequency he once had" (Prieto, 2007: 30).

Commentators looking back on the war have found it difficult to approve of the reporting of Matthews and his colleagues. Philip Knightley, for example, believes this type of reporting did a disservice to war reporting. Their "personal involvement made the war correspondents unable to fulfil their duty because they had lost their objectivity", and they "oversimplified a very complex situation" (Knightley, 2003a: 234), failing to report the "imperfect face of the Republican side" (233). Their 'I' witnessing in some circumstances provided a threat to professional integrity and the reliability of the news outlets they worked for. A balance had to be struck and in one case this led *The New York Times* to print two contradictory accounts of the nationalists' capture of Teruel in 1937 (Zelizer, 2007: 418). Many editors were concerned by the tendency as they saw it for "newspaper reporters to go Red" (quoted in Deacon, 2008: 54). This concern was not so much motivated by political bias but by the way in which many reporters did the job. Personal witnessing in the interwar years heightened the professional risk of reporting from the war zone.

Witnessing and the Second World War

The professional risk associated with 'I' journalism melted away during the Second World War. Reporters were encouraged to take sides, and in the fight against fascism many signed up to the Allied cause. Close connection with the fighting man was epitomised by the journalism of the award-winning correspondent Ernie Pyle. Pyle witnessed the sacrifice and suffering of American soldiers sent to help liberate

Europe. He had a free hand from his editors to roam the battlefield, looking for stories, storing them up to write once he had left the scene of the fighting. He did not have to file daily but had the time and space to produce columns on the tragedy, comradeship and personal fortitude that constituted the soldier's experience. Pyle did not conceive of his role in political terms. He was not interested in politics or holding the powerful to account or giving a voice to the victims of war. He reported on the heroism and hardships of the American soldier, and his first-hand battlefield reports provide insight into what it was like for 'our boys' at the front. As his colleague, the novelist and correspondent John Steinbeck, wrote, his reporting was of a

> war of the homesick, weary, funny, violent, common men who wash their socks in their helmets, complain about the food, whistle at Arab girls [sic] or any girls for that matter, and bring themselves through as dirty a business as the world has ever seen and do it with humor and dignity and courage – and that is Ernie Pyle's war.
>
> *(Schneider and Schneider, 2003: 121)*

Pyle's journalism constituted another kind of risk, that of becoming too close to those you report on. This is apparent in his uncritical and heroic reporting of the soldier. Many of his critics contend that "Pyle deliberately ignored and smoothed over the bungling of American commanders, the avoidable tragedies, the full horror of battlefield carnage and such ugly incidents as the slapping of two shell-shocked soldiers by General George S. Patton" (Browne, 1997). James Tobin (1997), in his appraisal of Pyle's reporting, draws attention to the dilemma between the need to tell the truth and the need to give his readers what they want to hear. Pyle was adored by millions of Americans; his fame was cemented by his Pulitzer Prize in 1944, and he was the subject of the Hollywood movie *The Story of G.I. Joe*. Pyle became trapped in his persona as the ordinary soldier's friend, and his capacity to provide eyewitness accounts of war was increasingly trammelled by his audience's expectations. His premature death in 1945 perhaps rescued his reputation from a dilemma which ultimately would have questioned the quality and accuracy of his war reporting.

During the Second World War, correspondents took every opportunity to accompany soldiers at war, queuing up to participate in bombing missions over Germany, parachute drops, glider missions, naval convoys and army operations. The new medium of radio facilitated the reproduction of the actuality of war. This increased the risk to the reporter. Two BBC reporters, Guy Byam and Kent Stevenson, were amongst a number of correspondents killed in air raids. The effort to get close to the action put correspondents in greater danger, but it also set up a close bond with the fighting men with whom they shared the risk. As many, if not more, reporters were killed during the Second World War as in Vietnam. The collaboration between reporter and soldier, their sense of being on the same side, led more reporters to share battlefield experiences with the military. Reporters at the front, however, had a fine line to tread between meeting audience expectations of 'live' battlefield reports and the need to get the tone of the coverage correct. For example, Charles Gardner's pioneering account of a dogfight over the channel brought criticism from some listeners. His overt enthusiasm for the demise of the German aircrew was disparaged; according to one listener, he was "likening grim reality to that of a Derby scene" (quoted in Elmes, 2013: 118). Getting the tone wrong risked alienating sections of the audience.

Challenges to witnessing

The problems of witnessing were drawn into relief by the reporting of concentration camps and Nazi Germany's treatment of minority cultures. In 1945, with victory in sight and weary from the travails they had gone through, correspondents were confronted by the greatest horror of the conflict. Nothing prepared them for what they found in the concentration camps liberated in the last weeks of the war. There had been some awareness during the war that the Nazis had been rounding up Jews and gypsies as well as their political opponents and systematically murdering them. Reports were filed from the World Jewish Congress and the Polish government in exile about the deaths of Jews in German-occupied Europe, and CBS' Ed Murrow told his listeners in 1942 of "mass murder and moral depravity unequalled in the history of the world" (quoted in Moseley, 2017: 301). However, talk of genocide and slaughter in such large numbers, the legacy of distrust left by the atrocity propaganda from the First World War, and a reluctance to accept that a nation with such a history of culture and civilisation as Germany could descend to such degeneracy made it difficult for people to come to terms with the scale of what was happening. On entering the camps, correspondents were confronted by sights, stories and behaviour they were not prepared for and could not comprehend. Some – initially – were in denial. Marguerite Higgins of the *New York Herald-Tribune*, suspecting the horrors were part of a propaganda campaign, began interrogating inmates (Moseley, 2017: 303). Alan Moorehead spoke of "having no stomach for this sort of thing" (quoted in Collier, 1989: 188). Correspondents struggled with how to represent what they were witnessing.

Most of the reporters who went to camps shared Ed Murrow's experience; one of his colleagues said, "he felt inadequate, defeated by his inability to handle what he saw" (Collingwood, quoted in Moseley, 2017: 302). He told his listeners, "I have reported what I saw and heard, but only part of it. For most of it I have no words" (Murrow, quoted in Moseley, 2017: 302). The reporters were worried about their ability to convey what they saw and whether they would be believed. On entering Buchenwald, Richard Dimbleby was profoundly affected by what he saw, but his highly charged report was initially not believed by the BBC, which refused to broadcast it. They demanded confirmation from other sources; Dimbleby threatened to resign, and the report was broadcast albeit in a truncated form (Collier, 1989: 188). Zelizer (2000: 84) comments on the inappropriateness of news language, the problem of putting such scenes into words and "generic inadequacy" of the eyewitness report when faced with such horror. Reporters, she writes, were "unable to concretize the story and ended up chronicling their own insufficiencies at the same time as they reported on what they saw" (Zelizer, 2000: 85). If the horrific scenes of the camps could not be put into words, photographers had similar problems taking pictures of the scenes (see Chapter 8). Many of those who photographed the camps talked about the personal impact it had on them (Zelizer, 2000: 87). For some, the effect would last throughout their reporting career. Martha Gellhorn writes of a "darkness" entering her spirit which eroded her belief that truth, kindness and justice would always prevail (quoted in Moorehead, 2004: 282) and subsequently shaped her capacity to witness future conflicts. The problem of witnessing the concentration camps was highlighted by a former Havas reporter who had been an inmate. He stated that "to write about this you must have been here at least two years, and after that ... you don't want to write anymore" (quoted in Kurlansky, 2002: xxviii). The inadequacy of words to describe the horror of war has subsequently confronted war correspondents in many post-war conflicts, particularly those in Bosnia and Rwanda, which one reporter described as "beyond explanation, beyond human reasoning" (quoted in de Burgh, 2000: 76).

Witnessing the post-war world

Witnessing became more problematic as the post-war world evolved. Many of the immediate post-war conflicts were primarily the outcome of decolonisation. In countries such as India, Algeria, Palestine, French Vietnam, Cyprus, Suez, Malaya, Kenya, Borneo and Indonesia the collapse of empire found the European powers struggling to maintain their increasingly anachronistic hold over their overseas territorial possessions. Initially patriotism prevailed and the reporting was "couched in an old-fashioned jingoistic, nation-superior style" (Moorcraft, 2016: 98); but as the price of maintaining empire began to rise, public opinion in the metropolitan centre became divided and it was more difficult to adhere to this approach. The nature of these wars and the way in which they were fought also had an impact. They were 'dirty wars'. The Algerian War of Independence was the exemplar. The French poured more and more troops into the country to retain its hold on Algeria, and the liberation movement resorted to a bombing campaign primarily aimed at the civilian French community. To 'pacify' the country, the French Army resorted to a counter-insurgency policy that included kidnapping and murder. Many Algerians – and some of their French supporters – disappeared or were tortured. The French press struggled to expose the illegal and immoral practices of the army. Censorship, intimidation and harassment were used to ensure the official version of events prevailed. At first, only a few individual reporters attempted to stand up to state intimidation. Reporters were expelled, newspapers were seized, newsreels were prevented from being shown in France, books were banned and levels of personal harassment were high (see Knightley, 2003a: chapter 15). Some French-Algerian journalists were tortured, and it is estimated that at least 70 journalists were killed (Freedom House, 1998). Foreign journalists were not welcome, but representatives of the international press sought ways to report the plight of the civilian population and stories of atrocities and the excessive use of force began to seep out. Correspondents resorted to a variety of undercover activities that came to characterise investigative journalism in the 20th century. American photographer Dickey Chapelle,[2] for example, was smuggled into Algeria by the rebels to report on the tactics of the French Army, and she provided a photographic account of their activities. She used deceit to gain access to the war zone dressed as a veiled woman (Moorcraft, 2016: 98). Operating in such a way, journalists like Chappelle put themselves at considerable risk during this "savage war" (Moorcraft, 2016).

The motivation of a growing number of correspondents was political and humanitarian, part of an anti-colonial sentiment that was blowing through the 1950s. The public was tired of war, and editors operating in the reduced circumstances of post-war austerity and rationing were reluctant to deploy resources to cover these conflicts. It took considerable individual strength or committed political partisanship to initiate and follow through reporting on conflict. For some, the attempt to witness what was happening led to detention and torture (see Erickson, 2013). Reporting of French military excesses often resulted in the government trying to discredit individual reporters and news organisations. Georges Chassange, a Fox Movietone News cameraman, filmed a gendarme shooting an Algerian prisoner. He was accused of paying the policeman to do this while he filmed what happened (Kuby, 2012). His footage was deemed too sensitive to be shown in France, but to much outrage in the country, the centre-left paper *L'Express* printed stills from the film in the lead-up to the 1955 election (Kuby, 2012: 46). Ironically the report engendered anti-American feeling and led to increased restrictions on reporters. This episode as well as the reports by Georges Penchenier, the Algerian correspondent of *Le Monde*, highlighted the "blind repression" (Kuby, 2012: 49; Knightley, 2003a). Strict censorship and rigid restrictions on access to troops and countryside were crucial in ensuring that relatively few reports of the excesses of the French Army appeared in the French press. Self-censorship was also a factor. Emma Kuby, in her analysis of Chassange's footage, highlights the reluctance of the film company to embarrass the authorities. Entitled *Cold Massacre of European Settlers Avenged by French*, the two-and-half-minute report was "intensely apologetic" and "justificatory" in framing an appalling act of violence (2012: 53). It was only the commitment of a number of French and international journalists to investigate what had happened that brought the suffering to light. Reporting the Algerian struggle threw into sharp relief the tension between loyalty to one's country and the professional duty to tell the truth of what one witnesses. Exercising a patriotic duty could be understood in a war of national survival; but in a struggle in which there was no direct threat to the nation, this was less straightforward.

Chappelle's reporting of the suffering of civilians at the hands of the French Army was not matched in the reporting of the last days of the British Empire. British actions, most notably in Malaya and Kenya, which included torture, mutilation, mass detention and systematic brutality against civilians, went largely unreported. The counter-insurgency campaign deployed to combat the Mau Mau rebellion in Kenya saw the incarceration of 1.5 million Kenyans and the execution of more than 1,000 individuals, more than in Algeria (see Elkins, 2005). Few British correspondents attempted to travel to the country to seek out the rebels' views despite the calls from missionaries and backbench Labour MPs for inquiries into alleged atrocities committed by the police and army. Similarly in Malaya the murder of civilians went unreported; the worst-known example, the killing of 24 villagers by Scots Guards in 1948, was not exposed until 22 years after the event (see Moorcraft, 2016). This failure is often attributed to these struggles taking place in inaccessible places, difficult and costly to reach. Malaya was a 22-hour flight from London, and on arrival the reporter had to travel on to remote jungle areas where transport was usually organised by the authorities; most correspondents usually went on trips facilitated by the military and filed stories on patrols with the British Army in an inhospitable environment (Royle, 1989: 254–5). It was easier, less risky and more efficient to report what the Colonial Office or the colonial authorities stated. Confronted by public opinion that was either indifferent to or supportive of what their government was doing and at a time when editors operated on tight budgets, making the case to travel to these war zones was difficult. Few reporters at the height of the rebellion had either the commitment or courage to risk their careers by going against the consensus.

There were exceptions such as James Cameron, who visited Kenya, travelled to the most affected parts of the country and reported on the trial of the nationalist leader Jomo Kenyatta. He was critical of British policy, police tactics and the settler community (Anderson, 2011: 90). Using the authority of the 'man on the spot', he challenged the editorial stance of the newspaper that sent him to cover the conflict. The *Daily Mirror* had by and large shared the official view in the lead-up to the declaration of a state of emergency in 1952, but as it gradually moved into opposition to the Conservative government, it became more open to criticism of colonial policy and Cameron "clearly swayed his editor" on the reporting of events in Kenya (Lewis, 2003: 235). As Britain's best-selling newspaper, the *Daily Mirror* had advantages over its competitors in the years of austerity after the Second World War, including more resources to devote to investigating stories abroad. Cameron's capacity to report the brutal facts of the war reflected the "potential for an individual journalist to shape press coverage" as well as the willingness and ability of the *Daily Mirror* to commit more correspondents overseas on investigative assignments.

The loss of moral compass that characterised the military's role in these dirty wars was partly responsible for undermining the relationship between the media and the military that had grown up between 1939 and 1945. The rigid approach of the military and authorities in handling war correspondents means that many of the wars and conflicts of the late 1940s and 1950s are characterised as 'forgotten wars'. At certain points the uprisings in Kenya and Cyprus dominated the headlines, mainly to report the plight of the settler communities in these parts of empire. Stories of the brutal attacks on isolated white farmers in Kenya and the attacks on

British servicemen and their families in Nicosia on what was dubbed Cyprus' 'Murder Mile' figured prominently in the British press. However, the suffering of the civilian populations was not witnessed by many war correspondents. These new kinds of war were more difficult to witness: a new type of enemy, guerrilla or insurgent, emerged, who infiltrated rather than engaged and whose activities had the connotations of criminality and random acts of violence. Many of these conflicts were never referred to as 'wars' by the authorities but were instead described as 'emergencies', and they took place in circumstances which were not conducive to journalistic scrutiny. As the decades progressed, these conflicts saw the terms 'bandit' and 'terrorist' preferred in labelling the insurgents, and they were eventually boiled down to 'communists' or 'Reds' as these dirty wars, whatever their causes and conditions, became embedded in the Cold War.

Cold War witnessing

American journalism had by the early 1950s become obsessed with Communism. This obsession had domestic roots with McCarthyism and the rise of the Red Scare, but internal paranoia was fuelled by what was seen as the inexorable march of communist forces overseas. American news stands were full of stories about Chinese cities and provinces falling to Mao Tse-Tung's People's Army. In 1949 the 'fall' of China and blockade of Berlin paved the way for the beginning of the Cold War. The 'Cold War frame' ultimately shaped the nature of the reporting of war and conflict between 1945 and 1989, subsuming local struggles including those surrounding the 'end of empire' discussed above. This process of incorporation developed gradually throughout the 1950s to establish itself as the dominant prism for understanding and reporting international events in the 1960s – even though an alternative perspective was adhered to by some correspondents, including many in the Global South. The war that was crucial to the transition – and perhaps the only conflict in the 1950s that received sustained attention from the international press corps – was the UN intervention in Korea (1950–53). This war, again, was often dubbed a 'forgotten war' by those who participated in it (see Huxford, 2016), but it received more press attention and representation in popular culture than any other conflicts in this period.

Witnessing is shaped not only by the personal observations of those who are there but also by the broader context in which the events take place. The 'zero-sum journalism' that characterised the Cold War confused the process of witnessing. Accounts of the plight of others could be, and were, dismissed as giving succour to the communist cause. Edward Herman and Noam Chomsky (1988) distinguish between worthy and unworthy victims based on the prism of the Cold War. The former suffer at the hands of communist regimes and their allies, while the latter are abused by their own states and their followers and supporters, backed by the US. The mainstream Western media paid more attention to witnessing the 'worthy victims' as they conformed to the ideological framework of the Cold War. Journalists who tried to tell the full story of what was happening, failing to differentiate between worthy and unworthy victims of warfare, were subject to disapproval, condemnation and career-threatening consequences. The fate of James Cameron and Bert Hardy and their editor at *Picture Post*, Tom Hopkinson, during the Korean War is an example of the price that was paid for witnessing the Cold War era. The journalists lost their jobs for a story documenting the appalling treatment of political prisoners by South Korean forces. Hardy, Cameron and Hopkinson were prevented from publishing their story by the magazine's owner, Edward Hulton, because it 'undermined' the Western cause in the Korean War. Cameron and Hardy were aware of the political sensitivity of their story but believed that the evidence of what they saw with their own eyes would be sufficient. They did their utmost to write the story with "the best restraint and care" and to "drain it of emotion", documenting the facts from their pictures and other sources (Cameron, 1967: 143). Cameron, one of Britain's leading post-war reporters, acknowledged after the event that he had to keep his head down; "one or two more of these journalistic crises would make me virtually unemployable" (Cameron, 1967: 147). The risk of losing one's career became the price for not witnessing the Cold War according to the official storyline.

The thin line between the media and the military that had developed during the Second World War was re-established with the Cold War. War correspondents operated within a closed environment (see Aronson, 1990; Fainberg, 2017). Those critical of official policy and sceptical of popular anti-communist sentiments or who challenged official accounts or attempted to paint a fuller picture of the protagonists were marginalised. The Cold War bred a sort of orthodoxy in the reporting of war and politics, and any deviation too far from prevailing attitudes led to rejection, as the celebrated American investigative journalist I. F. Stone experienced. He was blacklisted for his 'left-wing leanings' and found it difficult to work. Others were less fortunate; George Polk of CBS was murdered in 1948 after exposing the US government's links with right-wing authoritarian elements in the Greek civil war. Stepping out of line was a high-risk policy, but as the Cold War waned and a new generation of reporters emerged in the 1960s, a new moral imperative slowly came to guide the process of witnessing.

Modern witnessing

The Cold War may have formally ended with the collapse of the Berlin Wall in 1989, but the unravelling of this way of seeing the world had had started as American power faded with the progress of the Vietnam War. The correspondents who covered Vietnam were younger and had grown up in a different social environment from their colleagues who had reported the Second World War. Less deferential, more critical, were described by one military officer as "young men in a hurry, not willing or having the time to check the facts" (quoted in Mercer *et al.*, 1987: 240). The profession was changing with the rise of what some labelled 'advocacy journalism', which pitted the journalist against official accounts. Objective journalism for many of these reporters "almost always favours establishment positions and exists not least to avoid offence to them" (Wicker, 1979: 39). It was inevitable that a more interpretive form of reporting emerged which not only changed the relationship with the military but also ushered in a more aggressive and committed form of witnessing.

This form of witnessing accentuated divisions within the news media. The men and women in the field found themselves in conflict or competition with their colleagues at home. On one level, this manifested itself in a traditional way: reporters complained about the difficulty of getting their editors to accept their version of events. War correspondents have always objected to the rewriting of their copy by subeditors who were not there and could not grasp the nuances of the circumstances on the ground. They had to learn what their news desk wanted or "otherwise risk being confined to page 20 alongside the truss ads" (quoted in Mercer *et al.*, 1987: 243). War correspondents in Saigon had to fight against their colleagues assigned to the Washington 'beat', who were more positive and optimistic about what was happening. Witnessing is not just about seeing; it is also about saying (Peters, 2001: 709). During the Vietnam War correspondents often had to hedge their accounts of events in the field in response to editorial pressure and counter interpretations from their colleagues at home.

Losing the Vietnam War empowered many war reporters to believe that witnessing could change the course of war. It was not only the military that made the claim that reporting had brought about the end of the Vietnam War. It was the mantra of news executives and a large number of correspondents that, in the words of a vice-president of the US news network ABC, "by showing war in its stinking reality, we have taken away the glory and shown that negotiation is the only way to solve international problems" (quoted in Mercer *et al.*, 1987: 223). The evidence to support this claim is at best thin (see Hallin, 1986), but it became the perceived wisdom. Rippling through the reporting community, it established a new dilemma for witnessing. The perception that by witnessing modern war and warfare journalism could change the course of a conflict had a profound effect on war correspondents, combatants, particularly those in the non-Western world, and Western audiences. The lesson for the military and governments was that correspondents had to be more effectively controlled. For many war reporters, Vietnam became a template by which to judge the reporting of subsequent conflicts. Witnessing became proactive as correspondents were encouraged to seek out violations of human rights, military misdemeanours, war crimes and government cover-ups. Post-Vietnam journalism became more investigative, with reporters such as Seymour Hersh, who broke the My Lai massacre in 1967, adopting a more interrogative approach. Such reporting demanded time, resources and an outlet. News organisations in the 1970s and 1980s were willing to devote the manpower and money, and the crusading journalist was a figure of respect for the audience. This type of journalism carries high risk, financial, personal and political. There are costs to the news organisation if stories do not materialise, which became an increasing concern for correspondents as competition increased and market-driven journalism prevailed. It enhanced the expectations of many actors involved in conflict that publicity could assist their cause. Investigative war journalism was driven by the growing commitment to humanitarianism and the reporting of human rights abuses. As the BBC's George Alagiah (1999) notes, "the defence of human rights is a principle" to which leaders and government "ought to be held accountable".

Correspondents' desire to expose was matched by the hopes of those involved in conflicts that media coverage would bring about change. The rise of the 'CNN effect' corresponded with the new morality that pervaded global news reporting. Whether you accept the effect or not – and there is considerable difference of opinion within the scholarly literature – there was a growing perception in the 1990s that 24-hour news media had an impact on policymakers and public opinion. In particular, policymakers had to respond to the initiatives of the news media and journalists. Images of events on the ground forced decision makers to take action to alleviate suffering. Martin Shaw notes that in the wake of 1991 Gulf War, television forced world leaders to intervene to support the Kurdish rising in northern Iraq by putting them "on the spot, linking them directly to the visible plight of miserable refugees" (Bahador, 2007: 24). The failure to do anything about the Shi'ite rebellion in southern Iraq is attributed to the lack of pictures of the suffering of Shi'ite refugees. In the era of globalisation, many people in the Global South believed that global news coverage could change the course of their war. As a citizen of Juba, South Sudan, put it: "It may be a blessing to be in front of the camera – then at least the world will get to know about it. But it is painful to die or be killed, without anyone knowing it" (Olsen et al., 2003: 39). Armed intervention on humanitarian grounds came to be associated with regime change: David Rieff, a journalist specialising in humanitarian issues, stated that these interventions "have to be about regime change if they are to have any chance of accomplishing their goals" (quoted in Bajoria and McMahon, 2013). This connection with political change inevitably heightened the risk of practicing war reporting as governments in many parts of the world became more suspicious of the presence and objectives of reporters coming to their countries. This was acutely experienced and articulated during the conflicts in Bosnia in the 1990s.

Journalism of attachment

The small wars which broke out in Eastern Europe and the former territories of the Soviet Union in the wake of the melting of the Cold War had a major impact on war reporters. The trend to moral witnessing, according to the accounts of many of the leading correspondents who covered these wars, was accentuated by the sheer wrongdoing involved in these conflicts. Bosnia epitomised this wrongdoing and led reporters to question how they were doing their job and to openly challenge the usefulness of the basic tenet of the profession, objectivity. The BBC's Martin Bell is credited with articulating the "journalism of attachment". He argued that war correspondents had a "moral obligation" to distinguish between "good" and "evil" and make judgements about wrongdoing when they came across it in a war zone (Bell, 1997: 8). Perpetrators of war crimes should be called to account and the human and emotional cost of war should be documented, and it was the reporter's job to do this. Bell was eager to ensure that it was "harder for government to remain inactive or indifferent" (Bell, 2012b). His declaration that war reporting should be a "moral enterprise" confronted the notion of journalistic objectivity. Reporters, he asserts, "do not stand apart from the world. We are part of it" (Bell, 1997: 8). His disagreement with established journalism was shared by many of his colleagues, notably CNN's Christine Amanpour (1996: 17), who states that "objectivity means giving all sides a fair hearing but not treating all sides equally". By being neutral in Bosnia, she continues, you risk "drawing a moral equivalence between victim and aggressor" (Amanpour, 1996: 16–17). This approach generated considerable debate (see, for example, Hume, 1997; Tumber and Prentoulis, 2003; Lloyd, 2004; O'Neill, 2012). The problems of operationalising objectivity in the reporting of war and conflict is, as we have seen above, nothing new. The difference in the 1990s was perhaps the growing frustration of correspondents in the face of the difficulties of reporting and understanding the complex and brutal conflicts that took place following the collapse of the Cold War. The genocides and ethnic cleansing in Bosnia, Chechnya, Rwanda and the Democratic Republic of the Congo presented a challenge to reporters which left an indelible mark. The desire for something to be done to stop the slaughter of innocent victims led many correspondents to advocate intervention. Action, they believed, was necessary to bring an end to the plight of the victims, and objective reporting was impotent in the face of this challenge. Bell's experience of the horrors of Sarajevo led him to believe that in "our anxiety not to offend and upset people, we were not only sanitizing war but even prettifying it" (Bell, 1995: 214). In the case of Bosnia, Bell's critics argue the journalism of attachment had a corrupting effect on its proponents. They became propaganda tools for US and NATO interests in the same way as those who adhered to conventional practices (see Brock, 2006; Hammond, 2000). The journalism of attachment is deemed to be predisposed to this because of its simplistic framing of war as good versus evil (Hammond, 2002: 180) or its depoliticised approach to war reporting (von Oppen, 2009).

The ramifications of the journalism of attachment for modern war reporting are considerable, but for the purpose of discussion on the risk culture of war reporting, the crucial point is that it accentuates the risk of doing the job. By emphasising that the truth is based on subjective experiences as much as objective facts, the journalism of attachment highlights the number of ways that a war correspondent can conceptualise her or his relationship with the 'war zone'. It does not mean that journalists "no longer believe in the existence of truth" or that truth is "unattainable by journalism" (Lloyd, 2004), but that there are different ways of attaining the truth. This has been the case throughout the history of war reporting, but now the complexity of modern conflicts, the marketisation of news and the speed of mass communication has led to a re-evaluation of the balance between the objective and subjective components of the job (see Chapter 3). By placing more emphasis on the subjective, the expression of emotion and making judgements, reporters put themselves at greater risk. Moral witnessing requires that the reporter must not only witness 'evil' but also experience or at least risk experiencing suffering (Margarlit, cited in von Oppen, 2009: 25). Bell's journalism of attachment locates the correspondent as a witness between good and evil, and the authority to make a judgment is provided by being at the centre of what is happening. By conceptualising war correspondence as a moral enterprise, the demand is that journalists should be closer to the conflict, to the action, with all the dangers that entails.

By asking journalists to speak of their personal experiences, their fears and their feelings, an increasing burden is placed on the reporter. Dealing with the trauma and the emotional costs of war and conflict has confronted correspondents since the early days of the specialism. Developing mechanisms of coping is a feature of the work. The demand that correspondents pay more attention to their personal experiences of and emotional responses to what is happening on the ground makes this more difficult. Studies have shown that close proximity of correspondents to war and conflict can result in post-traumatic stress disorder, depression and/or emotional distress (Feinstein *et al.*, 2002; Feinstein, 2013). Correspondents have expressed their unease about "moving *into* the story" and how "emotion was deftly encouraged" to make the news "more accessible" (Adie, 2002: 415). Many have nevertheless embraced the encouragement to communicate in emotional terms. Reporting the emotional cost of war leads war correspondents to pay more attention to sources who have suffered or who have witnessed suffering, thereby forcing them to deal with the pain and suffering of others. Their responsibility to tell the stories of these sources, experiencing their plight, enhances the sense of responsibility they feel to them. An extreme example of taking responsibility was the rescue and adoption of a young girl from war-torn Sarajevo by ITN correspondent Michael Nicholson (2011). Making moral assessments and expressing emotions forces reporters to become more engaged – Nicholson also energetically campaigned for the evacuation of children from Sarajevo. The risk is that this level of engagement will result in them being perceived as combatants and turn them into targets (O'Neill, 2012). The line between journalism and propaganda is porous, as Knightley has shown in his seminal history of war reporting, and much war coverage has been shaped by the practice of 'patriotic journalism' which takes sides. According to one US reporter in the wake of 9/11, "I am an American first, a journalist second" (quoted in Ruigrok, 2008: 311). By choosing the role of moral agent, war correspondents have, if not taken sides qualitatively, changed the practice of war reporting, placing further emphasis on the risk of doing the job.

Digital witnessing

Witnessing in the digital age emphasises the question of making moral judgements without being there, and technological change has increased the possibilities and opportunities to bear witness (see Chapter 4). David Carr (2014) argues that witnessing today "becomes something different delivered in the crucible of real time, without pause for reflection". The rapid speed of modern communication demands instant judgement, which enhances the risk of getting things wrong. More crucially, digital witnessing has had an impact on the expectations of those involved in conflict. Their plight is not only made available for immediate public reproduction on a global scale but it can also be communicated in their own terms, in their own language and understanding. The boundary between the production and consumption of personal testimony has been blurred. The citizen's voice is no longer subordinate to that of the journalist but, as a result of social media, sits alongside that of the war correspondent in providing visual and verbal evidence (Frosh and Pinchevski, 2014; Chouliaraki, 2015). There has been a dramatic upsurge in the visual images available to the public, transforming their access to conflict (Mortensen, 2014: 2). Ordinary citizens and combatants are usually the first on the scene, and how they interpret, show and disseminate their first-hand experience of observing what has happened has changed the nature of war reporting and thrown the process of witnessing into "crisis" (Allan, 2013). The exact nature of the crisis is the subject of much scholarly discussion (see Chouliaraki, 2010), but the emergence of citizen witnessing has implications for the risk culture of war reporting.

Citizen witnessing challenges the authority and authenticity of war correspondents in acting as eyewitnesses. Scholarly conceptualisation of citizen witnessing emphasises the provision of "fresh perspectives" which fill in "the gaps, silences and fissures" and offer an alternative form of witnessing to that of mainstream media reporting (Allan, 2013: 94, 151). Citizen witnessing is "raw, immediate, independent and unapologetically subjective" (Allan, 2013: 94). War correspondents are confronted not only with the capacity of ordinary citizens to provide images from war zones more directly and more rapidly but also with the way in which war, conflict and suffering is represented and reported online. News organisations are increasingly outsourcing the role of eyewitness to private citizens with digital cameras and phones. This enables them "to claim that they 'have been there' as witnesses of events they have not witnessed" (Zelizer, 2007: 425). For correspondents, the collaboration poses difficulty as they have to reconcile the editorial values of accuracy, impartiality and objectivity with the immediate, uncensored and vivid content of the blogosphere (see Hermida, 2009; Sacco and Bossio, 2015). The countervailing pulls of objectivity and subjectivity are further heightened. Correspondents spend more time in front of screens gathering and processing more information about what has happened from a wider range of sources, mainly non-official. They are becoming more immersed in the events they are reporting, and their immersion in the emotions, propaganda and spectacle of the online world encourages them to speculate, pronounce and make moral judgements. The "bearing witness – at a distance" (Allan et al., 2007: 373) leads to emotions being placed alongside facts in establishing the authenticity of the various accounts from the war zone.

The process of accommodation between the professional and the citizen journalist has led to war correspondents having to spend more time interpreting civilian testimony, with all the problems this suggests. Using social networking sites provides correspondents with more information and evidence, but it presents more problems in verifying the authenticity of what is posted (see Bennett, 2011).

John Peters (2001), in his influential essay, highlights the problems of bearing witness accurately, citing the difficulties of memory, honesty, presence, perception and scale.[3] These are magnified online. Syria is the most socially mediated conflict in history, and it is hardly surprising that reporting of the conflict is regularly qualified by the use of the phrase, "*despite the difficulty in independently verifying reports from Syria*" (see Chouliaraki, 2015). The motivations of the citizen journalist differ from those of the professional correspondent. Attention is usually drawn to the political motivations of bloggers and the way in which social media are used as propaganda and promotional tools. There are a variety of reasons to generate film and copy. Many simply want to tell the world what is happening in their neighbourhood. One activist in Syria said,

> I filmed my feelings and wanted to document my neighbourhood, my area. I filmed a lot of injured people and martyrs and bombings but not with in [sic] the back of my mind to be able to use it as evidence.
>
> *(Quoted in Wessels, 2016)*

For others, producing your own content from war zones is not simply about information. Studies of YouTube indicate that "uploaders strive for view counts" and "viewers come for entertaining rather than educational experiences" (Silvestri, 2016: 32). Witnessing in these circumstances is reduced to spectacle, sometimes spoof or even parody.

The key point is that the nature of eyewitnessing is changing as, through online communication, correspondents become more involved, more emotionally and personally engaged. A number of interpretative repertoires – resistance, resignation and renewal – have been identified in the response of correspondents to the use of citizen journalism and user-generated content in their reporting of crisis events (Anden-Papadopoulos and Panatti, 2013). It is clear, however, that there is a growing "professional–participatory tension" (Lewis, 2012). Correspondents increasingly want to be the "eyes, ears and nose" of their audiences, and are encouraged by their employers to report what they see, hear, feel and smell so that "the readers could experience this with me" (Loo, 2006: 105). Their personal and emotional experiences are as much part of a more subjective world of witnessing as those of the people involved in the fighting. Correspondents have to ensure their collaboration with citizen journalists flourishes while also minimising the risks and challenges that it presents (see Johnston, 2017). Coping with the intensity of the pressures and complexities generated by social and new media comes at a price.

The rise of citizen witnessing has been accompanied by the decline in the number of full-time war reporters and by more people in the world's war zones expressing doubt about the capacity of Western war correspondents to act as credible witnesses. The war in Syria appears to have cemented the view that correspondents are, in the words of one of their most celebrated, the "epitome of cynicism, charting the depths of depravity and suffering knowing full well that our record would neither bring good nor redress" (Loyd, 2015: xvii). Personal testimony is increasingly associated with career aspirations and winning awards. Eyewitness accounts not only serve to get reporters noticed; they are also the stuff of Pulitzer Prizes. Nora Mellor (2012a, 2012b) describes how the act of witnessing is a practice which locates the correspondent as part of a journalistic community. It has become central to the identity of the modern war reporter and something that is asserted, to bring attention to the plight of those caught up in war, in the face of the challenge posed by the claims of others. It accounts for the increasing propensity of war correspondents to take risks in order to experience and share the suffering of the victims of war. Testifying against those accused of war crimes, human rights violations and crimes against humanity is one way of doing this.

Testifying

In the 1990s three major international tribunals were created: The International Criminal Tribunal for the former Yugoslavia (ICTY); the International Criminal Tribunal for Rwanda (ICTR); and the International Criminal Court, which became permanent in 2002. Witnessing acquired a political dimension as journalists faced the possibility of being called to provide personal testimony in war crimes trials. Whether to appear before war crimes courts divided opinion between correspondents (Tumber, 2008). Many European journalists were willing to give evidence, while their American counterparts refused to testify. US news organisations believed testifying compromised their neutrality and threatened their safety. Jonathan Randal, *The Washington Post* correspondent covering the Balkan wars, refused to appear before the ICTR, arguing that in future sources would view reporters as instruments of the UN or other official bodies and journalists' independence would be undermined, reducing the opportunity to interview combatants. Journalists, he argued, would be put at risk and the fear of being called to testify would reduce the amount of information reported (see Bernstein, 2002; Gutman, 2003; Spellman, 2005). Robert Fisk (2002) defended his decision not to testify with the argument that journalists should not be policemen and it would make it more dangerous to do this job: "A reporter's job does not include joining the prosecution. We are witnesses and we write our testimony and we name, if we can, the bad guys. Then it is for the world to act. Not us" (Fisk, 2008: 395).

Even amongst those journalists who did appear, concerns were expressed about the effect of doing so. Lindsey Hilsum, international editor for *Channel 4 News*, testified before the ICTR, attributing this to her responsibility as a human being rather than as a journalist. However, she believed that testifying against a specific witness could compromise her effectiveness as a journalist. BBC reporter Jackie Rowlands, the first journalist to appear as a witness at Milosevic's war crimes tribunal, did not believe that giving evidence would make it significantly more dangerous for journalists in the future, asserting that no journalist should be exempt from moral obligations or international justice (Day, 2004). Perhaps one of the most powerful advocates of testifying is award-winning reporter Elizabeth Becker, who, nearly 20 years after reporting the mass murder of nearly 2 million people by the Khmer Rouge, returned to Cambodia to testify against the officials responsible. Her unease at testifying was assuaged by the faces of the people brutalised by the regime and being told: "You're doing this for us" (Becker, 2015).

The extent of danger for journalists who testify is recognised by the tribunals. In 2004 the ICTY ruled that war correspondents have a qualified privilege not to testify because of the possible physical dangers that they might find themselves in if they are perceived to be future witnesses in war crimes trials. The tribunal admitted that war correspondents should be considered as independent observers rather than as potential witnesses for the prosecution, stating that "journalists reporting on conflict areas play a vital role in bringing to the attention of the international community the horrors and realities of the conflict" and that they should not be "subpoenaed unnecessarily" (ICTY, 2002). It was only if information could not be obtained by other means that they should be summoned to appear. This ruling only applied to war correspondents[4] and is only binding to the ICTY (Tumber, 2008), but it has set a precedent for the obligation of the correspondent to testify.

The risk of being seen to take sides is commonly seen as the main problem of testifying before war tribunals. However, in terms of the capacity of correspondents to do their job, testifying is perhaps more significant for the threat it poses to the relationship between the source and the journalist. Privileges have developed in liberal-democratic societies to protect journalists because of the belief that there is a public interest which justifies the exclusion of testimony by professions such as journalists, doctors and therapists against others. The International Criminal Court (ICC) *Rules of Procedure and Evidence* (ICC, 2013) recognises the immunity of judicial testimony,[5] but there is no specific international convention regarding freedom of information, and the journalistic privilege not to divulge sources varies from country to country. The European Court of Human Rights recognises that journalists cannot be made to give evidence concerning confidential information or sources, 'unless it is justified by an overriding requirement of the public interest' (ECoHR, 2018: 1). Testifying opens up problems of verification and scrutiny. Subject to cross-examination, reporters have had to defend their practice and profession and open up their confidential notes or make available unedited footage, with consequences for their sources (Gutman, 2003). It opens up challenges to the testimony of witnesses as a result of the inconsistency in the ways in which journalists asks questions and the problems people have in retelling their stories of being involved in traumatic events. Testifying can increase the "risk of contamination and the undermining of a witness's testimony" (Tumber, 2008: 266). In the age of the Internet and social media, questions arise as to who is a journalist and who can claim the privilege of protecting sources. Journalists are not defined by membership of a professional body; they do not have to undergo formal training and they do not have to be employed by a professional media organisation. As more freelance and non-professional information gatherers cover war, the definition of a journalist becomes more difficult and the subject of immunity more problematic. The emergence of moral journalism and the arrival of the digital age highlight the dilemma that has been at the heart of war reporting since its inception: whether correspondents should be indifferent to or care about to the plight of the people they cover.[6] Getting the balance right is not easy, as both aspects of the work have to be satisfied. This has always incorporated risk, but this has been heightened in the digital world.

Notes

1 For a debate in the US context of the development of the byline and the merits of naming reporters as opposed to anonymity of reports, see Campbell (2006).
2 For a detailed evaluation of Chappelle's reporting of the Algerian War, see Webb (2005), who argues that her reporting of the war was "unique" amongst American correspondents in its partisanship and that her identification with the cause of Algerian independence was motivated by her role as an outsider, the result of being the only female war correspondent in the field. This perhaps ignores the extent to which a growing anti-colonial sentiment developed in the press during this period; Chappelle's sympathy for the rebels was in keeping with the approach of journalists in other media systems.
3 These can be summed up as the problem of remembering what you saw, being truthful in your account of what you saw, being there at the crucial moment in the events unfolding, all the important things being seen and heard and the extent to which the witness is overwhelmed by the scale of what has happened.
4 Journalists who have not been credited as a 'war correspondent' are in a more difficult situation.
5 Rule 73 states that

> communications made in the context of the professional relationship between a person and his or her legal counsel shall be regarded as privileged, and consequently not subject to disclosure, unless:
> (a) The person consents in writing to such disclosure; or
> (b) The person voluntarily disclosed the content of the communication to a third party, and that third party then gives evidence of that disclosure.
>
> *(ICC, 2013: 25)*

6 For specific discussion, see Wiesslitz and Ashuri (2011).

3

ORGANISATIONAL AND OCCUPATIONAL RISKS AND WAR REPORTING

The capacity of war correspondents to understand and navigate the risks presented to them is shaped by the organisational context and occupational culture they work within. As we saw in the discussion of the development of 'bearing witness' in Chapter 2, this context and culture are dynamic. In recent years this has been underlined by the increased personal 'bodily' risk to the war correspondent. Although correspondents and news organisations are more concerned with how personal safety can be enhanced and improved through means such as hostile environment training, a series of changes are taking place in the organisational and occupational culture of war reporting that are fuelling risk-taking. The market-isation of the news media has led to a shift in the burden of managing the heightened risk from the news organisation to the individual reporter. The changing nature of employment has meant the work of the war correspondent is more precarious than it has ever been. Increased competition has sharply added to the demands on the individual reporter. War reporting, just like the nature of war, is more complex, and as a result managing risk is more problematic. Alongside organisational change, correspondents sense of who they are and what they do is undergoing a transformation. Their working environment now includes new actors, new ways of newsgathering and new forms of interaction with audiences. This is responsible for a crisis of identity as correspondents seek a new role, a new sense of purpose and new ways of doing things, which are changing their approaches to risk and risk-taking.

This chapter examines the changes in the organisational and occupational culture that shape the construction of risk in reporting from war zones. The focus is on the growing importance of economic and commercial factors in the production of war news and the increasingly precarious nature of the employment of war correspondents. New types of people are becoming war reporters today, and their relationship to the job and the news organisations that use their copy has impacted on the propensity to take risks. Relations with sources of information have also been affected, and the changing ability and capacity of sources to provide information has made newsgathering a more difficult and uncertain process. The expectations of audiences and news organisations of the role of correspondents have also altered working practices, placing more emphasis on taking risks in the daily routines of the war reporter. The 'habitus' of the war correspondent is shifting, making their work more risk inclined. Barbara Korte (2009: 24) draws attention to how the memoirs of war correspondents show them "playing up to a certain image". She argues that a range of factors such as audience expectations, organisational demands, group identity, role models, occupational culture and the representation of correspondents and their work in popular culture shape their performance, predisposing them to behave and act in certain ways. The behaviour of individuals is not uniform, straightforward or consistent, but a predisposition to certain actions is discernible among this group. The 'performance' is changing as the profession becomes more precarious and uncertain, and at the heart of the change is a greater propensity to take risks.

Economic logic

The war correspondent's performance is anchored in the organisational context in which he or she works. This context has evolved over the years, but in the post-war period it has undergone a radical transformation as a result of economic, technological and political developments. The changing economic realities that face war reporting have had a significant impact on the organisational structures within which correspondents operate. Two particular areas have a direct bearing on the construction of risk. First, the changing nature of employment has made war reporting, like other forms of journalism, more precarious. Not only are more of the correspondents who report war and conflict working on a freelance basis, but the dwindling number of permanent correspondents face greater instability in their daily efforts to do their job. Second, the commercialisation of news has led to a different kind of product, a product more geared to entertainment and ratings than truth and analysis. This product places more emphasis on reporters being closer to danger.

War reporting has always been undertaken by full-time and freelance correspondents. In the past this was primarily a matter of choice; today it is a necessity. In recent years the rising costs of gathering news has made the maintenance of full-time staff correspondents a costlier undertaking. Numerous scholars have discussed the conglomeration of the media business, the savage cuts in news budgets, the closure of foreign news bureaus and the laying off of full-time correspondents (for example, Sambrook, 2010). The new economic realities have led to news organisations depending more on outsourced labour, and there has been a proliferation of freelance war reporters (see Palmer, 2015). Reporting war and conflict today depends on freelance reporters more than it ever has, and the increasing death toll amongst reporters is often attributed to the growing number of freelance reporters.

The way in which freelance war correspondents work is seen as making them more susceptible to risk-taking. Jill Carroll (2005: 54) emphasises that the freelancer is a "different breed of journalist" from the staff correspondent. Working outside the remit of the news organisation, they do not have the financial security and personal protection that is given to full-time reporters. They have to "pay for their own accommodations, translators, food and health insurance" (Carroll, 2005: 56) and often lack the training and preparation given to staff reporters. This means they stay in places that are considered less salubrious and safe. Cutting back on the costs of transportation and personal security, for example, puts them at greater risk of being kidnapped in war zones (see Picard and Storm, 2016). They are "a uniquely vulnerable class of journalists" (Creech, 2015: 1016) which has been recognised in recent years with the establishment of organisations such as the Rory Peck Trust and the Frontline Freelance Register, that have tried to provide basic training courses and support mechanisms for freelance war reporters. These independent organisations stress that the lack of resources and the absence of institutionalised support and security means the freelance war reporter experiences risk differently.

The bottom line is that freelancers have to sell their stories. No matter what their commitment to journalism, whether it is to bearing witness or providing a voice for the victims of war, their primary goal is earning money on a daily basis. It is this imperative that drives them to take more risks than their staff colleagues. It leads them to take on the riskier assignments. The conflict in Syria has been referred to as a 'freelancers' war' due to the reluctance of staff correspondents to risk their lives and the unwillingness of editors to assign their best reporters. More than half of the 50 or so Western journalists killed in Syria were freelancers, and the Committee to Protect Journalists calculated that in 2013 almost two-thirds of the journalists killed in combat or crossfire were freelancers (cpj.org/data). Many mainstream news organisations have become concerned about encouraging inexperienced reporters to take unacceptable risks. Some have stated that they will not buy material from independent reporters in high-risk conflict zones (Pendry, 2013). It is not only a question of the risks that freelancers face. Concern also stems from the admission to the battlefield of untrained, unsupervised, inexperienced and highly driven reporters, which is seen as heightening the risks faced by all war correspondents. Many freelance reporters are dismissed as 'war tourists' who pose a headache for correspondents and the military alike. The degree of recklessness and naivety is highlighted by some going to Syria "to learn to become a war correspondent" (Patel, 2012). Reporters working under increased pressures, having to prove themselves, are "seen as careless and put themselves and other colleagues in danger" (Kramp and Weichert, 2014: 29). By stating they will not accept freelance copy from dangerous war zones, news organisations have recently acted on their concerns; but in a highly competitive market, driven by the economic needs of reporters and news organisations, this has not proven successful. Such an approach is difficult to maintain in the face of a major story and the growing capacity of freelancers to find a conduit for their stories in a world of burgeoning news sites and more recently established news organisations such as Vice News and BuzzFeed.

Freelancers have also objected to what they see as a restriction of their ability to work. It is not simply the inexperience of freelance reporters that is contributing to an increase in the overall risk for reporters working in war zones. It is driven by a media economy which encourages outlets to hire such reporters to reduce their costs of production.

The level of rewards in freelancing should not be ignored. Reporters such as Francesca Borri (2013) draw attention to the low pay of freelancers, highlighting that the rate of remuneration does not vary "whether you are writing from Aleppo, Gaza or Rome". The struggles to make ends meet, including covering the cost of the basic equipment needed to report war, have been well documented (see Borri, 2013; Crane, 2014). Borri's assessment that freelancers are "second-class journalists" has to be put in the context of the potentially considerable reward for success. Astrid Gynnild (2005: 113) describes the rise of a "relatively small international group of extreme risk-taking freelancers, in a physical and mental sense". She cites as example of this type of war correspondent the Norwegian reporter Asne Seierstad, whose international renown reflects how fame and fortune can be attained if one is willing to take risks. The best-paid cultural worker in Norway in 2004, Seierstad's 'winner take all' career reflects the changes media technology and the transformation in media business practices that have taken place in recent times. She was the only Scandinavian reporter in Baghdad in 2003 and was able to brand herself journalistically at national, regional and international level. Her reports filed across multimedia platforms during the first three months of war, added to by a documentary released a few months after the war and a book published later that year on her war experiences, reaped considerable financial reward. Her 'brand' established, Seierstad was able to proceed with her lucrative freelance career in subsequent wars. By taking the risk of staying in Baghdad and casting around for buyers, her personal gain was considerable. Often the realities of low pay for the many are forgotten by the considerable financial rewards for the few.

The uncertainty and unpredictability of freelance work adds to the stress of journalists (see Gollmitzer, 2014; Cohen, 2010). Freelancers are "underpaid, under protected and can be discarded at any time" (Palmer, 2015: 228), and their precarious conditions of employment are closely associated with physical and mental health problems and issues. Feinstein's pioneering study of war reporters and post-traumatic stress disorder (PTSD) did not find that freelancers are more likely to develop PTSD or exhibit more prominent symptoms of the disorder, but they are more prone to psychological distress including depression and social dysfunction (Feinstein, 2006). This is attributed by Feinstein to their working conditions, "financial worries, anxieties over selling work, inadequate or absent insurance, sleeping on floors, bumming lifts, scrounging satellite phones – in short, all the impediments of a stand-alone existence" (Feinstein, 2006: 98). Putting aside this correlation, the working conditions of freelancers influence their reporting of war. Not only do they have fewer resources but they also have less time to devote to their reporting. They have to spend more of their working day managing their business and organising the basic logistics of doing their job. The constant wear and tear of worrying about money, logistics and security increases the risks of doing the job and impacts on their health (see Ertel *et al.*, 2005).

Changing nature of freelancing

Freelance war reporters fall into different categories, which has a bearing on the risks they face. The assumption is that they are young people in a hurry, starting out on their careers. However, freelance war correspondents come in many shapes and sizes. They can be distinguished by the nature of their relationship with news organisations; some have a guaranteed contract with them; others occupy an arm's-length relationship with no assurances. Today more and more of them are experienced correspondents who have been laid off due to the downsizing process. Mostly they are local journalists from the areas engulfed by war and conflict. They usually work for small news outlets locally and supply international news organisations with stories. They are increasingly employed by large news organisations for their local knowledge and skills. Soomin Seo (2016) has documented the increasing number of local reporters hired by news agencies to cover worldwide events. These stringers have come to play a more important role in covering war and conflict as the dangers and complexities of war reporting have increased. The extent of their importance is highlighted by the number of local journalists who make up the growing casualties of war reporting. All but 3 of the 45 journalists reported killed or having died in action in the year prior to September 2017 were 'local' reporters from the Global South (see IFJ, 2017b). Not all were killed covering war and conflict – reporting corruption proved just as dangerous.

Local individuals, including reporters, have long played a part in the work of foreign correspondents. As fixers, they are part of the "underground economy that makes foreign news reporting possible" (Palmer, 2016: 5). Scholars have ignored their contribution in this capacity to war and crisis reporting (Murrell, 2014). However, since the 1990s local hires have become a prominent feature of the global news media. This expansion has been driven by several factors including the globalisation of the market for news, the need to compensate for downsizing, the increasing difficulty of accessing war zones and, with the demise of the long-stay correspondents, the necessity to understand complex events and places. Local knowledge is required for parachute journalism to function effectively, and strin-gers and fixers contribute to the servicing of Western star reporters who appear when events reach crisis proportions. According to Martin Bell (1995: 85), "the most important member of any TV team in an unfamiliar war zone ... is not the reporter or cameraman or producer or videotape editor, but the local contact with reality". Colleen Murrell (2014) notes how fixers and stringers contribute editorially as well as logistically. In some situations they have come to take over the role of regular reporters, and in the coverage of conflicts such as Syria, Afghanistan and Libya, Western news organisations "disproportionately rely on stringers" (Crane, 2014).

The risks of employing more local reporters to report war are articulated in different ways. From the perspective of many Western reporters, which is where most of the scholarship in this area is located, the growing dependence on local reporters is seen as accentuating their fears in a number of ways. Palmer and Fontan (2007), in their study of the period following the 2003 invasion of Iraq, stress concerns about the reliability of translators and interpreters and the impact that using stringers has on the quality of information coming back from the war zone. Several risks are attached to translation: mistranslation can lead to misinformation or worse, and there is the potential for the omission or loss of useful information. Stringers and fixers are seen as having their own agendas or being locked into particular networks of contacts which lead to certain interpretations of events. The greatest risk calculation concerns assessment of the security considerations in going to particular areas or doing specific interviews. This is acutely felt by freelancers who do not have the institutional backing to make judgements about the trustworthiness of the local assistance they engage. The onus for hiring locals is on individual reporters, freelance or full-time, who have "regularly recruited fixers at the last minute, sight unseen" (Murrell, 2014: 130). This is another example of what Creech (2017: 3) sees as a process that "shifts risk from a collective concern to an individual one" as news organisations attempt to remain flexible and cost-effective in the new market economy.

From the perspective of those employed as stringers or fixers, the risks inherent in working with Western reporters are highlighted. They draw attention to the problems that emanate from reporters' naivety or lack of care in negotiating cultural differences and mores. Palmer's study of fixers cites several examples of how "correspondents' culturally insensitive or naïve behaviour" placed their lives at risk (Palmer, 2016: 9). The lack of cultural understanding was compounded by a limited knowledge of local issues, which many fixers believed was responsible for poor quality of reporting. The ability of the local fixers to correct errors or misunderstandings was limited by what many of them saw as the greater weight of trust editors placed in their reporters. The lack of knowledge was less likely to be attributed to apathy or complacence than to the predisposition that reporters bring to the story (Palmer, 2016: 10). It was the "narrow views" and "preconceived notions" that generated impoverished and imbalanced coverage (Palmer, 2016: 11). Whereas correspondents express their anxieties about stringers skewing their stories, fixers see their job as being to educate correspondents – hence the tensions in the relationship.

For most war reporters the relationship with local fixers and stringers is close, even if it is not fully acknowledged. Those specialising in reporting particular conflict zones such as the Middle East have forged strong bonds with their fixers, and this dependency encourages a duty of care which is reinforced by the arm's-length position often taken by news organisations. The general attitude of large news organisations to local employees is highlighted by their action at the end of the Vietnam War when they "ordered the members of their staff to leave Saigon and left their bureaus in the charge of freelancers for whom they would have no great responsibility, financial or legal" (Simpson, 2017: 236). Many reporters feel they have to compensate for the lack of appreciation and value given to fixers and local personnel. Protecting their identity and their sources and covering stories in such a way that there is no fallout for the local reporter once the journalist has left are some of the ways in which this has been done. This onus places a greater burden on the individual war correspondent in calculating the risks attached to the stories they cover and report. They feel they have a particular duty of care that is denied to fixers not only by news organisations but also by their own governments. The case of Ajmal Naqshbandi highlights the vulnerability of local reporters. Kidnapped in Afghanistan with an Italian journalist, the Afghan government bartered for the release of the Westerner but not its own citizen. Naqshbandi, who described his job as "taking one enemy to another enemy so that they can talk to each other", was executed by the Taliban (Olds, 2009).

Ever since the 19th century, war correspondents have relied on local contacts and connections to gain access and facilitate the logistical side of their work. In the early days these contacts were servants, drivers and couriers who knew the best routes to get copy back to the nearest telegraph office, hired by correspondents to accompany them to the front. Since the end of the Second World War, the international environment has accentuated the need for professional assistance and heightened local knowledge to support correspondents as war and conflict has become more complex. Wire agencies led the way as speed, trustworthiness and colour became the dominant characteristics of news. In the broadcasting era, reliance on local stringers has become more pronounced, expanding beyond transportation, translation, making connections and safety to include story tips, leads and in some cases filming and reporting. This development has led to a shift in the relationship. Always involving a process of negotiation, the relationships have become more complicated in the era of globalisation. Maria Armoudian (2017) distinguishes a fundamental difference between the parties in the dialogue. The news story is the goal for the reporter, while reporting is far more personal for the fixer. Not only is it a source of income, a livelihood in an increasingly squeezed economic situation in many parts of the world, but it is also a means of redressing perceived wrongs in their societies. Fixers, local reporters, are "more inclined to focus on untangling and exposing local vexing issues" (Armoudian, 2017: 139). An emotional intensity is often attached to this undertaking as it is "their family, friends and neighbors who are among the fallen, their cities that are destroyed and their countries that have come apart" (Armoudian, 2017: 140).

The growth of precarious employment is associated with heightened friction between full-time and freelance correspondents (Tumber and Prentoulis, 2003: 218). This relationship has been widely discussed with the focus on the relative 'autonomy' of freelance correspondents. Kathleen Ryan's study of freelance television reporters in the US found that they exhibited a greater degree of job satisfaction than staff workers in relation to their autonomy in the workplace (Ryan, 2009). A similar finding emerged from a study of British freelancers, who placed considerable emphasis on the initiative they are able to take in their work (Storey *et al.*, 2005). These findings are based on interview surveys and perhaps do not tend to tell the whole truth. As Colleen Murrell (2014: 2) notes, "journalists are skilled at penning their own myth-making, and much of the autobiographical work by foreign correspondents has emphasised the joys of independent newsgathering in crisis-torn lands". Negotiating autonomy carries different risks for full-time and freelance reporters. Freelancers stress their ability to follow up stories in the ways in which they want to. This allows them to cover conflicts that other correspondents cannot reach, and they are able to spend more time reporting, often filling in the gaps that are ignored or neglected by full-time reporters. They are less dependent on the newsroom and its agenda and have more "latitude ... to ignore those who urged [them] to stop [their] investigations" (Thayer, 2001: 29). However, free-lancers invest considerable time, money and resources with no guarantee of their stories being published. They risk losing out considerably if their story is not run. Established full-time reporters in many cases have more cultural capital within their organisations, allowing them to exercise some degree of independent discretion in doing their job, which helps to manage the risks of the work.

The rise of the network megastar is a feature of contemporary media culture. Celebrity status is nothing new. Ever since the beginnings of the specialism, war correspondents have been public figures and some have attained fame; on his arri-val in the US to cover the civil war, Russell was described by *The New York Times* as "the world's most famous war correspondent". In his diaries Russell wrote of the fickle nature of fame, comparing his status to a "great firework" which "com-mences with some small scintillations" before it "blazes up and flares out in blue, purple and orange fires, to the intense admiration of the multitude" and then dies out suddenly and "is thought of no more" (Russell, 1863: 555). Television ele-vated the cult of celebrity in war reporting, with certain journalists acting as icons of particular conflicts (Markham, 2012). It was said in military circles "that until Kate Adie turns up it is not a war"; her appearance at a trouble spot was an acknowledgement that an event was now a big story (Leonard, 2003). Regular correspondents complain about 'big-footing' when they are edged out by celebrity correspondents as a story escalates into a major news event (Bell, 2017: 246). Fame is a double-edged sword and depends on the accord of the audience and the news organisation. Personality-led reporting means sometimes the reporter can become bigger than the story, and the fallout for a reporter's celebrity status from his or her actions and reports carries risk. The determination to get the story and be on screen can lead to increased tension with colleagues and producers, which can undermine the capacity to do the job, particularly in the broadcasting environment which emphasises co-operation and teamwork.

Commercialism and editorial control

The work of war reporters, freelance or full-time, has to be seen in the context of the commercial imperatives of the modern news organisation. Care has to be taken in generalising about news organisations in the contemporary media system. There are clearly differences between organisations in their treatment of correspondents and the extent to which commercial factors prevail over professional ones in the decision-making process. How commercial factors shape news organisations should be distinguished between mainstream media organisations, news organisations such as Vice, GlobalPost and BuzzFeed as well as various start-ups like NewsFixed, GRNlive and Worldcrunch. The traditional distinction made between public service and commercial news organisations is perhaps less significant than it was. Public service broadcasters such as the BBC struggle today to maintain their commitment to their principles in the face of the deregulation and liberalisation of markets. Brian Creech (2016) draws attention to a trend towards the commodification of risk that has accompanied the marketisation of international news. The rise of television incentivised correspondents to take greater risk to produce stories that were closer to the action, but in the digital world proximity to danger has become "an economic incentive for news organisations" (Creech, 2017: 10). A highly competitive market leads to an "impulse to entertain" which places correspondents at the forefront of their stories. It is through their subjective experiences that the dangers and risks of war are communicated to the audience. Reporters, camera workers and photographers are increasingly at the centre of the 'bang-bang' footage that newsrooms crave. Their brave or reckless behaviour, depending on how you characterise it, is increasingly driven by the compulsion of the market.

The extent to which freelance and full-time war correspondents are involved in negotiations with news organisations is often ignored. Expressions of loneliness or being on your own in war zones are common in correspondents' memoirs, but they hide the extent to which correspondents have to accommodate the needs and requirements of newsrooms and editors. This accommodation depends on the status of the reporter. There is a 'pecking order' amongst war reporters. Pedelty (1995) differentiates between powerful full-time staffers, Western stringers and freelancers, and marginalised local journalists in the reporting of the war in El Salvador in the 1980s, all of whom who experienced risk differently. Today the distinctions are less clear-cut; political, personal and economic pressures to produce eyewitness stories from more dangerous war zones have given increased prominence to those on the spot. These tend to be local journalists and increasingly non-journalists, or as some people refer to them, 'citizen journalists', whose reports have become more important with the advent of new media technology. Reporters of all types speak of the erosion of their autonomy, which they believe adds to the risks of doing the job. ITN's Michael Nicholson (1992: 3) wrote in the late 1960s of "more and more everyday editorial decisions … taken away" by editors who "had seldom been abroad" and "whose worldview came from an ageing *Daily Telegraph* wall map". Editors in the comfort of offices far away from conflict zones are making decisions based on limited knowledge and understanding, often adding to the difficulties and dangers correspondents face.

Questions of editorial intervention have exercised war reporters since Delane instructed Russell to tell as much of the truth as he could. The history of war reporting can be seen as a struggle between the special correspondent in the field and his or her editors at home. Technology has had a major impact on determining the outcome of this clash (see Chapter 4), but the means by which news organisations arrange their newsgathering processes is also significant. Much of the research into the organisational context highlights the problem of direct editorial intervention, but many journalists understand the limitations of their autonomy in relation to the structure and routines of their work (see Skovsgaard, 2014). Deadlines and competition between reporters inside news organisations are identified as important constraints on the freedom they have in their daily work. Bell (2017: 238–9) refers to his hatred of being "spiked" (having your story dropped in favour of another) or "ooved" (not appearing on screen). The intensity of such feelings accounts for correspondents' susceptibility to the pressures from editors and news desks. In response to the demands from the home office, correspondents have been known to fabricate, falsify and overdramatise their reports to make for a better story to 'sell' to their news desks. Instances where things are made up are "not endemic, but they occur too often to be entirely accidental" (Bell, 2017: 168). Bell describes a number of routine practices in TV news that may mislead the audience, such as editing footage of an event outside a war zone into action sequences shot by another camera worker under combat conditions or passing off reconstructions as the real thing (169, 171). "Shading the truth", as Bell refers to these acts, is encouraged – or perhaps colluded in – by newsrooms operating in an entertainment-driven, competitive TV news market. The risk of being found out is carried disproportionately by the individual reporter, as is highlighted by the sad case of James Forlong of Sky News: having passed off a drill as combat action, he then resigned and eventually took his own life.

Editors are adamant that decisions about logistics can only be made in the context of the value of the story. Editorial influence over the reporter in the field increased in the electronic era. Previously, distance allowed more initiative, time and independence in the newsgathering process, but as it has shrunk, editors have been able to set the news agenda for their men and women in the field. Several authors distinguish between news organisations in terms of the extent to which editors exert influence over their correspondents. Bell (2017) singles out US TV reporters as being more heavily controlled than most. They are subject to "a process of script approval" which lets editors check their reports before broadcast for style and accuracy (Bell, 2017: 173). A documentary on the coverage of the peace accords in Central America in the late 1980s shows ABC editors in New York, including anchor Peter Jennings, vetting down the line the script of their crew in Nicaragua and imposing their news agenda on the events reported on the ground (The World is Watching, 1988). The story was made to fit what New York wanted. The risk of not giving the editors what they want has increased with the greater pressure and control they can exert over their correspondents.

Collectivisation of war reporting

War correspondents work together in close proximity. This is perhaps best summed up by the term 'hotel warriors', reflecting that in most wars and conflicts certain hotels serve as the loci for the majority of war reporters. Whether it is the Hotel Caravelle in Saigon, the Hotel Palestine in Baghdad, Beirut's Commodore Hotel or the Hotel Florida in Madrid, there is a propensity amongst war reporters to share watering holes. In recent years it seems that many war correspondents have spent most of their tours of duty on hotel rooftops conducting two-ways with the studio. Besides being "detrimental to first-hand newsgathering" (Murrell, 2014: 17), this is also seen as leading to the phenomenon of pack journalism. Experienced correspondents are aware of the dangers of spending too much time together; socialising can blunt the competitive edge (Simpson, 2017: 148). But the camaraderie of war correspondents is something that younger reporters believe singles them out as a group. According to Sam Kiley of Sky News, "we're a small tribe but we look after each other" (quoted in Hilsum, 2013). Photojournalist Kate Brooks places greater emphasis on the close-knit community of those who cover conflicts when she states that

> It's a very small group of people who work in conflict zones. We basically all know each other or are connected in one way or another. After many years of shared experiences, we're bonded in ways that make us like a family.
>
> *(Quoted in Curry, 2014)*

The motivation to collaborate is driven by calculations of risk. The risk of not getting the story is a crucial consideration. Editors in a highly competitive environment are always keenly watching their rivals' output and are worried if they do not have the stories their competitors have. This worry is today more quickly conveyed to the reporter in the field, and sticking close to one another is a way of managing the risk of not getting the story. As one correspondent puts it: "if everyone has the same story, more or less, things are okay, more or less, professionally" (Tufekci, 2011). There is also safety in numbers, a feature of war reporting since Russell's days. Travelling in unfamiliar terrain in strange parts of the world with concerns about personal security encourages collaboration. Freelance reporting encourages greater co-operation and collaboration. Travelling with colleagues, particularly in regions where kidnapping and abduction is common, provides some security. But more importantly it means resources can be pooled, transport shared and costs saved. Strong bonds are constructed, particularly between freelancers, who are seen as developing a shared understanding of events which, in the view of some scholars and commentators, leads to "groupthink" (Janis, 1982).

Pack journalism encourages not only lazy reporting, the loss of independent reporting and the narrowing of sources consulted on a story, but also the development of a "herd mentality that renders news coverage one-dimensional" (Matusitz and Breen, 2007: 58). War reporters are seen as particularly prone to the phenomenon. The hostility of the environment in which they operate accentuates the normal inclination of journalists to socialise and co-operate with one another in foreign parts. Former AP correspondent William Dorman and his colleague Mansour Farhang (1987), in their gripping description of the press coverage of the fall of the Shah in Iran, provide an excellent account of how proximity can lead to a shared sense of what is happening and how it should be covered. The idea that the majority of a press corps accept the perspectives of a few dominant members is a relatively common theme in accounts of war reporting. This charge was most famously levelled at the Saigon press corps in the early days of the Vietnam War when, it is argued, the 'pessimistic view' of leading reporters such as David Halberstam, Malcolm Browne and Neil Sheehan exerted a disproportionate hold over the construction of the story. More recently the coverage of the 2003 war in Iraq is portrayed as a collective failure on the part of the US media for uncritically accepting the case for going to war and not reporting fully, fairly and accurately the conflict. In his assessment of the reporting of the 2003 conflict, Douglas Kellner (2008: 310) argues groupthink was the product of the "highly competitive nature of corporate media where no one dare gets out of line or stray too far from conventional wisdom, as their career would be endangered". Echoing Herman and Chomsky's propaganda model, he highlights the importance of "flak from the right wing and attacks from the Bush administration" for keeping journalists in line (Kellner, 2008: 310). In 2003 the intimidation of critics, the denial of access and charges of a lack of patriotism constituted the government flak, aided and abetted by the system of embedding reporters with the military, which encouraged reporters to see events unfolding through military eyes.

The embedding system deployed in 2003 highlights some of the problems in exploring groupthink amongst war correspondents. Pedelty (1995: 32) notes that in spite of their expressed antipathy towards collaboration in group activities, most journalists, even the most independently minded, participate in them because the "risk of getting scooped [is] too great". The dynamics of the 'small tribe' of war reporters are a strange mixture of collaboration and competition. Whereas the search for the 'scoop' or exclusive occupies much of the recollections of reporters, the co-operation and sharing between correspondents is less explicitly discussed. The combination of the professional compulsion to get a scoop and editorial pressure to obtain the same stories as competitors provides the group dynamics of war correspondents with particular characteristics. It is a balancing act between the need to co-operate in a difficult, dangerous and unfamiliar environment and the commitment to beat your colleagues to the story. Understanding pack journalism at war is dependent on the nature of the particular war, the composition of the press corps, the newsworthiness of the story and the logistical problems that confront the reporting. Vietnam has been described as a tale of two press corps – Saigon and Washington – who represented two different interpretations of what was happening on the ground. The notion of groupthink fails to fully grasp the nuances of how war reporters work collectively.

The pressures on war correspondents to conform are considerable, but the capacity to dissent from the collective approach is also apparent. The professional and personal values of war reporters place emphasis on going it alone and getting the exclusive story. Most correspondents' recollections emphasise their 'rugged individualism', individual initiative and satisfaction with being first with the news (see Korte, 2009). News organisations encourage competition between their correspondents as well as with those of other organisations. The BBC, for example, is described as "Darwinian" in "letting its correspondents fight it out between them" (Bowen, 2006: 70). The failure of or resentment towards pooling systems established during various conflicts attests to the strength of the competitive element in the reporting of war. Even when pooling arrangements are made to reduce the threats to the personal safety of reporters, they are disliked and often undermined. The Sarajevo pool was an example of an initiative set up to reduce the risks of covering fighting in the besieged city (Bell, 2017: 197–8). It lasted for three years and, in theory, shared the risks of filming and reporting. It was not popular as it went against the competitive ethos that pervades the profession. Managers and news organisations were most hostile. Reporters on the ground had reservations, but they could see that it made their job less risky. On the ground the practical and logistical requirements of the work demand as much co-operation as competition. The team effort required to generate war stories may clash with reporters' self-perception as scoop-driven individuals. It can also contradict audience expectations of war correspondents, but the reality of doing the job involves co-operating with colleagues and competitors. Hostile environments accentuate the tension between co-operation and competition, which is central to managing the risk of reporting war.

Whether the development of a "herd mentality" is the result of "more efficient resource sharing" (Pedelty, 1995: 32) or shared ideological values (Herman and Chomsky, 1988) or succumbing to pressure from official sources (Kellner, 2008), it can be seen as having a bearing on the risks and uncertainties faced by correspondents. Differing from or disagreeing with your colleagues is not easy in any walk of life. Conformity often results from the tendency of the individual to look to others for information about events and issues they are unsure about. Newsworthiness and what makes a good story is often learned from more experienced colleagues and second-guessing the news desk. Unfamiliar and pressurised circumstances increase the tendency to conform. Elite news organisations such as the BBC, *New York Times*, the international news agencies and CNN as well as the star reporters tend to exercise disproportionate influence over identifying what the story is, who are reliable sources and what angle should be taken. Technology has enhanced the ability to know what your colleagues are doing; contemporary pack journalism no longer requires the physical proximity of the hotel as journalists can monitor and imitate each other via the World Wide Web. As the pressure to conform increases, the consequences of nonconformity grow more risky. During the 2003 Gulf War unilateral or un-embedded reporters were criticised not only by the military but also by their own colleagues. They also worked under more difficult and dangerous conditions, and often their copy never saw the light of day. During the 1991 Gulf conflict Jon Alpert, a freelance reporter contracted to NBC, was the first correspondent to bring back uncensored footage from inside Iraq of the effects of American 'surgical strikes' on the Iraqi population. Just before his report was due to air, Alpert's story was spiked and he was fired (Variety, 1991).

Sources and security

The closeness of reporters' relationship with their sources of information is another example of how proximity poses risk in covering war. War correspondents are perhaps more reliant on their sources than journalists in general. The confusion of the battlefield and the problems of accessing war zones require correspondents to build good working relationships with those who are able to guarantee safe passage and provide knowledge. These usually are the parties to the conflict, particularly the military.

News organisations have since the latter part of the 19th century negotiated military accreditation for their correspondents, which has usually involved agreeing to commit to a set of rules about the copy they file and the conditions under which they access the front. The overwhelming consideration from the military perspective has been 'operational security'. Avoiding the putting into jeopardy of military operations or the safety of troops by giving information helpful to the enemy has been central to the military regulation of reporters on the battlefield. Reporters by and large have accepted the censorship of their copy on these grounds, but the history of war reporting can be seen as a struggle to determine what constitutes operational security. With the greater use of the policy of embedding reporters with the armed forces, this struggle between reporter and soldier has become more acute. The risk involved in breaching operational security has intensified as reporters embedded with the military can be put in routine danger. Several reporters in Afghanistan have died while embedded with the military (see Keeble and Mair, 2010). Sharing the daily risks while being present with troops can bring reporters and sources closer together. It also humanises the nature of the risk. John Shirley, who covered the Falklands/Malvinas war for *The Times*, tells of unfairness of criticising those on whom you depend on for your safety and well-being. There is much evidence to indicate that reporters find it difficult to criticise the soldiers they accompany into war (see Hastings, 2000).

The relationships between war correspondents and their sources have changed in recent years with the increased ability of sources to organise their information strategies and the growing technical ability and capacity to supply their views of events directly to the public. The approach deployed by military authorities of direct communication to the audience is designed to bypass critical journalists and to avoid the media as a channel of communication. This approach is supported by the allocation of greater resources to the propaganda and PR operations of official organisations, particularly the military. Military information management has become more skilful, pervasive and co-ordinated in the post-war period. Combatants today are described as 'media-savvy'; for example, ISIS has displayed "a deft command" of the media (Shane and Hubbard, 2014). However, it is Western propaganda and PR that exerts the greater influence over the daily newsgathering routines of most war correspondents today. As the media has become integral to the military's war-fighting capability, the war reporter has become central to information policy (see Miller, 2004b). During the 2003 Iraq conflict many reporters accredited to cover the war were unable to directly access the battlefield. They were embedded at media centres in Kuwait and Doha, Qatar, where they received daily briefings. Michael Wolff of *The New Yorker* describes his job as "not to cover war but to cover the news conference about the war" (Wolff, 2003). The quality of these briefings has been subject to much criticism (see Wolff, 2003; Keighron, 2003); isolated and dependent on the regular flow of official information, reporters risked being overwhelmed by the official view of events. Their capacity to make sense of the broader picture was reduced.

The growing risk of sourcing information about war has been made worse by the greater involvement of a wider range of sources in the process of news-gathering and dissemination. War correspondents justified their existence on the basis of their monopoly of the flow of news stories from the battlefield. For sources, they were the indispensable channels for communicating to the public. Today there are many more channels through which sources can communicate. With the difficulty of gaining entry to war zones such as Syria, alternative sources such as local bloggers can help solve the problem of lack of access. The proliferation of sources has generated a blizzard of information online which is often difficult and always time-consuming to verify. Correspondents, at the same time as searching for a new role in a rapidly changing information environment, face increased challenges and difficulties in managing their relationships with their sources. The problems of verifying information in a 24-hour news culture, growing concerns about official information management and the growing reluctance of combatants to facilitate access has led reporters to take greater risks.

Concerns about access to and reliability of official sources have led many war correspondents to develop relationships with other parties who can facilitate their ability to report from war zones. NGOs have played a considerable role in enabling the reporting of difficult and dangerous conflicts such as in Syria, Libya and Iraq. Humanitarian organisations such as the Red Cross, Medecins Sans Frontieres and UNHCR are involved not only in broadcasting the plight of those caught up in conflict but also in facilitating reporters' access to war zones. Christoph Meyer and his colleagues describe how NGOS are "increasingly filling a supply gap left by government sources that have lost credibility and a demand gap created by the difficulties of media organisations to provide direct reporting and verification from highly volatile and dangerous conflict settings" (2017: 16). Their "reporting capacity has increased substantially and now rival the resources found in major news organisations" (Powers, 2016: 401). NGOs supply information from war zones and make agreements with news organisations for their personnel to gain access to conflicts, combatants and victims. The consequences for war reporting are a matter of discussion. Simon Cottle and David Nolan (2009) argue that NGOs are "packaging information and images in conformity to the media's known predilections". Several studies refer to NGOs following the "media logic" and aping the agenda and approach of mainstream news organisations (Fenton, 2009; see also Waisbord, 2011). More controversially, Cottle and Nolan refer to "beneficent embedding", which they see as a positive development facilitating supportive networking on the ground and in-depth analysis and investigation (Cottle, 2013; Cottle and Nolan, 2007, 2009). This evaluation is supported by NGO representatives who believe closer working relations between NGOs and news organisations are creating "stronger" reporting (Abbott, 2009). NGOs provide "information subsidies" in a world in which the resourcing of international newsgathering is declining (see Gandy, 1982), but the risks of beneficent embedding should not be underestimated. Monika Kalcsics of the Austrian Press Agency notes that journalists' immersion with aid agencies and humanitarian organisations is as problematic as their being embedded with the military (Kalcsics, 2011). Any form of embedding leads to the risk of gaining access to "the stories the agency chooses" and telling those stories from "the perspective of the particular institution" (Kalcsics, 2011: 22). Many freelance war reporters actually work for both NGOs and news organisations, blurring the boundaries between journalism and humanitarian bodies (Wright, 2015, 2016). This collaboration is driven by financial, personal and political considerations. Brigit Mathisen (2017) distinguishes between freelancers driven by entrepreneurial considerations, making money and running businesses and those "idealists" who produce independent in-depth journalism that has a social and/or political impact. Many freelancers work for NGOs whose values and aims they are in sympathy with. The consequence is that the balance between activism and journalism is changing; agendas and approaches are mixed, and stories and ideas generated for NGOs are sometimes used by newsrooms.

The practical value of NGOs to war correspondents in an era of dwindling resources cannot be underestimated. They are helping journalists to get the story and understand the story. The help comes in various forms – most significantly, assistance in gaining access to war zones and the peoples displaced by fighting and military operations and help with the provision of materials including videos, photographs, case studies and interviewees (see Wright, 2015). They even provide training programmes which extend to fixers and translators. The growing involvement of journalists with NGOs has led to increasing criticism from reporters of the ability of agencies such as these to set the agenda in news reporting (see Magee, 2014). Developing a close – some say "incestuous" – relationship with the media (Styan, 1999: 292) is comparable with becoming embedded with the military, and freelancers run a greater risk of this happening to them.

The issue of proximity also applies to the relationship between correspondents and the people caught up in war zones. Getting close to those impacted by war depends on a number of factors, many of which are banal and have nothing to do with the politics of the situation. Jeremy Bowen (2006: 143) draws attention to how, in Bosnia, wearing a flak jacket was a "barrier between journalists and the people we were reporting on". The benefit of wearing flak jackets is a matter of debate amongst correspondents. Martin Bell (2017: 254–5) believes they are bulky and can "endanger your health and safety" in situations where fleet-footedness is required. Alsumaria's correspondent Mustafa Latif similarly states flak jackets are very heavy and restrict the movement of journalists and camera crews in the thick of conflict (Sa'adoun, 2017). Wearing them amongst civilians can be "discourteous" as it can "advertise you are safer than them" (Bell, 2017: 255). For Robert Fisk (2012), the flak jacket gives the impression that "the lives of Western reporters are somehow more precious, more deserving and, more inherently valuable than those of 'foreign' civilians who suffer around them". In addition, they can single you out as a target and, in some cases, make you feel "very uncool" (Bowen, 2006: 143). The flak jacket, however, has become a symbol of the glamour and heroism of the correspondent, and often, in spite of the reservations they have expressed, TV reporters don their flak jackets to do their pieces to camera. This satisfies the health and safety advisors and editors as well as meeting audience expectations. Professional bodies are critical of news organisations and reporters who take the risk of dispensing with the flak jacket, but the demands of information gathering and audience expectations often encourage reporters to eschew its protection.

Objectivity

One of the central tenets of reporting is objectivity. Much attention has been paid to the socialisation of journalists into accepting this ideal, but the challenge for the correspondent in the field is to put this commitment into practice. The problems and issues involved in being objective are acutely experienced by war correspondents. The value of objectivity in war reporting has regularly been questioned by correspondents as they attempt to resolve the dilemma of involvement and dispassion. Reporters of the interwar years wrestled with the collective failure of the news media to fully and accurately report the catastrophe, death and destruction of the Great War (see Chapter 2). They emphasised the need to tell it like it is, stressing the value of their own experiences, both what they saw and what they were told. The commitment to objectivity has become deeply engrained in the operation of the modern news organisation, and since 1945, particularly as a result of the development of broadcasting, it has become a professional and organisational expectation. Correspondents' concerns about the impact of objectivity on their operation in the field have increased as news organisations have asserted the importance of 'objective coverage' in branding their product. In the world of 'fake news', news organisations have had to 'beef up' fact-checking mechanisms and assert their commitment to objectivity to stave off growing criticism and suspicion of their output. The countervailing pressure on correspondents arises from the changing political economy of news production. The market demand both for correspondents' expression of personal feelings about the battlefield events they are caught up in and for receiving instant dispatches from the war zone challenge the commitment to objectivity. This is reinforced by the increased professional commitment to bearing witness. These pressures place the correspondent at the centre of the news narrative; what she or he feels or experiences has to be balanced against the organisational need to be seen to be detached. These tensions acquired an acute expression during the wars in the Balkans in the 1990s, which resulted in leading correspondents publicly debating the merits of objectivity and detachment in war coverage.

Managing emotion and personal feelings has always been challenging. How to keep your emotions and feelings in check as you do your job is a theme that runs through the memoirs of war reporters. Getting personal is part of showing the 'human face of war', but expressing one's emotions is not easy, straightforward or compatible with the tenets of the profession. Jon Snow of *Channel 4 News* expressed a passionate plea about the suffering of children in Gaza. He showed he cared about what was happening and his monologue became a 'hit' on YouTube. Emotion and tears on camera can attract viewers and stimulate public reaction for something to be done. It also brings criticism from those who believe the act of sympathy condones one party to the conflict. The risk in expressing emotion is that trust can be weakened or lost. TV is a medium of emotion rather than elucidation, and TV war reporters such as Bell (2017) describe the difficulties of real-time television, which places the journalist at the centre of the viewers' gaze. It differs from the impersonal newspaper byline, which to some extent preserves emotional distance.

Operationalising the concept in wartime is fraught with risk. The era of television has placed emphasis on telling both sides of the story as a means of providing objectivity. In covering conflicts in the late 19th century, newspapers attempted to accredit reporters to the various parties involved in the conflict. However, as wars became more ideological and complex, such a policy became a challenge to many newspaper outlets. Today the onus to balance accounts is more dangerous. One American correspondent has written about the need to balance his account of the war in Afghanistan by interviewing a Taliban commander and the "extreme risk" he took to proceed with this assignment (Rohde and Mulvihill, 2010: 2). Taking risks such as these are often seen as the product of inexperience. For other commentators, the real risk posed by the practice of objective journalism in modern war is not to personal safety but to professional standing. The conventions of objectivity, the dualism of balanced reporting and the dependence on official sources lead to conformity which "create[s] a virtual reality that reporters and readers alike must inhabit if meaningful transmission of news is to take place" (Pedelty, 2002: 166). Breaking the conventions is riskier in professional terms: "the greatest bravery a war correspondent can show is to report differently at a time when news conformity is the norm" (Pedelty, 2002: 166). Increasingly in the world of breaking news, with the decrease in the time for fact-checking or research, reporters are "servilely following the news agenda" instead of making decisions about what to cover, what to investigate and who to talk to (Marthoz, 2016: 23). The conventions of objective journalism help some media workers to accept this situation; as a former diplomatic editor of the *Daily Telegraph* puts it, the correspondent's job is simply to reproduce what he or she is told and to acknowledge the source; it is not their job to determine whether it is true or not (Standard Techniques, 1985). Challenging editors or seeking to set the agenda is sometimes seen not only as requiring too much work or carrying too many risks but also as assailing the conventions of objective journalism. The risks of practicing objective journalism should also be seen in the context of reporters' growing awareness of their audiences. Technology enhances war correspondents' contact with and knowledge of their audiences and what they believe, know and want. This has not been a salutary experience for many in relation to the practice of objectivity. Jackie Spinner speaks for many when she says that "people are going to find their truth whatever I report" (Spinner, 2015). Prior to the Internet there was little opportunity for the audience to check the sources of information used by war reporters – there was what David Weinberger (2009) describes as a lack of "transparency". Today viewers, listeners and readers can examine where the news comes from and how it is produced. They no longer have to trust the correspondent. Content is "linked, public, discussed and always subject to dispute and revision" (Weinberger, 2009). Whether war reporting has ever been objective is a moot point. Various studies have shown that as correspondents are "caught up within the rising tide of national sentiment or patriotic fervour" (Cottle, 2006: 84) or "confronted with the often-horrific realities of war", the belief that it is possible to remain detached and objective "tends to go out of the window in a hurry" (Zelizer and Allan, 2002: 3). However, in a world in which transparency is present, the practice of objective journalism is fraught with more risk and pressure.

4

TECHNOLOGY AND RISK MANAGEMENT

Telegraph, telex and Twitter

Technology plays a crucial role in determining the decisions war reporters make on the battlefield. Advances in media technology have facilitated the ability of reporters to get closer to the action and provide near live reports from the front. Since the Crimean War media technology has gradually made war more 'real' and 'live'. From the development of the telegraph in the mid-Victorian period to watching the real-time bombing of Baghdad during the second Gulf war, not only has the audience attained the ability to watch war unfolding but also correspondents have been able to report more of the story of war. Since 2003 the rise of social media has qualitatively changed the work of the war correspondent, for some making the need to have a reporter on the spot redundant. Advances in technology have continually changed the practice and performance of war correspondents and their coverage of war. These advances have "extended the scope for more independent and critical news media" (see Robinson *et al.*, 2010: 25) not just in the digital age but throughout the history of war reporting. For many war correspondents, these have added complexity to the process of newsgathering and reporting and increased the anxieties they face in doing their job.

This chapter explores the impact of technological developments on risk-taking and the ways in which war correspondents have understood and managed risk. It traces how new technologies such as the telegraph, photography, radio, cinema, television, satellite, videophone, and Twitter and other social media have, in their turn, impacted on the working environment of war reporters. The consequences of "digital war reporting" have been explored (see Matheson and Allan, 2009), but more attention is required to how technology has influenced the practices of war reporters. For some observers, "the basics of news gathering in times of conflict have changed very little" (Lederer, 2001: 19). Continuity in war reporting practices should not be ignored, but the enhanced capacity and ability to report instantly from the battlefield has influenced how war correspondents work and the risk culture he or she works within. Technology has made it easier to get the story and, more significantly, to get the story back, but it has also increased the pressures on the war correspondent to turn material around more rapidly. More risks are taken, and some would say more corners are cut, particularly with checking the reliability of what correspondents are told. Audiences today are accustomed to getting information quickly: according to an Associated Press news editor, "we are reporting for a public that checks back with their favourite websites, four, five or six times a day and they expect to see updated news" (quoted in Campbell, 2001). They can scrutinise and comment on correspondents' output in unprecedented ways through blogs, Twitter and other social media, adding to the burden to get the story right. Reporters increasingly have more of their time taken up justifying and defending their reporting to their audiences. Technology has made it easier for the war reporter to be in touch with his or her fellow correspondents in the field, and never before has the correspondent been as aware of what competitors are writing about. Technology has increased editors' expectations of what their reporters send back from the front – copy and images that are more vivid are demanded – as well as having strengthened the capacity for governments and other actors to manage war news. These factors have amplified the risks that are taken in the reporting of war.

Culture of distance

Warfare traditionally distinguished between the battlefield or front line, where the fighting took place, and the home front, where the domestic consequences of combat had to be addressed. During the early days of the war correspondent, the distance between the home and front line was clearly delineated by the time it took for dispatches from the front to return home. Russell's letters took around three weeks to get back from the Crimea (Furneaux, 1944: 38). These were the last days of the age of horse and sail; the telegraph had just begun to develop as a means of public communication in the 1840s, but the world had yet to be fully wired up. The mail coach was still the primary carrier of news and information. Better canals, roads and bridges improved the speed of the mail service, but land and sea travel were confronted by many obstacles and characterised by great uncertainty. For correspondents trying to get their dispatches back from foreign parts, the main risks they faced concerned the delay or destruction of their corre-spondence. Letters were often delivered by the Post Office in a bundle, a mixture of letters from different dates. As a result, correspondents often entered into arrangements with third parties for the safe and speedy return of their copy. Reporters in the Crimea used a variety of official channels – military, diplomatic or other official mailbags – or relied on individuals who were returning home to carry their prized copy. There were telegraph offices on the periphery of the conflict areas at, for example, Constantinople, Varna and Vienna to which correspondents could go to send short notices of events – the telegraph was at this stage an expensive means of communication. In 1855 a cable was successfully laid from

Varna to Bucharest, which brought London within 12 hours of the Crimea (Furneaux, 1944: 39), but dispatches still tended to be sent by land and sea. Edwin Godkin of the *Daily News* wrote of the futility of sending telegraphic accounts from the 'seat of war' as the telegraph "did not come further east than Budapest". Russell's reluctance to use the telegraph is attributed to his desire to check his stories before committing them to transmission (Royle, 1989: 20). It was also the case that "poor … lines" and "incompetent operators" could sometimes lead to "garbled telegrams" (Read, 1992: 30).

The risk of dispatches going astray or being delayed or being miscommunicated determined how war reporters worked. Editors required a flow of material from their special correspondents, but they were cognisant of the difficulties that faced their reporters in the field and hence expectations of the ability to get material back were lower than they subsequently became. One leading early 20th-century war correspondent, Ellis Ashmead-Bartlett, describes newspapers in this era as being "in no great anxiety to receive news almost before the event to be described had taken place" (1913: 59). Correspondents worried about ensuring the accuracy and inviolability of their correspondence rather than its earliest communication. Their reports would have to compete with official communiqués, which would usually reach home more quickly. For example, official news from the War Office took ten days to come back from the Crimea to Britain (Furneaux, 1944: 38). A distinction was made between public and private correspondence. Public letters were compiled for inclusion in the newspapers, but things that could not be said were included in private dispatches. Russell's private correspondence was much more critical and unequivocal in apportioning blame, and this is what Delane shared with members of the Cabinet. The task of ensuring that both public and private correspondence found their way into the correct hands exercised correspondents. Getting things wrong could not only damage reputations but, in Russell's case and that of his newspaper, it could have been detrimental to the campaign to improve the lot of the ordinary British soldier. Alan Hankinson (1982: 54), in his biography of Russell, draws attention to the correspondent's willingness "to correct any mistakes he made in subsequent Letters", which "increased the trust of his readers". The balance between accuracy and speed favoured the former and the risk of getting it wrong weighed more heavily on the correspondent than being first with the news. The arrival of the telegraph changed this.

Telegraphing risks

The introduction of the telegraph was met initially with "scepticism" and "resistance" by the press and politicians, and it was left to the military to first recognise its value in gaining a tactical advantage on the battlefield by allowing faster communication (McLaughlin, 2016: 64). The extension of the telegraph speeded up the process of civilian communication; time and space were annihilated in what was the transition from a "leisurely pace to instantaneous touch" – as fundamental a change as anything we are experiencing today with new media (Neuman, 1995:

26–7). Correspondents now cabled rather than transported their reports, and soon government was first learning of events on far-off battlefields from newspaper accounts rather than their own officials. US President Polk initially heard about the fall of the Mexican stronghold of Vera Cruz in 1847 when it was sent to him by *The Baltimore Sun* after they had informed their readers (Neuman, 1995: 36). As the telegraph network expanded and the world was cabled up, war reporting began to embrace the tyranny of speed. It is commonly agreed that during the Franco-Prussian War (1870–71) the telegraph established itself as central to the organisation of the newsgathering activity of the war reporter.

The telegraph fundamentally realigned the logistics of war reporting. Less reliant on military and postal services, it was now the job of the war correspondent to locate the nearest telegraph office to get their stories home. The importance of the telegraph to war reporting was recognised by the government and military authorities. During the American Civil War, the government attempted to seize control of commercial telegraph services and equipment to limit the transmission of information that could be detrimental to their cause. Correspondents became highly worked up about getting copy back as they had to make crucial decisions about when to leave the scene of action to send their dispatches. Being first with the news started to exert its hold over battlefield reporting, and haste in getting copy back became the defining goal of the war reporter. The correspondent who typified the new breed of reporter was Archibald Forbes, whose 100-mile "Ride of Death" across inhospitable terrain amid hostile forces to the nearest telegraph station to communicate the first news of the battle of Ulundi in 1879 grabbed the attention of the British public (Wilkinson-Latham, 1979: 155). As a 'telegraphic correspondent', Forbes spent a considerable amount of his working time arranging a string of horses to reach nearby telegraph stations; he also had ridden non-stop across the Carpathian Mountains, 140 miles in 30 hours, to dispatch news of the siege of Plevna in 1877. As Wilkinson-Latham (1979: 135) notes, "the increased use of the telegraph made it vitally necessary for the correspondent to be a good rider" or at least to be able to organise a system of couriers to dispatch reports. Competition reinforced the efforts to be first with the news. But as the technology facilitated the capacity of correspondents to file scoops, it accentuated the danger of the work. The risk involved in making decisions was calculated not only in terms of the personal threats and dangers of travelling across hostile and unknown lands; leaving the battlefield when potentially significant developments could take place was also a consideration. This was recognised by editors. Mowbray Morris, managing editor of *The Times*, encouraged Russell and his other special correspondents to use the telegraph freely, but he also drew attention to the problem that "something important may happen in your absence" (Furneaux, 1944: 185). Often correspondents fearful of missing a story would employ couriers to take their reports. Finding reliable individuals to undertake such potentially perilous ventures was not easy, and there was no guarantee they would be able to deliver the dispatch. The history of 19th-century war reporting is full of episodes when dispatches went astray, were not delivered or not delivered on time or when couriers were impeded or imprisoned. The uncertainty led many reporters to take on the risk of delivering their own stories.

Use of the telegraph in the late Victorian period was encouraged by most editors, increasingly mindful of competition in the newspaper market. Reporters were more wary. Between the end of the American Civil War and the Franco-Prussian War, the merits of using the telegraph to communicate war news were the subject of differences within the profession. Established reporters such as Russell and Godkin were loath to use the new technology. This is often portrayed as a reluctance to engage with change or as the result of age; one of Russell's biographers places considerable emphasis on how it was not possible for "a man of fifty" to race from the battlefield to telegraph his copy (Furneaux, 1944: 203). It also represented a difference of opinion about how to practice journalism. Some editors were initially sceptical of using the new technology on the grounds of the costs involved, but many correspondents were concerned that accuracy and literary competence would be sacrificed for speed and "scoops" (Weiner, 2011: 85). Godkin refused to use the telegraph, sharing the judgment of one of his colleagues that the "pestilent wire" was "utterly destructive of style and too often lends itself to inaccuracy" (Weiner, 2011: 99). The pressure to be first with the news led correspondents during the American Civil War to make up stories or to rush copy out before verifying their facts, which had major implications for their reputations and those of their newspapers. They were responsible for sensationalism and exaggerations as well as outright lies and conjecture including reporting battles that never happened (see Risley, 2012). Concerns about accuracy, however, could not prevent the industry from becoming fixated with the primacy of speed.

The Franco-Prussian War saw the demise of the 'old' journalism as telegraph accounts dominated the coverage. Russell's accounts of the major battles of the conflict were a matter for complaint from the management of *The Times*. Delane expressed disgust at having to publish letters from his star reporter of battles days after they had been reported in rival publications. Morris complained of being "beaten" by the *Daily News* "on several important occasions, both in speed and in quality" (Furneaux, 1944: 184). The most important example was the battle of Sedan, the decisive confrontation of this war. Russell delayed his return to London to check his facts and perfect his information on what had happened. The delay allowed the *Daily News* to publish the news of the French defeat first, and as a result of cabling the story to New York, readers of the *New-York Tribune* read the story before readers of *The Times*. Russell's despatch might have been "fuller and gave more details", but its news was 48 hours behind its competitor (Furneaux, 1944: 183). Speed rather than accuracy or the 'felicity of expression' was now the means by which war correspondents were judged, and it was those who skills lay in organising a system to get copy back to the home office more quickly than his rivals who prevailed. According to Forbes (1895: 225), "in modern war correspondence ... the best organiser of the means of expediting his intelligence, he it is who is the most successful man – not your deliberate manufacturer of telling phrases, your piler-up of coruscating adjectives".

The telegraph changed the way in which war was reported and how it was written about as the "need for economy … led to a drastic pruning of words" (Weiner, 2011: 96). Some of the basic features of modern journalism are attributed to the use of the technology, but the crucial development in the working lives of war reporters was that it placed more pressure on them to get stories back to their home offices. Taking more risks became a more significant feature of the work. Forbes describes the wear and tear on reporters of "long wearisome rides on dead tired horses" which are part of a job "calculated to make a man old before his time" (Forbes, 1895: 22, 46). Ashmead-Bartlett (1913: 60) depicts the war correspondent during the 1912–13 Balkan wars as being in "in a state of nervous unrest from the moment he arrives at the scene of the hostilities" due to the competition to obtain a scoop facilitated by the telegraph. He distinguishes between the Anglo-Saxon and European press. The French and the Germans, he states, "go in very little for cabling, they do not spend nearly so much money on their work, and, therefore, they are hardly in a position to compete for speed with ourselves" (Ashmead-Bartlett, 1913: 61). He emphasises the success of the war correspondent as being dependent on "the preparations he has made for sending off news from the front, before he actually starts on the campaign" (Ashmead-Bartlett, 1913: 61). It was critical to be able to identify the quickest means of getting news to the telegraph stations as well as having the ability to distinguish between stations from which to send censored and uncensored news. Ashmead-Bartlett's recollections of the Balkan wars relate in detail the risks attached to the purchase and use of a car to ferry news. The "endless trouble and bother" (Ashmead-Bartlett, 1913: 66), which included mechanical problems, unreliable chauffeurs and unsuitable roads, was pitted against the need to compete with the *Daily Mail* and *The Times*, who had also purchased cars and had the opportunity to send off news ahead of rivals. The cost and energy consumed in organising this means of transport were ultimately seen as detrimental by all who attempted to use it during this conflict. Subsequent wars have seen numerous accounts of correspondents' lack of preparedness in organising transportation. Making sure transport is in good working order is crucial to minimising risk. Few camera workers go into war zones without making sure their equipment is in good working order, but many fail to check the roadworthiness of the cars they hire. Many crews "will still go into dangerous conditions with a vehicle that does not work", and many deaths in the field are due to "bad practical organisation" (Beckett, 2006).

Making reporting easier

As the telegraph became the primary means of getting the story back to the office, a series of technological innovations at the end of the 19th century supposedly made the correspondent's work easier. The portable typewriter, for example, became indispensable to the production of copy in the field. The Blickensderfer portable typewriter first made its appearance in the 1890s. Described as the 'war correspondent's best friend', it was small, easy to carry and cheap. Lionel James, war correspondent for *The Times*, used it in the Sudan in 1898, and by the Boer War most reporters depended on the machine to produce their copy. All that was required was a basic technical knowledge to change ribbons and find paper. By the Second World War, no war correspondent would travel anywhere without his or her typewriter. They were now equipped with a small tripod, which made it easier to use them in the field. According to Alan Moorehead (2000: 96), "we could write anywhere at any hour of the day or night – anywhere, that is, except during a bombardment". The typewriter had become part of the technology that supported a "new kind of reporting … exasperating, exciting, fast-moving, vivid, immense and slightly dangerous" (McCamish, 2016: 78). The flexibility of the typewriter can be contrasted with the writing table, ink and pens that Russell had to transport. The portability of the typewriter allowed correspondents to travel more rapidly and independently, with a corresponding increase in risk.

If the typewriter facilitated the writing of copy, reporting was assisted by the advent of the telephone. The relationship between the telephone and war reporting has been little discussed compared to other technological advances. The first long-distance telephone call was made in 1876, and by the end of the century the mechanism was a feature of most newsrooms (Mari, 2017). By the Great War, both the telegraph and telephone had been incorporated into the military infrastructure, and the interwar years saw the telephone and typewriter established as emblematic of the profession. Will Mari (2017: 1–2) describes how the telephone led to a "bifurcation" in the newsgathering process between the gathering of news and its writing, editing and dissemination. Just as with the telegraph, the take-up of the technology was dependent on the development of an exchange network, and its impact on the working routines of war correspondents was not fully felt until the 1930s. Perhaps the key consequence was the creation of the 'tethering effect', which tied reporters to editors, a feature that was to accelerate with subsequent technological developments. The telephone contributed to the speeding up of communication. Stories could be sent much faster by telephone; 75 words a minute could be processed compared to between 40 and 50 words by telegraph (Mari, 2017: 6). It furthered encouraged reporters in their efforts to be first with the news, but its vulnerability was apparent in wartime – until the 1920s the exchange network was mainly wired up by overhead lines, which could easily be cut when fighting began.

For reporters, the telephone enabled easier checking of what they were being told, thereby helping to minimise the risk of getting stories wrong. It also added to the ability of journalists to gather news and information without leaving their desks. Other technical advances such as the telex, developed in Germany in the 1920s, facilitated a desk-bound approach to reporting. But if the telephone had become an essential tool for the reporter, it did not solve the problems of corresponding from the battlefield. During the Korean War, newspaper reporters faced considerable challenges in finding and using telephones to get their stories back to Tokyo so they could be put on the wire; sometimes 10 or 20 reporters struggled for one telephone line to phone their stories through (Anderson, 2009: 408).

Phone lines were scarce outside the Western world, and it was slower to get news back from Korea than it had been during the Second World War. The telephone made the work of war reporters easier in some ways, but it had implications for their autonomy and added to the complexity of the decision-making process on the battlefield.

The arrival at the beginning of the 20th century of the lightweight and compact Leica camera is regarded as having enhanced the autonomy of the war reporter as well as improving his or her capacity to cover war. Small enough to fit into a pocket, this camera could take pictures in rapid succession. It changed photography, taking it out of the studio and onto the streets, and its invention coincided with the outbreak of the Great War. It meant that anyone could photograph war, and ordinary soldiers in the trenches became war photographers (see Allan, 2011). Ordinary soldiers' photographs of the battlefield were rarely reproduced in the press due to strict wartime censorship and the threat of the death penalty if found carrying a camera. The technical problems of reproducing photographs in newspapers remained a barrier until the 1920s when the wire transmission of photographs was developed. The introduction of the lightweight camera was nevertheless a "definitive moment in war reporting" – it was the first step on the way to the democratisation of image-making in wartime as well as the emergence of the photojournalist (see Wilson, 2016). During the interwar years photojournalism thrived with the development of the means to print photographs without the intervention of an engraver and the birth of photo-magazines such as *Life, Vu, Picture Post* and *Berliner Illustrite Zeitung*. These magazines gave an impetus to the growth of photo agencies which supplied pictures from around the world (Wilson, 2016: 137). Modern photojournalism played a considerable role in the reporting and representation of war and conflict in the 1930s, with Robert Capa and Margaret Bourke-White achieving prominence; but it was during the Second World War that some photojournalists gained celebrity status. Their war work became a story in its own right as publications such as *Life* played up their adventures to capitalise "on the brand value of its intrepid band of photographers" (Wilson, 2016: 145).

The high profile of war photographers such as Bourke-White, Lee Miller and Capa accentuated their risk in doing their job. The branding, in which many photographers colluded, emphasised the heroic stereotype of the intrepid photographer who plunged into the unknown to bring vivid pictures of ordinary people at war to their readers (Wilson, 2016: 141). Living up to this image proved to be a risky challenge. Looking through the lens of the camera impacted on reporters' judgement in warzones and had long-lasting effects on their well-being. Finding methods to deal with death and dying on the battlefield has long challenged war correspondents (see Chapter 8). The camera lens, first still and then moving, assisted in this process. Peter Beaumont sums up the view of many war reporters: "By an act of will, I make the observation of violent death a deliberately mechanical process. Blink. An emotional curtain comes down like a camera shutter. The distance is preserved while I go about the business of looking" (2010: 82). The technology encourages the notion that war correspondents can be detached from the events they report on, thereby facilitating their work. Such a view, as Beaumont admits, is "delusional", and research has shown the traumatic effect that photographing war has had on men and women. The suicide of Pulitzer Prize-winning photographer Kevin Carter after failing to help a dying child who became the subject of an award-winning photograph is often cited as an example of the cost of remaining detached in war and crisis situations (see Kleinman and Kleinman, 1996). The high level of exposure to traumatic events has led to calls for "the inclusion of emotional risk in theories of the relationship between photojournalistic practices to the creation of images" (Newman *et al.*, 2003). However, seeing the world through the lens of a camera can also influence risk assessment. Robert Capa's death, treading on a landmine while accompanying troops in Vietnam in 1954, is often seen as highlighting the risk of getting too close or trying to feel too much. Others reflect on the possible psychological effects of using such technologies and the ways in which they inform risk behaviour (Cottle, 2017: 163). One BBC producer speaks of less conspicuous lightweight cameras encouraging reporters to take risks they would not usually take. Such equipment leads correspondents to be less aware of being a target and to be more complacent.

Broadcasting risk

The advent of sound broadcasting on the battlefield moved war correspondents even closer to the action. Growing suspicion of news in the interwar years was accompanied by a shift in the way in which people were receiving their information. Radio had established itself in the US by 1938 as the "preferred medium"; it was cheaper than buying a newspaper, and it communicated what was happening more quickly (Sweeney, 2006: loc. 1398). This took a little longer to happen in Britain, but a survey in 1940 found that three-quarters expressed more trust in the BBC than the press (Nicholas, 1996: 196). Radio was new to the reporting of war, and its practitioners were finding their feet during the Second World War; the intimacy of the medium posed new challenges about how to report war, including describing events as they unfolded live from the battlefield. During the Phoney War (1939–40), radio was technically limited for front-line reporting, and reporters had to contend with military restrictions as they developed the best ways to exploit the medium to report battlefield conflict. Military anxieties mainly focused on the capacity of sound broadcasting to compromise operational security, and there were worries about the impact of radio descriptions of war's horrors. As the war progressed, technical innovations extended the capacity of radio as lighter and better-quality recording equipment was introduced. Early in the war, transportable disk recording machines operated from a car or truck, but by 1943 the invention of the midget disc recorder meant recording equipment was portable enough to be carried into action; it could also be operated without an engineer (Hood, 2011: 79). These machines were used to capture the sound of war more easily, and they enabled radio reporters to get closer to the action. In January 1943,

Richard Dimbleby became the first BBC journalist to accompany the RAF on a bombing raid over Germany, capturing not only the sound of the raid but also the voices of the crew (Hood, 2011: 112). Live reports from the field were, however, rare. Most were recorded in order both to satisfy the censors and to avoid the risk of correspondents being killed live on air.

By facilitating the ability to get closer to the action, sound broadcasting increased the risk to reporters. Being closer to the scene of action also fuelled more emotional reporting. Ed Murrow might have delivered his account of a bombing raid on Berlin in a measured and calm voice, but his reports of Londoners under bombardment were impassioned. His commentaries went "beyond the current facts and dug into the emotion of the moment" (Conway, 2009: 100). Becoming involved heightened the senses and led him to become "absorbed in what was going on" (quoted in Cozma, 2010: 668). He could never be a detached observer but immersed himself in the action – for example, Murrow went on 25 bombing missions. He had to experience events, and sound broadcasting allowed him to communicate his experience in a conversational style to his audience. Radio encouraged the more personal, emotional and involved style of reporting which Murrow's journalism epitomised. It influenced the development of post-war radio news reporting, establishing the importance of reporting on feelings as well as facts. On the spot reporting facilitated a more emotional style of reporting in order to touch the sensitivities of the listener. But such reporting collided with the commitment to objectivity and getting the facts. Moreover, encouraging the expression of feelings had implications for risk assessment.

The use of film equipment during the Second World War highlighted the logistical difficulties correspondents faced in operating the new technology. Dimbleby had taken film equipment on the bombing raid of Berlin, but a combination of mechanical problems and the cold prevented him from filming the raid. Technical problems and issues influenced the capacity of newsreels to report war. Newsreels had established themselves during the Second World War, but their ability to report from the battlefield was curtailed by the heavy, difficult to operate camera equipment. "Ten minutes of film, a thousand feet, weighs pounds; the camera weighs twenty-eight pounds. Then there is lens, film magazines, camera cases and so on" (Noble, 1955: 71). This description of a newsreel camera worker's experience in 1942 resembles the tales told by William Dickson and his biograph during the Boer War. Various means of transport were used to move this equipment around, from mules and camels to jeeps and trucks with varying degrees of reliability. In moments of crisis when camera workers had to flee the scene of fighting in a hurry, "quick decisions on what to take and what to leave must be made" (Noble, 1955: 71). Such logistical considerations made the work of newsreel camera operators during the Second World War more risky and difficult than that of their print or sound colleagues.

These difficulties were accentuated with television, which replaced radio as the primary source of public information from the battlefield in the 1960s. The medium provided sound and pictures, giving the illusion of immediacy. Getting the pictures was a time-consuming and labour-intensive business. It involved at least three people carrying a welter of wires, cables and batteries. A limited amount of film could be carried into the field, which had implications for when to let the camera roll. This could lead to friction between reporter and camera worker if the pictures for the story were not taken. Due to their weight, there was also a limit to the number of batteries that could be taken into action. Overall, the technical logistics of television at this time worked against the production of long reports. In addition, getting pictures home was a longer-drawn-out process than today. For American TV networks during the early years of the Vietnam War, film either had to be put on an airplane and flown back to the US or to one of the cities in Asia, such as Hong Kong, Tokyo or Manila, where it was developed and edited and finally transmitted over one of the few satellite links to New York (Hirashiki, 2017). The need to fly or airfreight film home required considerable organisation, and the time delay had implications for what camera workers shot. Many of the early TV reports were ambiguous in terms of time so that they would not be dated when aired.

Technical improvement enabled television to show more vivid and "close up and personal" pictures as the Vietnam War progressed (see Hallin, 1991). However, editorial control remained a feature of the medium. It was not until the 1980s that the medium ceased to be cumbersome, heavy and expensive; videotape replaced film, enabling correspondents to edit in the field. Bell (2017: 83) describes the era of electronic newsgathering in the 1980s and early 1990s as a "phase of liberation". The technology, he argues, allowed reporters to "become our own news editors, deciding on the spot and usually without reference to higher authority what went into the report and what stayed out"; editors could decide not to broadcast a report but "they did not have the time to change it" (Bell, 2017: 84). Greater autonomy placed more responsibility on the reporter as the distance between the battlefield and the living room diminished. TV reporters, as Jon Snow (2005: 174–93) notes of his experience during the civil war in El Salvador in the early 1980s, were subject to more pressures. They had to determine on the spot what pictures to include and vet potentially gruesome images. Civilians sought their protection as the presence of cameras that could send pictures back quickly were seen as able to prevent violence. The perception of the power of TV led to death squads in Central America targeting television journalists. Bell perhaps exaggerates the degree of autonomy reporters acquired in this period, but he asserts control was re-established with the advent of the mobile phone in 1995.

Satellite communication became a feature of war reporting throughout the 1990s. It was this technology and its affordances that took centre stage for the reporting of the 1991 Gulf War (see Smith and Higgins, 2012). To begin with, satellite technology presented similar logistical problems to previous forms of technology in reporting from the field. It required a point from which you could feed your material via satellite to the home office. Getting to and from events, filming them, recording your audio and getting back in time to edit and send them via the satellite link required time; and with poor transport infrastructure, unsafe roads and limited internal communication in many countries, this added to the logistical uncertainty. The satellite phone to some extent disposed of these problems, replacing the team of trucks and technicians with the individual reporter, her digital camera and a satellite uplink. The increased mobility of satellite technology conquered the remoteness of many parts of the world (see Livingston and Van Belle, 2005). It shifted war reporting away from institutional newsgathering and processing to breaking news, encouraging the reporter on the spot to "rely more on their own observations" and access alternative sources to the official communiqués and accounts they had tended to rely on (Livingston and Van Belle, 2005: 47). Closed regimes immediately recognised the threat to their control of information from war zones from newsgatherers who operated uplinks; as a result, they placed more restrictions on the access to the territory they controlled. It took longer for correspondents to recognise the consequences for their newsgathering routines. The dependence on the new technology, the demand for – indeed growing expectation of – live reports from the battlefield and the competition from non-journalists in providing accounts from war zones had a profound impact. Some have dubbed this as the birth of "existential" or "liquid" war reporting (see Busch, 2012; Deuze, 2005, 2008). Others draw attention to the changing nature of control over what reporters can do and the growing emphasis on the performance (Bell, 2008). Most agree it has corresponded with reporters taking more personal, professional and intellectual risks.

Working digitally

It is the changes in media technology since the 1980s that have had the most profound impact on the work of war correspondents. For many observers, new media technology is assisting the ease with which war correspondents can access, record and report back the immediacy of war. Reporters in the field acknowledge this, but they also see the recent technological advances as increasing editorial control over their actions and activities. Permanent connection with the home office can be established through the mobile phone, laptop and Internet, reducing the capacity of the correspondent to make the news. The daily news agenda as well as the nature, tenor and content of news packages and reports is, as we discussed in the previous chapter, becoming more driven by home editors. Decisions are increasingly made by those not on the spot. Vaughan Smith of the Frontline Club argues that logistical matters must be separate from editorial considerations (Beckett, 2006). Assessing the potential risks to reporters, he believes, should be in the hands of suitably qualified people on the ground. They are in a better position than more distant home offices to make risk calculations.

The growing regularity of the demands made by the home offices on their field reporters has limited the ability of the latter to get out and find out what is happening. Rolling 24-hour news in the 1990s led to the emergence of the "dish monkey", the reporter tethered to his or her satellite dish, available to respond to questions from studio presenters and fill time with commentary and speculation

(Bell, 2017: 121). The emphasis was on 'being there' or at least being seen to be there, not actually knowing what was going on there. As Bell puts it, war journalism is increasingly about "packaging" than reporting the news. Field correspondents can now receive as well as transmit, and as a result they can present a "parcel of images tied up with words" without moving from their hotels, an exercise which "rewards the glib and plausible" (Bell, 2017: 122). Drawing on his experience of covering wars in Ossetia and Gaza, James Rodgers (2012) describes the experience of multiplatform storytelling where the reporter's day is taken up filing for a variety of different types of platforms, programmes and outlets. The time-consuming nature of providing different versions of the story for different platforms not only limits "your time to gather facts" but also undermines "a reporter's sense of self-worth" and "job satisfaction", leaving many reporters exiting the war zone with the feeling that they have not managed to tell everyone the full story (Rodgers, 2012: 91). Bell (2017: 259) equates the advance of technology with the retreat of journalism. While offering the opportunity to get closer to the fighting, new technology is seen by some old war hands such as Bell as bringing about the emergence of a new type of war reporter who covers war without going to where the fighting is happening or even travelling to the war zone. The Internet allows the man or woman in the field to access news film and footage from a range of sources inside and outside of the war zone he or she is reporting from. With the emphasis in television news on producing 'packages' for a variety of outlets, the risk for the TV correspondent is to stay in one place rooted to the technology, packaging rather than reporting (Bell, 2017: 122). The demands created by new media technology reduce the capacity of the reporter to gather information and gain knowledge and make local contacts, which are crucial to the story and for making judgements about their safety.

The increased use of technology on the battlefield demands reporters possess some degree of 'digital fluency'; according to one freelance war reporter, "you have to be Inspector Gadget these days" to get work (Palmer, 2015: 229). Facility with the technology often distinguishes freelancers from staff reporters, who are at best 'ambivalent' to the new media technology. The range of skills the man or woman in the field is required to possess today has considerably increased, making the work of the modern war correspondent more complicated. Maintaining the equipment is one skill which demands more of the journalist. Technology is not and never has been infallible. Malfunctions and crashes occur, and in hostile terrain technical knowledge is required. Local assistance and replacement parts are not easily found in places such as Afghanistan. Smartphones might decrease the amount of specialised equipment required to broadcast directly from the war zone, but they increase the technical know-how demanded of the modern war reporter. This has increasingly been associated with a decline in knowledge-based journalism and subject expertise. A sign in the Pentagon Press Office during the 1991 Gulf War drew attention to the military perception of correspondents' declining knowledge – it stated, "Welcome Temporary War Experts" (Sparrow, 1999: 58). Former marine and *New York Times* defence correspondent Bernard Trainor complained in

1991 of "reporters on the scene asking asinine questions" such as whether an environmental impact statement had been filed before the bombing of Baghdad had commenced (Henderson, 1994). This perception is not confined to the military. Scholars and sections of the public have also expressed concern at declining levels of knowledge in the profession, which it is argued makes reporters more vulnerable to manipulation by their sources. Despite correspondents having higher levels of educational attainment and the increased capacity to access a growing wealth of data and knowledge online, the ability to apply knowledge to daily working routines is perceived as diminishing (see Patterson, 2013). The amount of time required for primary research is not compatible with the speed of daily journalism, and this is compounded by the magnitude of the information available. The consequence is that journalists cut corners in assessing the information they collect and in making calculations of the risks in gathering news and generating stories.

Portable satellites and mobile phones are a threat to the personal security of those reporting on war and conflict. These have enhanced the ability to track the movements of reporters in war zones. Routine monitoring of the whereabouts of correspondents threatens their safety and their capacity to do their work in a number of ways. It facilitates the targeting of journalists by warring parties; one example is the deaths of Marie Colvin and Rene Ochlik by the deliberate bombing of buildings or areas where mobile phone signals were detected (Rayner and Spencer, 2012). Previously, during the 2003 Gulf War, the Pentagon threatened to fire on the satellite uplink positions of independent journalists in Iraq. According to veteran BBC war correspondent Kate Adie, the Pentagon made it known to correspondents that their telephones were detectable in order to discourage them for accessing areas they did not want reporters to go to (Sunday Show, 2003). Phillip Knightley believed that the Pentagon "may find it necessary to bomb areas in which war correspondents are attempting to report from the Iraqi side" (Sunday Show, 2003). The growth of surveillance doesn't only demand greater consideration of personal security; it also requires that more attention be paid to how correspondents protect their sources, gain access to data and make decisions about what to cover (see Bell and Owen, 2017). The implications for source protection have been highlighted by the current war in Syria. The Internet and social media have been used by Assad's intelligence operators to monitor journalists, activists and opposition forces. Those trying to document the abuses perpetrated by his government emphasise the importance of working anonymously. The "pseudonym helps me feel safe", says a citizen journalist working in government-held territory (al-Adnan, 2016: 28). The factional and fragmented nature of the opposition forces reinforces the need to work in secret. Sources are reluctant to be quoted and increasingly refuse to be filmed: "you media people take photos and rake in the money and we get bombed by Bashat al-Assad's planes because you take photos" (quoted in Al-Adnan, 2016: 30). The enhanced technological capacity to monitor what is reported has made independent enquiry into what is happening on the ground more difficult.

The greater opportunity provided by new media technology to disseminate information from the battlefield is dependent on reporters' ability to access and operate within that battlefield. Journalists in the field have always struggled to report the 'big picture' of a conflict. The advent of technology facilitating their ability and capacity to know what is going on is today mitigated by the increased dangers of operating on the ground. In Iraq in the years after the 2003 invasion, the inability of Western reporters to leave the Green Zone led to what has been described as a two-tiered level of reporting. Local Iraqis hired as fixers go out and do the on the ground reporting, and the Western reporters write up the story on the basis of the information their fixers supply (Anderson, 2009: 411). In recent conflicts, the advent of Web 2.0 technology has opened up the possibility of ordinary citizens communicating their views of what is happening in a war zone. Communication from suffering populations, facilitated by Twitter, YouTube and Facebook, perhaps more than any other technology has changed the relationship between the journalist and the citizen in the war zone and the way in which the war correspondent does the job.

Social media revolution

The advent of a new generation of media technologies such as blogs, Twitter and other social networking sites has enabled non-journalists to disseminate information about and comment on war and conflict to an ever-expanding number of online readers. Ordinary people – or at least those with access to social media – have been empowered by this technology in two crucial ways: they can produce content on social media platforms with no cost, and they can use these platforms to build networks. Web 2.0, unlike the first generation of websites, facilitates interactivity and allows individuals to be creators as well as users of content. For many commentators, this development has "irretrievably changed the way that wars are fought, reported on and consumed" (Patrikarakos, 2017: 9). Since the conflict in Kosovo in the 1990s, ordinary citizens have been more able to convey their experiences of war. Web pages devoted to accounts of being on the receiving end of NATO air strikes on Belgrade or description of life in Baghdad under the threat of imminent US invasion in 2003, provided by bloggers such as Salaam Pax, exemplified what many people represent as an alternative version of war. News organisations incorporated such stories into their coverage, providing what was seen to be a greater diversity of views and perspectives (see Matheson and Allan, 2009). The introduction of a new type of information producer and provider has changed not only where people get their news and information about war but the working practices of the war correspondent. Elite news outlets and correspondents retain their high status, but citizen journalists have attained credibility because of the immediacy of their accounts. The perception is that they are more authentic and unmediated than other sources (Johnson and Kaye, 2010). With the difficulties of accessing recent conflicts, such as in Gaza and Syria, such accounts have become an essential ingredient of the coverage of contemporary conflict, with many news outlets relying on them to provide first-hand experience of what is happening inside the country.

From the perspective of newsgathering, the opportunities presented by techno-logical advances have been accompanied by a fundamental reconsideration of how to find stories and what these stories should be about. For some critics, the thinking about the impact of technology on the process of gathering news has not kept pace with the changes that are taking place (Braman, 2003: 26). Most commentators believe that citizen-journalists present a major challenge to the way in which war correspondents perform their job, undermining the traditional hierarchies, with elite news organisations and elite reporters at the top, that have dominated the reporting of war and conflict for most of the 20th century (Sambrook, 2010). Power is "moving from hierarchies to citizens and networks" (Patrikarakos, 2017: 10), or to put it in a more hyperbolic way, "this is John Lennon's Power to the People, but turbo-charged and amplified. The people want a voice, and now they really have it. Their own voice, unedited and unfiltered" (McNair, 2006: 152). The extent to which this is happening is a matter of debate and conjecture, but it does mean that correspondents no longer depend only on military accounts. They can now check their phone or computer and access the latest accounts and posts on the Web to gain a fuller picture of what is happening on the battlefield (see Anderson, 2009).

Social media, according to Patrikarkos (2017: 86), has "greatly expanded the news net". The problem of gaining access to war zones is to some extent over-come by the army of tweeters and YouTube posters who can communicate their views of what is happening, allowing the correspondent to check what he or she is told by official sources. Accessing their Twitter accounts or checking Facebook is a feature of the activities of contemporary front-line reporters. Using social media gives the correspondent the ability to cover events he or she could not reach otherwise due to their inaccessibility, the cost of getting there, the difficulties of travelling in a war zone, official restrictions placed on them or the suddenness of the event (Sacco and Bossio, 2015: 66). The main challenge is that social media push out a vast amount of material, and the reliability of the accounts, pictures and images posted online is difficult to substantiate. The flood of unmediated and unverified stories raises the question of the capacity of correspondents to check the quality of the information. The assumption that citizen journalists or those caught up in the fighting provide independent and untainted accounts is doubtful. Putting aside the fact that their reports may act as propaganda for certain interests, citizen journalists, like their mainstream colleagues, are restricted by the circumstances they operate within. As Alexandra El Khazen of Reporters Without Borders says of the conflict in Syria,

> It is nearly impossible for anyone inside Syria to cover the war with distance and impartiality. Citizen journalists in Syria do not have the same access to information, each has [his or her] own reality. They depend on the local group who controls the territory they work in.
>
> *(Quoted in Baraniuk, 2016)*

The problem of verifying reports from non-journalist sources is accentuated by the susceptibility of social media to be used in information warfare (Ojala *et al.*, 2016: 299). Their low cost, ease of access and capacity for global dissemination make them a valuable tool for state and non-state actors. Despite their wide usage, social media are awash with detailed conspiracies and flooded with hoaxes, doctored images and fake news (Patrikarakos, 2017: 133). War correspondents using social media become deeply entangled with information wars. They are targets of online attacks, subject to hostile commentary and other efforts to influence their accounts and evaluations of what is happening (Ojala *et al.*, 2016: 299). Journalists are more accountable for their stories, increasingly forced to validate them in a news environment even though, as we have seen, they are provided less time and resources to do so. Several studies have found that in spite of the capacity of social media to bypass the conventional media, the credibility, authority and popularity of certain reporters make them influential gatekeepers of information flows in the digital world. A familiar brand such as a leading correspondent or elite news organisation gives credence to a report from a dubious source; hence the efforts to use Twitter, YouTube and Facebook to convince correspondents in the field of a particular interpretation of events. Correspondents' tweets may be limited to 140 characters (now 280) and may tend to describe actions, but what they decide to retweet and the hyperlinks they supply to their consumers can go further to shape perceptions and understandings of the conflict. These problems have not stopped the use of material from social media by elite news organisations and their reporters; they recognise the difficulties, and organisations like the BBC have set up reality fact-checkers (Jackson, 2017). However, it is perhaps other aspects of the new technologies that have made covering war more risky.

What is often the 'rawness' of the personal testimony from those present at the face of war, soldiers and civilians, can be seen as eliciting a more emotional and subjective response from correspondents. Markus Ojala and his colleagues, in their study of Finnish war reporters, found that the new media environment created by social media, in which "instant messaging, borderless interactions and information warfare" prevail, has led correspondents to reconsider or adapt what they report (Ojala *et al.*, 2016: 307).[1] The increasingly visceral nature of the visual representation of war is partly attributable to the impact of social media. No longer are news organisations able to manage the images that people see on their screens or view in the press. Alerted by the mainstream media, people today can go online to witness in full detail gruesome pictures and visuals, posted by the perpetrators or eye-witnesses to the events (see Huxford, 2004). In response to pressure from the availability of images online, newsrooms have had to reconsider their attempts to manage what they show, and reporters are now encouraged to convey the barbarities of war accompanied by their emotional response to what they have seen.

New technology has come to define modern conflict; for example, the Syrian conflict has been described as the first "Twitter war" or the first "YouTube war". This underlines the importance of technology for gaining access to a war which has remained inaccessible to most reporters. The Syrian authorities have restricted reporters' access to the fighting, which has led to efforts to enter the country illegally or to rely on local journalists and activists. Relying on the parties to the war, including the plethora of rebel groups, heightens the risk to Western journalists. The armed opposition groups are a mixture of extreme and moderate Islamists, secular groups of different political persuasions, and identifying the disposition of these groups has not proven easy. Gaining their trust is fraught with difficulty and danger, and once trust is won, convincing other factions that the reporter has not taken sides is far from straightforward (al-Adnan, 2016: 28). Entering rebel territory is considered a cardinal sin by the Syrian authorities, leading them to deny access to the government side (Vandervoordt, 2016: 313). Local reporters can fill a gap but they work under considerable restrictions – many rarely work at night or do not enter regions held by ISIS or government, their linguistic or journalistic skills are limited, and many people caught up in the fighting "do not look upon journalists favourably" (al-Adnan, 2016: 30).

Resorting to tools such as Skype to interview those they cannot reach physically minimises the threat to personal safety and overcomes the problem of access. Not only is it safer to use Skype, but it also enables reporters to continue to cover the war from both sides. The Syrian war is sometimes described as the "Skype Rebellion" as protagonists used this application to get around a near nationwide shutdown of the Internet in 2012 (Chozicknov, 2012). Armed with mobile satellite phones and dial-up modems, opponents of the Assad regime have used the technology to communicate with one another and the outside world. Correspondents based in Beirut and Turkey, unable to access the country, cover the war through a network of contacts, communicating with them via Skype, Facebook and WhatsApp (National Public Radio, 2016). A campaign of digital surveillance has been deployed by the regime to counter this communication, and a pro-regime group has used custom malware to target attacks on the machines of opposition activists (Roberts, 2012) and infiltrate several Reuters blogs and a Twitter account in order to post pro-government propaganda disguised as legitimate news content (Fitzpatrick, 2012).

Social media has allowed correspondents to overcome problems of access, and through its use, those caught up in the fighting – military and civilian – can provide their often more vivid accounts of what is happening in the war zone. Correspondents are under more scrutiny as the subjects of their reports can read or see or listen to what is said about them. Greater pressure arises from the enhanced speed of communication, the personalised nature of the information provided, and the increased capacity to access information on the front line. This has changed the amount and nature of the material available to the war correspondent, making her work riskier, not least by the way in which it pushes her to get closer to the fighting.

Note

1 Similar findings appear in studies of German correspondents; see Kramp and Weichert (2014).

5

THE MEDIA ON THE BATTLEFIELD

Risk and embedding

One of the features of modern conflict between nation states is that the war correspondent is embedded with the military forces on the battlefield. Embedding is not a new phenomenon, but it became part of the essential vocabulary of war reporting in Iraq in 2003. This chapter examines the practice of embedding in the 2003 Iraq War and explores the extent to which the risks to the journalists were lessened or enhanced by such a practice. Being 'in bed' with the military might help to safeguard the personal safety of journalists, but it increases the risk to an idealised form of objective journalism that pervades the profession's self-identity. It also introduces other types of hazards. The close co-operation with the military threatens the autonomy of the journalist, but other factors such as the expectations of news organisation, the physical demands on reporters and the personal stress that might accrue present other less obvious risks which in practice pose a greater threat to carrying out an ideal, if perhaps unreal, form of journalism.

There have been several studies of the performance of embedded journalists in Iraq in 2003 and subsequently (for example, Fahmy and Johnson, 2005; Kuypers and Cooper, 2005; Paul and Kim, 2004). These studies are based on particular understandings of the role of journalism in wartime that draw attention to the problem of defining journalism. There are several competing principles that "struggle over the dominant interpretation of journalism's social function and identity" (Hanitzsch, 2007: 370). Part of the confusion is whether journalism can be defined as a profession with a set of guidelines that influence how journalists should perform, similar to those enjoyed by lawyers or doctors. For Western scholars and commentators, the ideal form of news journalism is, as we have seen in previous chapters, linked to notions of factuality, impartiality and objectivity (Schudson, 2001) whereby objectivity is associated with neutrality, balance and reporting the facts. Journalists must be free and autonomous to be able to question power and act as watchdogs for democracy (see Deuze, 2005; Weaver *et al.*, 2007).

Numerous studies have pointed out the obstacles that exist to putting this ideal journalism into practice and the discrepancies between the ideal and *actual* performance (for example, Nord, 2007; Tandoc *et al.*, 2013), and it is acknowledged that journalism is at risk when this gap becomes such that the perceived obligations of journalism to society are undermined. Being embedded with the military, living and eating with them and being dependent on them for transport, food and safety, can be seen as compromising the basic ideals of journalism. It impairs the journalist's independence and neutrality and leads to the omitting or misrepresenting of certain facts because of her or his physical and emotional closeness to the military.

The chapter draws on personal experiences of reporting the Iraq War. In January 2003 the media was full of stories about imminent war in Iraq, and the BBC commissioned a 'landmark' documentary series in which seven documentary crews would follow the British military to war, if it happened. This series was originally intended to accompany the British mission to Afghanistan in 2002, but negotiations with the Ministry of Defence (MoD) had taken too long and the first fighting phase of the war was almost over by the time the necessary contracts were drawn up.[1] So when the next war came along, negotiations were already underway. If the British military was to go to war in Iraq, the film-makers would go with them. And so a small advance party[2] went to Kuwait to negotiate with the senior officers on the ground what military operations/actions it would be possible to film for this television documentary series. The series *Fighting the War* charting British involvement in the Iraq conflict through the eyes of the politicians and the military personnel who fought it, both at home and in the field, was broadcast on BBC2 in 2003.

The negotiated access the BBC agreed with the MoD might seem like a cosy scenario, but in the celebrated words of the German military strategist Helmuth von Moltke, "no battle plan survives contact with the enemy". Reference to the media as the enemy is something that pervades 'common-sense' attitudes inside the military to war reporting. As Barry Zorthian, a Pentagon spokesperson, said after the 1991 Gulf War: the war is over and "the press lost" (quoted in Engelhardt, 1994: 81). The relationship broke down in 2003 almost as soon as filming started; an indication of the complex relationship between the media and the military on the contemporary battlefield and the difficulties of squaring the ideals and practices of journalism. One of the primary reasons for the collapse was the difficulty of balancing a close working relationship with the military with the need to protect journalism's commitment to objectivity. For correspondents on the ground, the latter is interpreted in practical terms as the independence of reporters to film and report what they have seen. The agreement was made at an institutional level between the BBC and MoD, but it had to be operationalised on the ground between the soldier and journalist. In a wartime situation this is challenging. For news organisations such as the BBC, maintaining the commitment to the ideal of objectivity is crucial; but for reporters on the ground, this is understood in terms of their ability to do the job and their independence of action. Matters are further complicated by the medium the 'embeds' worked for. Press, photojournalists and

TV news reporters differed in relation to the demands their medium made on their work. The 2003 war generated a plethora of war documentaries, reflecting the revival of the media form and the increased mediatisation of war. More than 200 Iraq War documentaries and documentary series were made between 2002 and 2013, an output described as "unprecedented" (Culloty, 2014). Documentary film-makers operate within a distinct work culture. While the news attempts to present the facts as they occur, documentary film-makers seek to communicate what it feels like to be in the middle of a war zone, even though such a distinction is breaking down in the new political economy of war reporting. In the digital era nearly everything that is said on the air or off can be captured on camera and is available for documentary film-makers to use (Conway, 2005). Located somewhere between journalism and art, the documentary has been more creative in telling stories and providing alternative accounts. The BBC documentary team in Iraq signed a separate contract to that of the rest of the British media because the footage was not going to be seen until the team returned to the UK to edit the seven one-hour programmes. The lack of emphasis on immediacy distinguished the film-makers from their media colleagues in negotiating the experience of embedding.

Negotiating the relationship on the ground carries the risk that journalists become participants in war, either willingly or unwillingly (Taylor, 2000). Douglas Kellner (2008) describes three possible responses of war correspondents on the battlefield. They can simply describe actions, events and briefings, serving as a relatively objective conduit of information; they can debunk official accounts through their own investigations, or they can transmit lies or propaganda as part of a military information machine (Kellner, 2008: 300). Often the reporter can be objective, critical and propagandistic at different times and sometimes within the same report. Many reporters in 2003, in the post-9/11 climate, chose to be pro-pagandistic and militaristic (or as they would say, 'patriotic'), later apologising for reporting that *The New York Times* described as "not as rigorous as it should have been" (Kellner, 2008: 309). Correspondents also attempted to report what they saw, and in some cases their witnessing provided the basis for alternative and adversarial reports of the war. However, the ability to witness depends on where you are and what you can see. The 2003 Iraq War took place in the context of a highly managed and manipulated media war; the US and British military authorities deployed a sophisticated propaganda machine to control what journalists reported, what they published and, more crucially, where they could go. Of the journalists deployed to report the conflict, they were either based in Washington to receive briefings from the Department of Defense (DoD) and White House; at the Forward Operating Press Centres (FPICs) such as the Command Center in Doha, Qatar, just outside the war zone; and within the war zone attached to specific military units. Each of these locations provided a different perspective on the conflict and incorporated a different level of risk.

Embedding with military units or at command centres limits journalists' ability to witness what is going on. The risk of knowing less is matched by the danger of escaping this system by taking unilateral action. This was emphasised by the number of deaths of non-embedded reporters during the 2003 war. The capacity of war correspondents to tell the truth of what they witnessed in 2003 was not only restricted by the military's management of information and logistics but also by the caution of news organisations and editors and the personal disposition of reporters. The practice of embedding meant that information from the war zone itself was controlled by the military, but care must be taken in concluding that the reporting was "masterminded" by the military (Rid, 2007: 169). There was critical reporting such as Kevin Sites' account of the execution of wounded Iraqi fighters by US Marines. Sites' reporting of these events was shaped as much if not more by the attitude of NBC, the news organisation he worked for, and the response of members of the audience to his report. During the war in Kosovo, reporters attached to the UN Protection Force were able to report on atrocities (Hayward, 2010). Embedding does not inevitably lead to cheerleading journalism. Embeds' experience differs according to the unit they operate with, their location and the medium they work in. Their coverage of the 'grunt's eye view of the war' was skewed and partial, which was acknowledged by the news organisations that agreed to embed them. News organisations stressed that embedded reporting was only one element of their coverage (Tuotso, 2008; Hayward, 2010). However, the embedded reporting dominated the coverage of the up-close, first-hand experience of war that audiences demanded. Pressure from home offices to produce vivid copy and images as well as their own desire to find a good story, embedded reporters' calculation of the risks they faced were shared with, if not shaped by, the military on the ground.

Embedding

The US military registered nearly 2,500 reporters and their staff travelling to Iraq and neighbouring countries to cover the war in 2003; of these, an estimated 775 were embedded with military units of the US-led Coalition forces (Rid, 2007: 151). The US forces embedded the most journalists during this war as they had the largest military force, of roughly 150,000 troops. There were also 23,000 troops from other nationalities, but academic accounts of embedding (see Schechter, 2003; Brandenburg, 2007) often do not differentiate national practices of embedding the media. Justin Lewis and his colleagues (2006: 59) write that "American and British forces diverged significantly in their organization and handling of the media-embedding policy, both politically and operationally". There were also different experiences as documentary film-maker or as news journalist – print, television or radio – or as representative of organisations such as MTV and National Geographic who the Pentagon allowed to be embedded with military units. The experience of each journalist with various regiments diverged. Shahira Fahmy and Thomas Johnson (2007a: 107) note that "because of differences in access and contact, embeds reported differences in scale, context and perspective in reporting the conflict". There were also differences in the experience and practice of those journalists embedded at the FPIC located just inside Iraq, where many of the elite journalists were based. This group of journalists probably had the most frustrating time trying to persuade military Public Relations to take them, as a group, to different locations, as originally promised by the military.[3] Some of the most critical comments came from the reporters in the million-dollar press centre in Doha who complained that after being there for some time, "you know significantly less than when you arrived" (Wolff, 2003). Many left and joined various regiments on an ad hoc basis as the war progressed. Those embedded with specific regiments had to be resigned to covering the actions of that regiment, as embeds had to stay with the assigned unit for the duration of the operation. It was a gamble for the news organisation and caused much jockeying by the organisations when the journalists were assigned to regiments; if the unit was not engaged in any action, there would be little to report in news terms.

In Britain discussions between the MoD and the media about embedding began in October 2002. Each fighting unit was to have a maximum of five media placements, two for TV news and the rest print or radio. Embedding would be permanent, and many journalists had to sign up for a year as no one knew how long the war would last (Wyatt, 2013). The number of journalists who were embedded overall varies depending on the source consulted, but according to Taylor (2003: 186), there were 150 accompanying the British military. The difficulty in obtaining firm numbers for the embeds might be because some of the journalists initially did not embed, attaching themselves to military units or withdrawing as the dangers of the war became apparent, especially after the death of ITN's Terry Lloyd. For example, Jeremy Thompson initially travelled in an independent convoy of four vehicles, but after Lloyd's death, he joined the Deserts Rats (British 7th Armoured Division) (Lewis et al., 2006). It is estimated that only 50 to 60 journalists actually saw much action during the 2003 Iraq War (Tumber and Palmer, 2004).

The embedded reporters came from 22 countries, with 73 per cent of the participants from the US (Fahmy and Johnson, 2007a). In the UK, the MoD received over 900 applications, with 16 journalists from the BBC embedded. News organisations traditionally seen as hostile to Western interests, such as Russia Today and Al Jazeera, were allowed to embed. As mentioned, the documentary teams had signed a separate contract, but the rest of the British journalists had to sign *The Green Book*, [4] which states:

> The purpose of embedding correspondents with units and formation headquarters is to enable the media to gain a deeper understanding of the operation in which they are involved, particularly through access to personnel and commanders. They will be afforded all possible briefings and other facilities, including the opportunity to accompany British troops during war-fighting operations. Their individual requirements will be met wherever possible. In return, they are likely to be subject to some military orders and training, both for their own safety and that of the unit.
>
> *(Ministry of Defence, 2013: paragraph 22)*

Journalists were escorted by military officers and were required to make reports available to media operations staff in the military before sending them for publication, although the live nature of the reporting meant that much material was sent without being 'passed' by the military. They were not to compromise security by revealing details, such as locations, which might endanger the troops they were embedded with.

The risks to the concept of unimpeded, objective journalism from this particular practice are obvious. It was very difficult for embedded journalists in 2003 to balance their reporting, interrogate a variety of sources or interview the local population. The reliance on military sources meant that nearly all the information came from people who were, put crudely, "firmly in the pro-war camp" (Lewis *et al.*, 2006: 119). There were no embeds with Iraqi families, and hence few interviews were sought with ordinary Iraqis (Boyd-Barrett, 2004: 31). The dearth of information from the Iraqi side meant the main perspective on the ground was that reported by embedded journalists. Some correspondents are scathing about those who criticise them for not fully reporting the range of combatants. Channel 4's Alex Thomson (2010:14) points out the huge risk of covering the battlefield without negotiating safe passage with the combatants. For Thomson, while the use of the term 'embedding' may be new, it describes the way war reporters have always managed risk and kept themselves alive and well as they provide accounts of the fighting. Without embedding, it would not be possible to get into certain parts of the world and report on what is happening. He recognises the dangers of the approach – "the relative ease of doing embed journalism and in relative safety means there is simply too much of it" (Thomson, 2010: 15) – and argues it must be balanced by independent reporting and talking to the other parties as well as using local reporters in war zones to provide accounts of civilian populations. The problems of balancing embedded reporting with accounts from the 'other side' are ignored by Thomson. Contributors to a collection of essays on the reporting of Afghanistan talk of the problems of embedding with the Taliban and other opposition forces in the country (see Ramsay, 2010; Crawford, 2010). It is possible to undertake such reporting, but it is fraught with cultural and political problems and only offers a "rare glimpse of the war from the perspective of the Afghan insurgents" (Mackey, 2010). This form of embedding does not provide a view of the 'big picture' and, according to some critics, gives succour to the enemy (see Shachtman, 2008). It also reinforces a particular framing of war which focuses on military combatants and action.

Gathering information in war is a problem for any journalist, but it is particularly challenging for embedded correspondents. You could not stop to pop in to a village or a house to ask what Iraqis thought of the war. The documentary crew's experience of being embedded with a team that travelled with the battle group from Kuwait to Basra emphasised that the journalist is reliant on the military for transport and protection. The documentary crew was provided with a military soft-skinned Land Rover with a driver and an MoD press officer. They had to stay with the main battle group, and no vehicle could leave the convoy unless it had armoured protection. This meant that unless the soldiers that were being filmed encountered Iraqis, there was no transport or any means to go looking for other sources, as much as the team wished to do so. Thomson comments, "censorship is restricting someone's freedom of movement as much as it is restricting what someone can and cannot film" (quoted in Lewis *et al.*, 2006: 97). The problem was compounded in 2003 as most journalists did not speak Arabic and their appearance risked the possibility of being killed by Iraqis as they clearly stood out as Westerners and from the same nationality as the invading forces.

The documentary crew found one way to get around the logistical problem of being confined to a military Land Rover, which was to split the crew and negotiate transport with individual units within the regiment, thus ignoring the military minder. Much of the best footage obtained by the documentary team was when the cameraman managed to hitch a lift in a Warrior (armoured personnel carrier) and go out with one of the company commanders. Also, due to friendship cultivated with members of the Royal Electrical and Mechanical Engineers unit who drove a Chieftain armoured recovery vehicle (similar to a large tank), they allowed a member of the team to ride on top of it for some of their excursions. There was only room for one media representative in each vehicle, but by building relationships within the military and by using the different networks within the armed forces, some restraints were lessened through negotiation.

There is an issue of national compatibility in the embedding process. Most of the journalists were embedded with the military of their own nation or an aligned nation. The vast majority of reporters embedded with the British military forces were British. Only 20 per cent of the reporters embedded with US forces were from outside the US, and journalists from some countries, such as France, struggled to gain access to the Anglo-American preparations for the war (Miller, 2003). David Miller (2003) argues that the dominance of Anglo-American correspondents in the embedding system was part of the strategy. 'Supporting our boys' in action is a common theme exploited by the military in wartime. Fahmy and Kim (2008) concur that it is difficult to separate journalism and patriotism; journalists tend to become more 'nationalistic' in the reporting of international conflicts in which their host country is involved. Feelings of patriotism are an inherent problem for all journalists reporting on war, but this is particularly relevant for embedded journalists.

The problem of identifying with the troops you are embedded with is often reinforced by personal feelings. One embedded reporter in 2003 admitted "falling in love with my [his] subject" (quoted in Fahmy and Johnson, 2005: 303). He referred to how close personal attachments are formed "when you live with the same guys for weeks, sharing their dreams and miseries, learning about their wives and girlfriends … you start to make friends – closer friends in some ways than you'll ever have outside war". This is reinforced by sharing the same nationality of the soldiers that you are living with 24/7. Any 'anti-patriotic' inclination does not sit well with your comrades in war. In 2003 the *Daily Mirror*, having taken an anti-war position, saw its sales plummet dramatically and eventually had to tone down its anti-war coverage (Morgan, 2005: 391). John Mueller (1973) draws attention to the 'rally around the flag' effect at the beginning of a war which makes it difficult to express opposition to the policy of going to war. According to Phillip Rochot, embedded reporters in 2003 were "soldiers of information, marching with the troops and the political direction of their country" (quoted in Miller, 2003).

The extent to which patriotism shaped the reporting of embedded journalists in 2003 has to be put in the context of popular opinion on the war. Many of the journalists – and soldiers – encountered when making the documentary were in private highly sceptical of the reasons for the war and critical of the actions of the government. The perception of patriotic bias was shaped as much by the inability of embedded reporters to talk to Iraqis, which led to the presentation of the experience of the war from one side. Some differentiation needs to be made between the reporters on the ground and their home offices. Lewis and his colleagues (2006) make the point that it was the editors and anchors at home in the UK who provided bias with stories about Iraqis celebrating the invading troops, but that the embedded reporters presented a much more complete and some would say more balanced picture. Even so, as Thomas Rid (2007: 169) notes, by reporting accurately on the military developments on the ground, embedded reporters can serve up stories that provide an advantage for one side. The inability to put what they witness in a broader context highlights a general problem for the embedded reporter. The relative lack of access to knowledge and information makes it difficult to verify what they are told, and hence they are more susceptible to news management. This was highlighted by a BBC embed during the conflict who reported that he had to check each story with his media liaison officer who, if not sure about it, would check with his or her immediate superiors (Miller, 2003).

Doubts about the capacity of patriotism to bring journalists on side led the US and UK governments to justify the war in humanitarian terms. Much attention has been paid to the 'weapons of mass destruction' Saddam was supposed to possess, but the theme of helping the Iraqi people to escape the tyranny of the Saddam regime was equally if not more potent in shaping media coverage (Robinson *et al.*, 2010). The alleged brutalities committed by the Iraqi regime in the past and the apparent joyous reception of Coalition troops by the local population framed the reporting. Embedded reporters under pressure to vindicate the financial and other resource outlays of their news organisations had to respond to the demand for these types of stories. The dramatic nature of the reporting by embeds, gathered while accompanying soldiers, tended to exclude a more sober analysis. Tamar Liebes and Zohar Kampf (2009) attribute this to the advent of a new type of reporting. They argue that contemporary embedded journalism deviates from the traditions and norms of patriotic and professional journalism. What they refer to as 'performance journalism' is anchored in the 'live-ness' of modern television, which makes the correspondent more of a 'performer' than a reporter. Embedded reporters compete over "taking the most dramatic picture, showing the most authentic gesture, airing the hardest-to-get voices, and performing the most elusive live actions" (Liebes and Kampf, 2009: 247). The drama and spectacle of war with the reporter as a central figure or protagonist, risking his or her life to get back the latest pictures of what is happening on the battlefield, has replaced the effort to explain and evaluate the conduct of the campaign.

The risk of embeddedness is very much more tied up with the logistics of doing the job. The embedded journalist was aware of the need to manage the restrictions and limitations placed on his or her room for manoeuvre, dictated by factors such as lack of independent transportation and inability to wander away from their unit to find stories. This was acknowledged by correspondents and recognised by editors (see Lewis *et al.*, 2006). To compensate for the inability to gain a full – or at least a fuller – picture of what was going on by gathering information from a collation of sources, news desks sought to ensure that their reporters were assigned to a variety of locations as well as to the range of parties involved in the conflict. This includes making sure that civilian as well as military sources were accessed. Embeds, according to Sally Sara, who was the Australian Broadcasting Corporation's correspondent in Afghanistan, "are an important part of the story, but they're not the only story and it's important to have context with them" (quoted in Wilesmith, 2011: 40). She continues by saying that to get the story, "you've got to stay alive out there and there are some regions where the only way to go in is with the military", but "as long as you're balancing those stories out with civilian stories then it all fits into the bigger picture". In Iraq some broadcasters went to extraordinary lengths to balance embedded news. *Channel 4 News* set up a private company, called Out There News, which sent out small units of Iraqis to film around the country (Robinson *et al.*, 2010: 128). A riskier approach to providing balance is through embedding with the enemy – this did not happen in Iraq, but in later conflicts, reporters such as Sky News' Alex Crawford was given access to Taliban fighters (in 2009). Taking such risk is justified in terms of getting a broader picture of the conflict, but there are drawbacks in that it brings opprobrium from certain critics as well as the personal danger involved.

Following the story from either side is determined not only by logistical considerations and suspicions of military sources; often spotting a story is difficult because the correspondent is not sure what the story is. In November 2004, at great risk, embeds accompanied the US forces in their operation to retake Fallujah, and many stories and pictures ensued on the success of the American military. However, the real story was the seizing of Mosul, Iraq's third-largest city, by insurgents at the same time. Taking advantage of the concentration of US forces in Fallujah, the insurgents inflicted a "stunning reversal" on US-led forces, but as there were no US soldiers at Mosul, hence no embedded journalists, the story was completely missed by the media (Cockburn, 2010). It was only later that the strategic importance of a battle or event became clear. The dangers of reporting Iraq gradually led many editors to decide that the only way they could send their reporters to the country was to embed them with the military. Many reporters believe they are able to see through military propaganda and not regurgitate the official line, but as Patrick Cockburn (2010) states, the "most damaging effect of 'embedding' is to soften up the brutality of any military occupation and underplay hostile local response to it".

Fog of war

Many war correspondents refer to 'the fog of war' to describe their inability to find out what is happening on the battlefield. Writing about the 1982 Falklands/Malvinas War, David Morrison and Howard Tumber point out that "the problem was, rather, a logistical one. It was simply very difficult for them to find out at any moment who knew what" (1988: 120). This is the same for most war reporting, but embedding appears to have cemented the problem. Reliance on the military to tell you what is happening runs the risk of being able to use a story only on their terms. Often the military you are assigned to do not know what is happening. An example of this was highlighted in *The Guardian*'s War Watch column (Lawson *et al.*, 2003) which cited the reporting on Saturday 5 April, 10.53 a.m. by British soldiers of the discovery in a warehouse in southern Iraq of hundreds of bodies, believed to have been tortured and executed. It states:

> Dozens of wooden coffins are filled with the remains of an estimated 200 people. Troops also discover catalogues of grisly photographs of slain men, leading to speculation that the site was used as a torture and execution ground for dissident Iraqis opposed to Saddam Hussein's regime.

It then cites later reports that forensic examination showed the bodies were those of soldiers killed in the Iran–Iraq War. This is an example of the media not knowing what was going on. A *Fighting the War* documentary crew was with the Royal Artillery unit that discovered the warehouse. They wanted to film the firing of the AS90 guns, but the unit had been ordered to move to another location. The minder had gone back to the main battle group, so the crew had no transport and was swept up with the Royal Artillery as they moved closer to Basra. The next morning the cameraman had come down with the dysentery that was rampaging through the British Army, so the director had taken a small camera and gone out with the battery commander to the warehouse. It was clear that the remains had been carefully repackaged before the packers fled, so the story about the men being executed did not make sense. With no Arab speakers around to read the body tags or to question about the history of the place, it was difficult to piece together the truth of what had happened.

The story about the bodies being victims of the regime and the warehouse being a torture chamber was too good for the Army Press Office not to spin. The torture version had been taken up by some elements of the media before the forensics team verified the dates of the bodies. Donald Macintyre (2003) reported all the scenarios for *The Independent on Sunday*, but being based in Qatar, he could only rely on secondary sources in his investigation into the truth of the story. The warehouse and the bodies were filmed by the documentary team, but none of the footage could go into the general news pool and hence could not be used by other media. It was impossible to release the visual evidence of the carefully tagged bodies from the warehouse to any other media, and although members of the documentary team spoke to a couple of journalists, they could not offer them the visual evidence required to hold up the story.

The demand for instant news had led to a journalist filing the 'torture chamber' story without cross-checking or finding a second source. The report had to rely on speculation from the military. The risk of being used by the military, of giving inaccurate information, is immense under the conditions of limited time, editorial pressure and embeddedness. Michael Ware, who went to Afghanistan for *Time* magazine, stresses the importance of time in reporting a complex place like Afghanistan.

> It's lawless country, there's no safety net, no insurance, you're surviving on your wits and your instincts. Afghanistan was a journalistic nirvana. I had the name of one of the most iconic print publications on the planet, I had all the resources I could possibly have needed and that greatest of all resources, time, time to disappear.
>
> *(Quoted in Wilesmith, 2011: 11)*

Twenty-four-hour news coverage also raises the question of the information loop. Many British officers in Iraq listened to the BBC World Service or news from the UK to find out what was happening beyond their small patch of operations. On the evening of 23 March it was reported that up to 12 Iraqi tank squadrons were leaving Basra – the next day it became clear that it was in fact just 3 vehicles. This report seems to have originated from an embedded reporter with the British Marines and corroborated by ITN's Bill Neely (Lewis *et al.*, 2006: 79). The report was picked up by the Black Watch battle group, and as a result the forward section made a hasty retreat back to the border. It is not known whether they got the report from watching ITN or from the Marines, but the information loop confused the military. For some it was a planted story, an example of MoD misinformation; but it could also have been the product of embedded journalism in a 24-hour news culture. Such stories also affect any relationships between embedded journalists and soldiers if, at breakfast, the soldiers hear a critical report from the person they had spoken to the previous day and with whom they were expected to live for future operations.

Pressure from above

The embedded correspondent is, in effect, working to the demands of *two* organisations, those of their news organisation and those of the military. What these organisations want is mostly diametrically opposed. The media asks the journalist to push boundaries, uncover stories and pursue news. The military asks for obedience and silence and, in this war, needed secrecy to operate. Much effort was expended in Iraq, as in previous wars, in trying to fulfil the needs of the news organisations and find ways to escape the demands of the military. It was possible to differentiate between news organisations in the extent to which they directed their personnel in the field. Piers Robinson and his colleagues singled out Britain's *Channel 4 News* for demonstrating "the potential of journalists to overcome the constraints that are predicted to limit news media autonomy in wartime, notably sources, patriotism and ideology" (Robinson *et al.*, 2010: 128). They mention the programme's anchor, Jon Snow, who refers to the journalistic will to challenge authority. He believes that on its own this is not enough; it also requires an enabling environment, the news organisation's backing, which in the case of Channel 4 is helped by its remit to be 'alternative'. Journalists can provide innovative, challenging and different reporting, but to do so they have to have the backing of their editors.

The danger for reporters on the ground is that the material they send back is not chosen for transmission by the desk editor. In their study of the media coverage of the 2003 Iraq War, Lewis and his colleagues (2006: 103) refer to the "disparity ... between reporters on the ground giving a more nuanced account of Iraqi opinion, and reports from London inclining more toward the celebratory". What the journalist reports is not necessarily what is published, particularly if it challenges the orthodoxy. Attempts to present a differing viewpoint or perspective face greater obstacles. "Photographers may determine one aspect of a situation to be more salient as they work, but the editors who ultimately choose the photographs for publication may identify a different aspect to highlight" (Greenwood and Jenkins, 2015: 209).

This frustration with the editor or news organisation is a feature of all reporters in the field. It has a psychological impact on you if your story or material is not wanted but also if what you see as a good story that should be used is relegated to the cutting room floor or filed 'waste paper bin'.[5] It undermines your capacity to do the job, leading to the taking of more risks or suspending your judgement based on what you see as satisfying the demands of the newsroom. It also has implications for what you film or report on.

Censorship and self-censorship

The issue of what you can film or report exercises journalists in the field. The approach of the documentary team in Iraq in was to shoot first and ask questions about permissions or negotiate about transmission later (see Lewis *et al.*, 2006). Among the main skills of a war reporter are the ability to negotiate access, to placate opposition and to navigate the Scylla of the military and Charybdis of the newsroom. The immediate negotiation is with the military. Instruction not to report on matters of security and location are sensible in times of war, particular in modern warfare when instantaneous news reporting could result in you and the unit you may be embedded with being attacked. However, what constitutes operational security is often far from clear: "the looseness of the guidelines gives military commanders who are less sympathetic to journalists the discretion to remove unwanted reporters" (Tumber and Palmer, 2004: 28). The inconsistencies between units or forces in Iraq were a source of frustration as well as a matter of opportunity.

Most correspondents in the Iraq War do not recall attempts at direct censorship (see Lewis *et al.*, 2006: 95). The few efforts to intervene that are recorded are more to do with the attitudes of the commanders in the field than part of an official policy. The suppression of ITN's Romilly Weeks report on a failed water aid drop in Al Zubayr was done at local level by a commander who felt the report would have portrayed his unit in a poor light (Lewis *et al.*, 2006: 96). Such interventions varied; the documentary crew (and others) filmed water aid drops which came under fire in the same area without the imposition of military censorship. Reporters did not experience military control in the same way and to the same degree. Censorship takes many forms, and in Iraq in 2003 it was not so much direct intervention from the MoD or military command that was the obstacle but the individual whims of officers, whether a show of power or perhaps just a temper tantrum, which in many ways is more difficult to deal with. Ultimately if the commanding officer of the regiment did not want a team with his soldiers, even if the MoD wanted the media to embed, there was no way of negotiating or getting around that hostility. A more common experience was the military's attempt to facilitate "'positive' reporting" (Lewis *et al.*, 2006: 97). Military press officers took ITN reporter Carl Dinnen to film a training camp which the military believed connected the regime to terrorists (Lewis *et al.*, 2006: 98). Like Dinnen, the documentary team were taken to film an arms dump, but they refused to film, casting doubts on its authenticity; the weapons were antique and clearly too old to have been used in any present wars. The decision had consequences as the next time the crew wanted to film something that it thought was of interest, they were told they could not. Negotiation requires that you play the game, and in this case it would perhaps have been wiser to have filmed the arms dump and 'lost' the footage on the cutting room floor. The British forces started to use risk and safety as the reason to stop journalists going into an area as a form of censorship (Lewis *et al.*, 2006: 98).

The ability to negotiate is contingent on the elements that a journalist has to use as bargaining currency. The failure to navigate the relationship between military and the media is a major risk to journalism. It has been argued that the reporter's dependency and emotional ties to the military in 2003 allowed for a partiality towards the military (Miller, 2004a, 2004b: Tumber and Palmer, 2004). However, this has to be contextualised by the reporter's experience and understanding of what is happening. Many argue an experienced journalist expects and is used to manipulation. It can be argued that embedding is intrinsic to the practice of journalism. Gary Tuchman, who was embedded with the US Air Force in Iraq, acknowledges that "embedding happens on a regular basis; reporters are routinely 'embedded' with everything from sports teams to city councils" (quoted in Froneman and Swanepoel, 2004: 25). Embedding is an essential feature of the work of documentary film-makers: it is something they do frequently, and they are aware of the parameters they work within. If you have a close relationship to the people you are filming, you often get better access and better insight. Thomson identifies the difficulty of avoiding manipulation, but he also acknowledges it is something that reporters should be familiar with and able to resist. He states,

> You're always embedded with people to a lesser or greater extent. The difficult thing is how far it lets your brain get embedded … and how far you become a [public relations officer] for what's going on, which is essentially a game that the Pentagon and perhaps even more so the MoD clearly want people to play and it's depressing the number of journalists who are willing to go along with that.
>
> *(Quoted in McLaughlin, 2016: 145)*

There are also aspects of what happens on the ground that assist reporters avoid manipulation in their dealings with the military. An element that helped in Iraq in 2003 was the fact that on the whole, most soldiers, especially the non-commissioned officers, disliked journalists more than they disliked the enemy. Vaughan Smith writes about his experience of reporting on the military in Afghanistan: "As soon as you walk through the door as a journalist you understand that you are a sort of target, albeit treated much more gently than the Taliban" (Smith, 2010: 43). Competition is also a fear that drives journalists to ignore or seek to get around the restrictions in their quest to get the best news story. This provides some sort of safeguard from doing everything that the military wants.

Leon Sigal, in his seminal study of the relationship between reporters and officials which highlighted the dependency of the news media on official sources of information, draws attention to "the incentive to get the news first", which "makes reporters willing to play along with their sources in order to obtain disclosures on an exclusive basis" (Sigal, 1973: 56). Much of the academic literature on sourcing has reinforced the dependency on official sources and documented the advantages that official sources have in the production of news (see Hall *et al.*, 1979) and, in some circumstances, identified how certain strategies have allowed non-official sources to exert their influence (see Ericson *et al.*, 1989). More recently, attempts have been made to look at the different circumstances which have influenced the 'tug of war' between source and journalist. It is possible to distinguish between journalists in their capacity to exercise influence over this relationship – journalists with shorter deadlines face more disadvantages in their interactions with their sources. Documentary film-makers operate on longer deadlines and, on most occasions, cease their relationship with their subjects on publication. The working environment of the documentary film-makers differs from that of the daily news journalist. One film-maker refers to "a degree of schizophrenia" involved in documentary film-making; it has to "try and enter the subject, see the world through its eyes, accept its logic, while at the same time maintaining an aesthetic and often ironic distance from it" (quoted in Cousins and Macdonald, 2006: 451). However, in any film and TV documentary, disclosure is crucial. Documentaries such as *Fighting the War* (2003), *Restrepo* (2010) and *Armadillo* (2011), all of which used embedded crews, produced films questioning official versions of events, war's efficacy and the assumptions of the soldiers they were with – although they did not question the decision to resort to war.

A number of reporters believe that embedding does not blunt their professional practice as war correspondents. Geoff Thompson of Australia's ABC, embedded with the US transport corps, was able to report the killing of civilians while Lindsey Murdoch of Fairfax Media reported in *The Sydney Morning Herald* of the use of napalm by US forces (Dodson, 2010: 105). Perhaps the most famous example of critical reporting emerging from embedded reporting was Kevin Sites' report for NBC on the murder of a wounded Iraqi fighter by US soldiers. This provides an example of the embedding system producing some degree of transparency in reporting the nature of warfare – the 'soda straw view' of embedded war journalism might restrict the coverage of war, but it should not be simply equated with a sanitised version of conflict. It might be "very narrow coverage" but it is also "very rich" (Tumber and Palmer, 2004: 16). However, Sites' unease about damaging the military by releasing his footage and the revelation that NBC broadcast an expurgated version of the footage draw attention to the impact of embedding on the decisions made by correspondents and their editors (Sites, 2007). The failure of NBC to show the full footage, a decision followed by the other US networks – in contrast with other broadcasters around the world – resulted in US audiences getting a partial picture of the atrocity. Sites resorted to using his blog to screen the unexpurgated footage, highlighting that in today's technological environment the embedded reporter has other outlets to communicate what they witness (Matheson and Allan, 2009: 4–5). The flow of negative response to his post illustrates that the public does not always want to face up to the realities of modern conflict and provides justification for broadcasters' decision not to screen the gory details of warfare.

For the BBC's Kevin Marsh, the failings of journalism in the reporting of modern conflict are not the consequences of embedding but the product of the weaknesses of contemporary journalism. Commenting on the coverage of Afghanistan, he states the inability to fully and sufficiently report the conflict – its "complexity, cause and effect are indeed missing" – is "for reasons that have little to do with the constraints of embedding" (Marsh, 2010: 75). Embedding, Marsh argues, helps to report the war in Afghanistan, where the front line is inaccessible "without the protection as assistance of the military" (2010: 71). There are costs and risks with embedding but it is the failings of editors and "daily journalism's aversion to complexity; its centripetal tendency, dragging the apparent plurality of multiple outlets towards common framings; its inevitable preference for the striking event over the telling trend, and its eternal excuse, we're just telling stories" that are to blame (Marsh, 2010: 81).

Technology, risk and embedding

The new tools of journalism, especially the satellite phone and the videophone, as we have seen, precipitated the ability for reports and footage to be transmitted live and with much greater ease from any location (see Chapter 4). This meant that by 2003 journalists could now report live or send footage to their editors, which could be transmitted almost immediately. The move to 24/7 news also meant that news had to be turned around more quickly; the temporal space was now so close to the event that often no context or interpretation could be given, and without context there is no meaning. News is recycled every hour or so, offering less context or analysis with "endless speculations in order to fill up the ever-churning airtime" (Lewis *et al.*, 2005: 474). Embeds produced their reports in 2003 in a climate that emphasised the need to turn stories around rapidly. Paul Virilio reworked McLuhan's claim to state that "the message is not exactly the medium ... but above all the ultimate speed of its propagation" (Virilio, 1997: 6). "The Project for Excellence in Journalism calculated that 62 per cent of reports from Iraq shown on US news channels in 2004 were in live mode" (Matheson and Allan, 2009: 68). This focus on real-time coverage kept reporters tethered to their equipment; they could not stray far from their transmission gear and lost valuable time for information gathering while "cleaning out sand and recharging batteries" (Seib, 2004: 12). Embedded journalists did not have the time to check stories for accuracy. Most of the errors made in the reporting "could have been avoided if a bit more time had been taken to check out the information before delivering it" (Seib, 2004: 12).[6] The mistaken identity of the bodies (see above) is a story that also might not have been reported if there had been more time for further research.

The pressure to respond speedily is illustrated by the case of Brian Walski, a staff photographer for the *Los Angeles Times* who digitally combined two photographs taken when reporting from Basra in 2003. He wanted to 'improve' his picture, and with digital technology could do so, but he did not have the time to reflect on the consequences. When the forgery was spotted, he immediately confessed to merging the shots, but as Matheson and Allan (2009) point out, the lack of sleep and the stresses of being in a war might have clouded his judgement. While such pressure is not new, the shrinking of time to get things done and to reflect or check on what you are writing or photographing was a problem that was considerably increased in the 2003 Iraq War.

Real or reality war

Deborah Jaramillo (2009: 3) argues that TV coverage of the 2003 invasion of Iraq should be seen not as 'news', but rather as an orchestrated exercise in 'high-concept' film-making. The increasing liveness of broadcasts and the ability of embeds to film dramatic bellicose images from the front lines meant that the capture, understanding and use of the image became central to the work of the war reporter. There was a huge increase in the number of photographic representations of the 2003 war compared to the first Gulf war in 1991 (King and Lester, 2005). The ability to capture both the photo and the moving image was enhanced by the lightweight digital cameras and the freedom of movement that they afforded their operators. Andrew Hoskins and Ben O'Loughlin (2007: 32) point out that technological advances ushered in temporal and spatial transformations which changed the nature of news and the availability of the image, with the correspondent tending to linger more on the dramatic and the visual at the expense of context and detail. Embedded reporters provided far more vivid images of the battlefield than the more sanitised footage of the 1991 Gulf War (Lanson, 2003). Editors and camera workers in 2003 were looking for pictures to serve as a direct and iconographic representation of events and arouse an emotional response.

The increasing demand for dramatic 'war' images meant that reporters and camera operators put themselves into increasingly risky situations. By the end of 2011, nearly one in three of the reporters killed in Iraq were photographers or camera workers (Filkins, 2013). Susan Sontag notes that "the image must exist in the photographer's mind before he takes the photo" (1979: 91). This led to accusations about the filmic nature of the coverage of the war, such as the replication of images from past wars. Many soldiers and reporters compared the reality of the war they were fighting to the wars they had seen on screen. The night before a raid into Basra in March 2003, the documentary crew asked the Scots Dragoon Guards' squadron leader if it was acceptable to film his planning meeting. When the crew turned up at dusk, the soldiers had set the scene with a backdrop of a picture of Saddam Hussein hung from the tank and a hastily assembled 'bird table'[7] with subdued lighting, as no light was permitted at night in case it betrayed the location of the battle group. The reality of the scene was based pictorially on films about the Second World War, leading the film-makers to ask what was the reality being filmed. Comparison between the visual coverage of the 1991 Gulf War and the 2003 Iraq War found more 'fighting images' in the latter, as photographers were able to get closer to the actual combat (King and Lester, 2005). However, differences in the actual images of combat were not as great as might have been expected (Fahmy and Kim, 2008: 444). A cross-cultural study of an American newspaper and a British newspaper found that in 2003 more images of human and material destruction were published, including of the loss of civilian life in Iraq (Fahmy and Kim, 2008). While not necessarily representative of media coverage as a whole, this does indicate that in certain publications the human toll of war was represented, albeit in a limited way.

The closeness of embedded reporters, camera workers and photographers to the combat led to what some scholars depict as a 'reality TV' style of reporting. Thrilling footage of military vehicles charging through the desert and soldiers running through the rubble of battered buildings encouraged the viewer to share in the human interest stories of front-line soldiers. Sebastian Kaempf (2017) argues that the viewer was no longer a passive spectator but an engaged citizen soldier who experienced, through his or her screen, the realities of the battlefield. He points out the similarity of US TV coverage to a series, *Profiles from the Frontline,* which was aired by ABC just prior to the 2003 war. Filmed in North Carolina and Afghanistan and using footage provided by the DoD, it chronicles the military activities of US Special Forces in Afghanistan in their search for Al-Qaeda cells. The programme documented raids as well as the soldiers' feelings and emotions in doing the job. This, it is argued, laid down the model for the embedded reporting of the Iraq War which focused on the human interest stories of war, something reflected in the broader range of journalists embedded with the US armed forces. In 2003 it was not only representatives of major news organisations who accompanied the troops but also journalists from lifestyle magazines such as *GQ, Esquire* and *Men's Health*. This represented the efforts of the DoD to bring the war to a different public, the inattentive public who did not usually watch nightly news. The focus on ordinary people fighting the war was also encouraged through the embedding of reporters from local newspapers and TV stations with their local units. The intimacy and identification with the soldiers placed a new set of pressures on war correspondents as they attempted to report war in a news culture that encouraged information to be packaged alongside entertainment and emotion. For Kaempf (2017), this style of reporting meant that larger questions about the legitimacy of war were kept at bay.

Notes

1 Documentary makers are used to drawing up contracts with the organisations they film, to define where the filming can take place, with whom, for how long, health and safety measures, indemnities and what rights both parties have to the material filmed. The BBC does not give up editorial control, but in the cases of these films the Corporation will agree that if there are factual errors, the organisation being filmed can ask for changes, but it cannot change an edit because it does not like or agree with what the film is saying. This has been the experience of the films that Janet Harris has worked on.
2 In January 2003 Janet Harris, another BBC documentary director and the Deputy Assistant Chief of Staff, Media and Communications HQ Land Command, went to Kuwait to do a recce.
3 The documentary series *Fighting the War* (2003) had an assistant producer embedded with the journalists, able to record their many battles with the MoD press officers.
4 *The Green Book* sets out

> the arrangements for the selection of, and regulations for, accredited war correspondents. In return for protection and support, and access to other facilities, correspondents agree to undergo the necessary training and to abide by the operational security and safety measures required by the unit to which they are attached.
>
> *(HM Government, 2003)*

5 The documentary team was embedded with the Black Watch. Many of the soldiers were from Dundee and Perthshire and had strong Scottish accents, although the officers had English accents. Back in the cutting room, programme executives could not understand what the soldiers were saying and felt that it would be incorrect to subtitle them, so material was lost.
6 Luostarinen (1992) cites the announcement from Agence France-Presse four hours after the first attack of the first Gulf war on 17 January, 1991, that Allied forces had almost

totally wiped out the Iraqi air forces and the elite troops in Basra, that 18,000 tonnes of explosives were dropped and that as many as 2,500 planes took part in the first strike. However, Finnish military expert Pekka Visuri estimated that probably no more than 300 planes took part and that they didn't have the technical facilities to carry even 2,000 tonnes of explosives (Luostarinen, 1992).

7 This was a table with a map of the location with points of reference as seen in films about the Second World War. The screw tops from water bottles represented the tanks which were moved on the advance route.

6

ASYMMETRICAL RISK

Reporting post-war Iraq

The advance of military and information technology and the role of the media were at the heart of the changing nature of war and conflict since the Second World War. Several scholars have conceptualised the way in which the media have become central to military operations and the understanding of war and conflict. In the wake of the US-led invasion of Iraq in 2003, a state of "unprecedented ... chaos and flux" characterised the conduct of war and the reporting (Hoskins and O'Loughlin, 2015: 1320). Asymmetrical warfare is often defined as conflict between nations and groups which have disparate military capabilities; post 1945, conventional war has been increasingly accompanied by violent conflicts between state and non-state actors within and across borders. The end of the Cold War has witnessed a growth in these types of conflict, whether labelled guerrilla warfare, ethnic conflict or, more recently, the 'war on terror'. Since 9/11 the struggle between 'unequals' in which the weak use unorthodox methods such as suicide bombers, the indiscriminate shooting of people in public places or crashing civilian airplanes into buildings has advanced. A new level of asymmetrical warfare can be seen as having been reached in Iraq following the overthrow of Saddam Hussein. Hoskins and O'Loughlin (2015) label this as 'diffused' war; they stress the 'media-tisation' of war as the key battleground in asymmetrical conflict in places such as Iraq and Afghanistan.

This chapter primarily looks at conflict in 'post-war' Iraq and, to a lesser extent, Afghanistan, where reporting on a new style of asymmetrical war, the impact of globalisation and changes to journalistic practices all came together to impact on the risk culture of war reporters. Many of the hazards of reporting covered in the previous chapter remain, but as the tools and techniques of journalism change, so too do the problems and risks that the journalist must consider. The chapter draws on the experience of making a documentary for a four-part television series look-ing at what life had been like in post-war Iraq, exploring the character of Saddam

Hussein, what led to the war and speculating on what might happen next. It was commissioned by Middle East Broadcasting (known as MBC), a free-to-air, pan-Arab news and entertainment broadcaster that was set up in 1991 as the first privately owned and independent Arabic satellite TV station. The series was made under the auspices of an independent TV company which employed three British documentary crews to film in Baghdad. The chapter also draws on the experience of being embedded with the British military for a BBC documentary series about a British regiment in Iraq and their families in the UK. The issues of embedding are still relevant, but with the overthrow of Saddam Hussein, the number of embedded reporters fell drastically. The Pew Research Center estimates that by late autumn there were about 100 embeds; in 2005, 48; and by October 2006 numbers vary from 9 to 26 (Vaina, 2006). Now embedding took place in an entirely different context in which the reconstruction of Iraq took precedence. Operating with the military at this time had to take place alongside an engagement with Iraqi society, and in this period additional risks arising from dealing with fixers and ensuring their protection and that of Iraqi contributors became important considerations. These highlight, to an extent, some of the problems that distinguish working in the Middle East; the issue of trust and the lack of sources are particular factors to take into account. The risks raised by the increasing use of non-Western journalists, the use of material from citizen journalists and the impact of global journalism on the reporting of conflict are a significant part of this story.

The physical risks to journalists working in Iraq increased exponentially after 2003. In 2003, 14 journalists had been killed, but the number had risen to 32 by 2006 (CPJ, 2018). This was at a time when the number of embedded journalists in Iraq and Afghanistan had decreased. Even though the situation in Iraq was deteriorating and more British and American soldiers were being killed, there were for long periods, including crucial moments of the conflict, no British journalists present in Iraq. It is unclear whether this was because of decisions made by the Ministry of Defence (MoD) or because of the broadcasting organisations. As a result of the deterioration of control exerted by the occupying forces in Iraq, the MoD's influence over access became more vice-like. *The Telegraph*'s defence correspondent Thomas Harding stated that "dealing with the Ministry of Defence is genuinely more stressful than coming under fire ... we have been lied to and we have been censored" (quoted in Grey, 2009).

As attacks on the British military increased, the MoD became more intransigent. Even respected journalists such as David Loyn and Stephen Grey were barred from being embedded. The situation led to increased caution in other war zones; for example, a correspondent as experienced as Christina Lamb was not allowed to embed with the British military in Afghanistan between 2006 and 2008. Stephen Grey (2009) reports that he "was sent to a relatively quiet zone and his requests to visit bases where soldiers were engaged in combat were refused". *The Guardian*'s James Meek, who was embedded in Helmand in 2006, says he was allowed to speak freely and had no problems with minders, but he was told that "the priority was the tabloids and television because it was important for recruitment" (quoted in Grey, 2009). However, Tom Newton Dunn from *The Sun*, a newspaper which never flagged in its support of the troops, said he was frustrated: "I can get out only once a year, and only through kicking and screaming" (quoted in Grey, 2009). Major General Andrew Stewart (2009), commander of Multi-National Division (South-East) between December 2003 and July 2004, reported to the Chilcot Inquiry that he was more inclined to embed a reporter from Al Jazeera for a short period "because they reported what they saw". He "refused to have the BBC because they only reported what they wanted the people here to hear" (Stewart, 2009). Negotiations to gain access to Iraq were fraught, and for reporters the risks of annoying the MoD was that access to film the military, to talk to them, including talking ex-soldiers – most of whom will not talk to journalists unless they have MoD permission – was closed down.

The situation with the US military was similar. The US Department of Defense (DoD) hired a public relations company, the Rendon Group, to "'profile' journalists who wrote about the 'War on Terror'" (Paterson, 2014: 20). The journalist Jason Motlagh (2009) writes that his request to embed was denied by the DoD as they deemed 47 per cent of his published stories "negative". He found this out when the DoD's public affairs department mistakenly sent him a report with the information. The DoD denied the story (Motlagh, 2009). The same charge is levelled at the MoD, which manipulated "the parcelling-out of embeds to suit their own ends. … They use it as a form of punishment to journalists who are off-message or critical of strategy or tactics" (Grey, 2009).

When there are few alternative sources for the media to access in covering a war, the military have the upper hand. They can agree accreditation for whomever they want and organise locations for wherever they want. Media facilities "are organised on the basis of what the military want to show the media, rather than what the media want to see" (Maltby, 2013: 81). Falling foul of the military is therefore a risk that the journalist faces if she wants future access. This is even more problematic for freelance journalists who have no media organisation to back up requests to report on the military. The MoD Department of Public Relations will allow no access to programme makers without a commission from a broadcaster, but commissioners will not discuss a commission unless you have access.

Being embedded carries risks for the military in that the journalist is present continuously and can talk to soldiers when their minders are not present. They are present when events happen that the military might not wish journalists to see. This is not just events that are out of the control of the military, but those that may happen because the soldiers get used to the presence of a reporter and forget differences or are so used to a way of being that they cannot see events from an outsider's point of view. Lindsey Hilsum of *Channel 4 News*, who witnessed the second battle for Fallujah, said,

> Being embedded with the Americans for the assault on Fallujah was one of the most rewarding journalistic experiences of my life. It was extraordinary because they are so confident that what they are doing was right that they

really didn't care what you thought or what you saw. I found them incredibly open and, you know, if I was appalled, that was my problem.

(Quoted in Wilesmith, 2011: 27)

However, when they do not have the confidence or belief in their actions or when the war or conflict begins to go wrong for the military, opportunities to embed become more restricted (Maltby, 2013).

This was what happened as the conflicts in Iraq and Afghanistan developed. Fewer journalists were being embedded with the military. In both war zones, journalists not under military protection were finding reporting extremely difficult. The lack of telecommunications infrastructure, the reliance on fixers who often financially exploited journalists and the increasing danger posed by the Taliban as well as by robbers and kidnappers led to the Western press leaving Afghanistan by December 2001 (Carruthers, 2011). Some say that the war in Afghanistan was "a war that was lost from the start" (Nohrstedt and Ottosen, 2014: 23), while Chilcot (2016: 124), in the summary of his report, notes that the "UK forces withdrew from Iraq in 2009 in circumstances which did not meet objectives defined in January 2003". In both Afghanistan and Iraq most attention had been paid to the initial operations, but what came next had not been worked out. General Sir Richard Dannatt (2010), who led the initial UK involvement in Afghanistan, refers to the 'go first, go fast, go home' approach of British interventions abroad which, some argue, was reflected in the media coverage.

Hindsight is a useful skill to have, but even at the time it was clear to many that the British military was struggling. Their desire to control the media in general was increasing, as the story they wanted told was rather different from the one actually happening. The MoD was fighting two asymmetrical wars, one with the media and one with the insurgents. According to Tumber and Palmer (2004: 20),

> What the efforts to manage war coverage by those who wage it have achieved is to bolster the scepticism of reporters. It makes a cynical profession still more cynical when it notes the attempts of the military and official spokespeople to ensure that the media are "on side".

Sarah Maltby (2013) examines how the military are affected by and responsive to their experiences of working with the media. The "complex symbiotic relationship between the media and the military creates a dynamic of cooperation, manipulation and resistance" (Maltby, 2013: 64). Much of the material relating to the way that war reporters work with the military has been seen in the light of what McNair (2006) sees as a control versus co-operation model. This sees the state attempting to use the media as an arm of its public relations strategy, exerting a top-down influence on the correspondents in the field. The practice of journalism is seldom as simple. Another way of describing the world of conflict reporting stresses its complexity and the interdependent relationships of its constituent elements. It imagines war reporters and their world as an ecosystem (see Picard, 2014).

The conflict reporting ecosystem is constructed by the actors within it, the inter-actions they have with each other and the impact of landscape within which they are reporting (Pendry, 2014). Thus, access and stories are negotiated and influenced by the interactive relationships and demands of the military (which needs the media), the media (which needs the military), the actors' likes or dislikes for each other and the strictures of operating in a physically hostile environment. Caroline Wyatt (2013), who was embedded with the British Army in 2003, writes,

> We often talk about the media and the military. But really there are no such things. I prefer to think of us first as individuals, and then as tribes, rather than homogenous blocks. ... Just as any of those tribes can work together, and are part of a collective, each can also come into conflict with the other or within its own sub-tribes at any moment, and loyalties can be stretched in unexpected ways.

This dynamic presents a more nuanced understanding of managing risk in that some options of control can be negotiated and manipulated, but some cannot. This can be seen in the varying degrees of access offered to embedded reporters in the Iraq War (see Lewis *et al.*, 2006) depending on the attitude of the commanding officer of the regiment and the relationships with the non-commissioned officers within the general outline for access laid down by the MoD.

Blogging war

The relationship between journalists and the military have always presented risks to journalism, but during the Iraq War the rise in citizen journalism and the huge increase in blogs about the war presented journalists with new risks, as well as opportunities. "The Internet is brimming with so much Iraq war commentary that a crop of new directories has sprouted to help people sift through it all", observed Leslie White of *The Washington Post* (quoted in Webb, 2003). Not only was there an increase in competition for an audience, but there was also a threat to some of the traditional professional principles of journalism and the emergence of a different style of journalism.

The increasing popularity of war blogs during the post-Iraq War period was because they put a more "personal face to the war", allowed for readers to com-ment on news items and presented views from a range of sources and perspectives around the world (Kaye and Johnson, 2004: 292). They also allowed freelance reporters to raise funds for their reporting. Christopher Allbritton, a former Asso-ciated Press and *New York Daily News* journalist, raised $10,000, often through appeals on social media, to help fund a trip to Iraq. Like many other reporters writing from outside a news media organisation, he was free of organisational demands and editorial requirements. He notes: "It's not Associated Press inverted pyramid-style writing, but I didn't think people wanted that on a site such as this. My reporting combines the personal, the micro and the macro" (Allbritton, 2003).

It was the more subjective, opinionated and closer style of reporting that appealed to the readers of these blogs. They drew the reader into a world "unfettered by editorial restrictions, traditional media frames, news values and agendas" (Bennett, 2013: 39). The emphasis of the bloggers was on "prioritising the human element" and incorporating the concepts of community not just 'connectivity' (Kuhn, 2005). Readers commented, discussed and argued both with the author but also with each other, building a sense of a shared and interactive communication unlike the more traditional monologue style of reporting. The blog reading and reacting community was a new feature and had a considerable impact on more traditional practices. Where traditional journalists perhaps saw themselves as autonomous, having the authority and rigour of their practices such as fact-checking to inform people of what was going on, bloggers wrote what they personally thought and saw the truth as "emerging from shared, collective knowledge – from an electronically enabled marketplace of ideas" (Singer, 2007: 85).

Traditional media had to respond to this new style of reporting. Between April 2005 and November 2006 there was a "substantial growth" in user-generated content in the British press, with the number of blogs rising from 18 to 118 during this period (Hermida and Thurman, 2008). In a Pew Research Center study, nearly 60 million Americans, or more than a third of US Internet users, said they read blogs, and a sizable portion reported that they got their news from blogs (Lenhart and Fox, 2006). One of the developments of the Iraq War was the incorporation of blogging into journalists' traditional means of reporting (Matheson and Allan, 2009: 78). Former BBC News boss Richard Sambrook, in his study of foreign correspondents, concluded that "social media are leading, supplementing and complementing what professional news organisations offer, providing fresh source material for reporters, but also competing with them for public attention" (Sambrook, 2010: 2). The view of war shaped by personal experience, seemingly free of the strictures of the news organisation and journalism 'speak', was increasingly popular. "Not only were readers given insights into the individual's experiences or war, but the accounts gained a high truth value through a perceived authenticity to experience" (Matheson and Allan, 2009: 89–90).

The perception that truth lies more in the authenticity coming from the experience that the reporter felt or witnessed has the potential to accentuate the risks taken by war correspondents. It pushes them, as we have seen, to get even closer to the action as well as opening them up to further manipulation by their sources of information. In 2014 Stuart Little, chief executive of Storyful (a news agency which sources videos, identifies local witnesses and provides alerts to breaking news from the social media), stated that the growth of social media has meant that "authenticity has replaced authority as the new currency of this environment" (Dredge, 2014). Authenticity means more emphasis on the personal story of the journalist in wartime, with the emotions of the journalist or the sensation of what is witnessed becoming a central aspect of the war story. This new post-war environment was one of "images, not of letters; of stories not of issues; of people, emotions and actions, not of cognitive analysis" (Liebes and Kampf, 2009: 241).

Mohammad Soubra, who posted a video on YouTube of the July 2006 Israeli bombing of Beirut, criticised traditional war journalists for "reporting without passion" and lacking depth of understanding of the impact of war (Matheson and Allan, 2009: 94). Bloggers, he believes, produce accounts which are "more true to the lived experience of war than news reporting". They have encouraged an understanding of war that emphasises the personal experience of fighting. It is seen as having more value in the comprehension of conflict than the process of witnessing. The personalisation of war reporting in post-2003 Iraq may have challenged mainstream news media representation of Iraqis and the war, but it also initiated a shift in traditional journalism to sharing the first-hand experiences of those involved in the war. The risk of sharing the lived experience of war is much higher than any form of objective journalism.

The desire for emotion and sensation by editors, commissioners and audiences carries another risk which is allied to the demands for proximity and immediacy. The news reporting of war can be criticised as 'infotainment'. According to Thussu (2009: 113),

> Covering wars is inevitably a difficult journalistic endeavour but the demand for live 24/7 news, as well as competition among news providers, can lead to the sensationalism and trivialisation of often complex situations and a temptation to highlight the entertainment value of news.

The risk for war reporting is that the story takes precedence over the causes and events leading up to the story. This is a particular criticism levelled by military personnel. The commander of the invading British forces in Iraq, Air Marshall Brian Burridge, accused the media of infotainment, saying,

> If you look at what fills newspapers now, it's the equivalent of reality TV – it's superficial, there's very little news reporting, there's very little analysis, but there's a lot of conjecture. ... It's good that the public should see what we are doing. What has gone wrong is that the TV news programmes don't have the ability to lay a strategic overview.
>
> *(Quoted in Cozens, 2003)*

As the engagement with war becomes emotional, the politics and analysis of the war are left out. It is perhaps a threat not only to traditional journalism but also to the journalist at a personal level. They might lose the safety of detachment from the horrors of war but, at the same time, become personalities more defined by their response to war, something that encourages the audience to interpret a personal attachment to the side of victims or perpetrators being reported on. This can make them a target at home and in the theatre of war.

Social media can present a risk in that it provides a platform for personally directed flak. Darrin Mortenson, a US newspaper reporter, tried to defend the US television photographer Kevin Sites for filming a US solder killing an injured insurgent fighter (see Chapter 5). He became a target of abuse in the US media "to the point of fearing for his own safety and that of his family" (Mitchell, 2004). Mortenson acknowledges this 'blame the messenger' mentality, saying,

> When the news is good, everyone hails those hardworking reporters who live in the dirt and danger to accompany the troops, as long as their reports make us feel good. But when the images make us uncomfortable or force us to ask questions, we blame the media.
>
> *(Quoted in Mitchell, 2004)*

The case of Eason Jordan can also be cited; he was a chief news executive at CNN but resigned in February 2005 after a concerted campaign against him by bloggers (Matheson and Allan, 2009: 119). They had reacted to comments which they felt suggested that he believed journalists were being deliberately killed by US troops in Iraq. A campaign was also initiated by bloggers against Robert Fisk, coining the term 'fisking' to rebut anything written by the *Independent*'s Middle East correspondent (Redden, 2003). Those who did not like what he was writing could use social media to respond, highlighting the acute risk that journalists face from hostile forces when they become identifiable personalities. Social media make reporters in the field more vulnerable to pressure from those with a political axe to grind.

Different voices and pictures

The Internet and blogging challenges the traditional values of objectivity and neutrality of journalism, but the technology also enables journalists to broaden the scope of their war reporting (Bruns, 2009; Gillmor, 2003). Correspondents are using blogs as sources for their own reporting. Increasingly news outlets draw on citizen accounts not only as journalistic pieces in their own right but also as sources to find out more about a conflict. The picture of war in Iraq, particularly in the insurgency period, was constructed from many personal blogs. These included those of Iraqis such as Salam Pax, an unemployed Baghdad architect who posted updates on the war from Baghdad (Where is Raed?) and those of soldiers and ex-soldiers such as Lt. Comdr. Kevin Mickey (The Primary Main Objective), a US military officer in Kuwait (Webb, 2003). Academics such as Professor Glenn Reynolds (InsaPundit) and peace activists contributed during the Iraq War to sites such as Killing Goliath. Warblogs, a version of citizen journalism, provided "some of the best eyewitness reporting" of the fighting (Allan, 2006: 109). Within a few years of Salam Pax's efforts, Arab bloggers numbered 100 within Iraq and over 1,000 across the Middle East (Matheson and Allan, 2009: 78). Reuters' decision to include the contribution of bloggers as part of its news services on the Global Voices and Reuters Africa sites was not just to include different voices and redress the under-reporting of certain parts of the world, but aimed also to manage the personal safety of the correspondents and the rising costs of maintaining their network of reporters (Matheson and Allan, 2009: 112). In 2004 Reuters announced a programme, dubbed Fast Forward, for restructuring its newsgathering operations, which has led to the shedding of a considerable number of staff jobs over the last 15 years (Milmo, 2004). The capacity to maintain coverage of the world has relied increasingly on blogs and other forms of user-generated content, which has led, in the words of John Maxwell Hamilton and Eric Jenner (2004), to the "redefining of foreign correspondence".

The acceptance of the importance of citizen journalism was highlighted in coverage of events such as the hanging of Saddam Hussein and the London tube bombing, which were reported with uploaded videos and pictures from people who were on-site. They were simultaneously received by the audience. Sambrook (2005: 14) notes that within six hours of the London tube bombing the BBC newsroom "received 1,000 photographs, 20 pieces of video, 4,000 text messages and 20,000 emails ... the quantity and quality of contributions moved them beyond novelty, tokenism or the exceptional ... from now on, news coverage is a partnership". By 2006 CNN set up a site called iReport to gather and present news images, including images from the Israeli bombing of Lebanon in August 2006. The incorporation of blogging and user-generated content into the mainstream media not only influenced how war reporters work but also, it can be argued, transformed the nature of what is reported. The increased liveness and access impacted on the reporting. The pressure to be present at a story was lessened as media organisations were able to gather images and accounts of such events from social media. Blogging in particular was seen as changing how journalists worked (Bradshaw, 2008). It made them work more quickly, put reporters in a direct relationship with their audiences, changed the ways stories were generated and led to them writing more informally; and through interactivity and 'conversation', audiences were able to inform, educate and respond to what reporters had written or broadcast. Journalists could now see immediately what their audiences were interested in; via blogs, they could communicate directly with sources or request information. However, as the pressure to publish increased, it meant more reliance on rumours, the onus being on readers to check the facts (Bradshaw, 2008).

Malachy Browne, the managing editor of Storyful, believes that the ability to go straight to those involved in an event means that the news cycle today is much faster and more global (Browne et al., 2015). News also contains much more graphic content as it can include the footage from people directly involved in the events, what Browne calls the "very raw reality of the people who suffer in conflict" (Browne et al., 2015: 1340). This raises extra ethical risks for journalists who now have to make decisions about pictures that show what has happened in its entirety. Browne asks whether pictures of the disembowelment of a 10-year-old girl after a bombing in Syria should be shown. Previously the camera operator or professional reporter would have acted as gatekeeper to what was filmed, aware of editorial guidelines on the representation of graphic images. Now material from social media means the footage landing on the journalist's computer, though more broadly accessible, is often unchecked and anonymous. There is risk involved, particularly for those who eyewitness events; being identified as the source of material carries risk for individuals inside war zones, and there is also potential danger to those filmed, whose permission to reproduce or broadcast has not been gained. In the coverage of the violence and protests after the 2009 Iranian election, much of the reporting came from social media and activists' videos. After reviewing Twitter content from the first two days, Sambrook (2010: 92) concludes that

> If you relied on it, you might believe that all sorts of things had happened, which simply hadn't (tanks in streets, opposition members arrested, the election declared void, students killed and buried), running a high risk of being seriously misled about events on the ground. You might, at best, have simply been confused. You probably wouldn't have thought that [Iran's President Mahmoud] Ahmadinejad enjoys much popular support at all.

The supplanting of more traditional journalism by citizen journalism allows more voices to be heard in the reporting of war and conflict, but as Graham Mythen (2010: 52) writes, its real test is in the extent to which "it is able to give a voice to the excluded and disenfranchised". The danger to war journalism is that the use of these sources gives voice to those who shout in capitals and in the most emotional way. Zelizer (2007: 425) notes that in terms of eyewitnessing war and conflict, journalists and their reports have been excluded from the centre of reporting by technology and non-conventional journalists. She states that what drives eyewitnessing is proximity and immediacy, but without the fuller dimensions of eyewitnessing that help make it an integral part of journalism, it becomes formless and repetitive (Zelizer, 2007: 423). There is less accuracy and reasoned analysis, and reports are more open to defamation, rumour and malice.

Access

As seen from the conflict in Iraq, the news media organisation can take pictures from citizen journalists or social media, but the journalist will still want, if possible, to be at an event or location to witness what is happening. The problem is actually getting to where the action is taking place. Baron de Jomini (1838) defines logistics as "the practical art of moving armies", and this is equally applicable to journalists in conflict. If you cannot get to where the conflict is happening – especially for television, which relies on pictures – you cannot witness what is happening. Travelling safely around a war zone is, as we have noted in previous chapters, an essential part of the job. Whereas embedded correspondents have their travel and transportation arranged for them, the problems of movement and transportation raises a different set of problems for non-embedded reporters. In Iraq in late 2003, the documentary crew had two options: hire private security and travel in armoured vehicles with armed private security or 'go grey'. The former is very expensive. If the area was designated particularly dangerous, private security companies advised the need for two armed vehicles for a crew of two or three, with extra personnel in each. This was not only costly, but also meant that it immediately drew attention to the fact that the journalists were rich Westerners with something worth stealing or people worth kidnapping. The main security companies vet their employees, but the industry itself is unregulated. In 2014, four Blackwater Security Consulting (now Academi) employees were convicted in a US federal court on murder, manslaughter and firearms charges (Buchanan, 2016). Sometimes the last person needed in a potentially volatile situation is a young man, or a couple of young men, with a gun. In late 2003 the documentary crew in Baghdad decided to go grey and hire taxis. The drivers were hired by the fixer, and it meant they could travel around Baghdad relatively unnoticed. After 2004 when the country descended into civil war, the situation became too dangerous to risk going without security, although every driver in Baghdad had one if not two guns near to hand in their cars. The threat was not so much from insurgents, but from gangs who were kidnapping journalists for money. In 2012, BBC policy stated crews had to have security in Iraq. The BBC documentary crew were the only armoured car driving round Basra, so they stood out immediately. The vehicle was so heavy it could not travel off-road, as it would have sunk into the mountains of rubbish outside the city. The decision to go grey increased the reliance on local fixers during this period. Sometimes the fixers tell you what they think you want to hear. They claim to know an area, and for face-saving or job-saving reasons, they are reluctant to own up to a lack of knowledge. The potential fallout can be serious. Most of the fixers in Iraq, especially the younger ones, were city based and had to rely on contacts or family members to navigate villages or areas outside of Basra or Baghdad. This either slowed things down as they needed more time to organise the journey or increased the risk as they just went in blind. A journalist must be clear about expectation, and as in covering stories, it can be dangerous to assume without checking facts.

Fixers

As we have seen, changes in the international news market and the increasing danger posed to Western reporters have resulted in the role of fixers becoming more important in reporting war, conflicts and crises. Fixers in Iraq carried out a "mixture of relating the local news, translating, story generation, backgrounding and using their contacts to secure interviews, cars, hotels, petrol and story play-outs" (Murrell, 2010: 131). For the MBC series on Iraq, the documentary team hired a team of fixers to help make three one-hour documentaries, involving three separate crews. A main fixer was hired, who subcontracted separate fixers for each programme. He was a cousin of the bureau chief at AP at the time. Correspondents "would rather employ someone who was recommended or was a 'known quantity' to either another correspondent or to another fixer. If this wasn't possible, then they would approach media companies first and academics or teachers after that" (Murrell, 2010: 130). Word of mouth is very important in finding fixers as their role is vital to the success of not only the production but also the safety of journalists on the ground. The fixer for the MBC series was a former Iraqi

Brigadier General, had extremely good logistical abilities and spoke fluent English. The people he employed were relatives, close friends or associates. The documentary teams relied on this personal network to find stories, negotiate access and advise on security and life in general in Iraq.

At that time Iraq was still relatively safe for Westerners – compared to what was to come later – but the problems of sectarianism were beginning to surface. Employing fixers from certain communities had consequences, and relying only on Sunni fixers could be an issue. A major characteristic of many war journalists is their unfamiliarity about the country that they are reporting from, its culture and history. Lack of knowledge and ignorance of social structures accentuates the risk involved in what you ask the fixer to do. An added risk is that news organisations are not fully aware of the situation on the ground. In Iraq, sectarianism was an issue that could not be ignored. Main sources for one of the documentary programmes were Feyli Kurds in Baghdad. They had been targeted by Saddam Hussein in the 1980s as they were successful businessmen and he wanted to appropriate their businesses. Many of the families returned in 2003 to trace disappeared relatives and/or try to reclaim the properties that had been confiscated under the regime. Connections with them had been made in London, but because of the history of oppression by the Sunnis, the fixer would not go to the Feyli Kurd office in Baghdad. However, the fixer's uncle had been a general under Abd al-Karim Qasim, who was regarded as a hero by both Sunni and Shia Iraqis. Qasim had initially worked with the Kurdistan Democratic Party and Barzani, thus both Shia and Sunni Iraqis would speak to the fixer, his nephew and colleagues. When filming the story of the search for justice after the fall of Saddam, the documentary crew depended on this fixer for connections and contacts, and their ability to negotiate access can be seen as compromised by the relationship.

The reliance on fixers is seen by some as threatening the 'authentic news-gathering role' and weakening the traditional model of the correspondent (see Murrell, 2010). Reporters such as ABC's Peter Cave who either did not visit Iraq often or went as part of an embed mission tend to believe that "[i]t's very difficult to feel you're doing your job as correspondent if you are forced to report second-hand through a fixer or a local cameraman" (quoted in Murrell, 2010: 134). Long-term correspondents or documentary directors are more used to working in a team on the ground and see fixers as vital members of their team, similar to a production team working in their home countries. Locals fulfil the roles of researchers, assistant producers and sometimes, as in the case of the general, executive producers, telling directors and reporters what is possible to film and what is completely out of the question. As for shaping your story decisions, neither journalists nor TV producers nor film-makers lose their critical faculties. What to use, who to believe, the veracity of the information given, whether what is given is mistranslated or whether significant material is missing – these are all decisions that need to be made. This is the challenge in any conflict; it is just that in Iraq it all came with a higher degree of risk. As CNN's Michael Ware told Murrell, "[i]n the Iraq war as in all wars, everyone lies", and together with the restrictions, this made it very difficult but not impossible "to capture slithers or shards of the truth" in Iraq (quoted in Murrell, 2010: 135).

As the situation in Iraq became more dangerous and it was impossible for Westerners to venture out of their secure compounds in the Green Zone, fixers became the reporters and the crew. By 2009 it was impossible to venture into cities without having some sort of military escort, and Iraqi crews had to be given shot lists and interview questions. With the Western reporter sitting, less at risk, in a secure compound, the difficulty of assessing the quality of the information gathered and the interviewees accessed were more apparent. Assessing the credibility of what was being told to the local crew, whether the person chosen was the best contributor, and most importantly, what was not being said, was increasingly a challenge if you could not be there. In compensation for not speaking the language, experience and body language often helps alert the reporter or producer to something not being right; so, not being able to witness the knowledge transaction is less than ideal. The pressure of the constant knowledge that others were being sent out to face the dangers that they as the producers were not, weighed heavily on some reporters. Working out how to protect their fixers and support teams exercised correspondents, who increasingly chose not to select crews to film in the areas that they were from; in the case of Iraq, crews from Jordan were hired as they could leave the country and take themselves out of danger or retribution.

The danger to local journalists has increased exponentially with the war in Syria. In June 2016 in a video entitled *Inspiration of Satan*, produced and released by the local media branch of the Islamic State group in Deir al-Zour, Syria, five men confess to reporting for the media and NGOs and are then killed (CPJ, 2016a). In Syria, as we have mentioned, gaining access to the conflict posed many problems. The logistics of entering the country had implications for the capacity of reporters to travel within the country. Entering Syria meant making decisions about which side you would report from, either with a government-approved visa or in rebel-held areas. Robin Vandervoort (2016: 311) writes that "journalists who entered rebel-held areas without permission from the Syrian government were from then on considered to be collaborators and would no longer be granted an official visa". To establish a long-term presence, the BBC sought to get around this by sending a journalist to each side. This was perceived as "annoying" from the journalistic perspective and was regarded much like embedding, leading to similar frustrations in that the journalists felt they were only getting one side of a story, either from the regime point of view or from the side of the Free Syrian Army. The variety of opposition groups – secular, fundamentalist, separatist and the like – made the efforts to gain access more difficult and risky.

The increasingly sectarian nature of the war and the mediatisation of the conflict led to a situation in Syria in which the fixers could not be disentangled from the conflict. The situation in Syria was "more complicated" than in Iraq (Vandervoort, 2016: 318). In Syria fixers are themselves strongly dependent upon their network within particular rebel groups.

In other words: there are no "ordinary Syrians" left out of the civil war: the only way to access them is not through an unconsciously biased fixer, but through the increasingly professional communication staff working for particular movements involved in the conflict.

(Vandervoort, 2016: 318)

But even in Iraq, finding a fixer meant finding someone who knew how journalists work; and most journalists worked for a particular news organisation with a particular affiliation – few are 'neutral'. The ties might not have been as extreme as in Syria, but the nature of journalism in the Middle East made not knowing the allegiances of your fixer potentially a huge risk, likely to infect your own reporting and possibly jeopardise your security.

The safety of the fixers themselves has become more of an issue in the confused world of asymmetrical conflict. A foreign crew can leave when things get difficult, but a fixer cannot. Many translators in Iraq wear masks over their faces so they cannot be identified. It is nevertheless difficult for a fixer to maintain their anonymity when they have to organise interviews and filming and be clear about who they are working for. Moreover, they use contacts who know who they are or familiar networks where people know them and the others in that group. The UK media has extensively covered the issue of military translators abandoned by the US and British military after years of work with the forces, but it has not paid less attention to its own practice of the treatment of fixers. As we have seen (Chapter 3), fixers are usually undervalued and under-protected by their employers. As in all journalism, the root of this problem lies in finance. Training, insurance and contracts all have cost implications. In all the visits to Iraq, the documentary crews were provided with flak jackets and helmets but the translators and fixers were not. Crews have to complete hostile environment training and pay huge insurance sums, but the fixers and translators on the whole did not. The risk to fixers is as great as it is to reporters, but their safety and well-being seems less valued. In 2012 during a recce for the BBC documentary on Iraq, the BBC documentary team hired a local journalist and a translator in Basra. When they got back to London, the translator contacted the BBC to say he had received death threats warning him not to work with the Western media. He was released from his contract and another translator was found, even after explaining the risk that he was expected to undertake. In this case the BBC was sensitive to the situation, but for other, less well financed media organisations or for freelancers, the means and ends of telling the story becomes a dilemma fraught with risk. Taking responsibility for others in a team is increasingly part of the job of a journalist, and as the person negotiating between the organisation at home and the team on the ground, a reporter or director is always challenged by a series of ethical responsibilities which can determine how the story is covered.

Distant war, distant reporting

The increasing use of mediators in the reporting of news, both human and technological, echoes the military's increasing use of weapons at a distance. The use of satellites, rockets, cruise missiles, robots, drones and cyberwar mean wars can now be fought at long distance. Wars can be fought and reported on without face-to-face contact. The increasing use of drones, or unmanned aerial vehicles, increases the difficulties of reporting war. In traditional war, the journalist could be embedded with the forces and their weapons; but access to where the drones are controlled is highly limited, and being at the other end is not advised. Around 86 countries have some drone capability, with 19 either possessing armed drones or acquiring the technology. It is claimed that "since taking office, President Barack Obama has attacked more countries than any president since World War II, launching drone strikes against at least seven nations and killing thousands of people, many of them innocent civilians" (Bamford, 2016). Much of the drone warfare conducted by the US is overseen by the CIA counterterrorism agency as this type of warfare was initiated originally to take out Al-Qaeda operatives in Afghanistan. "Between mid-2008 and mid-2013, C.I.A.-operated drones waged what amounted to an undeclared, remotely controlled air war over North and South Waziristan" (Coll, 2014), but most of the evolution and conduct of this war is an official secret.

The US government does not acknowledge many strikes, and finding out about this type of conflict is problematic. Institutions such as the Bureau of Investigative Journalism keep a database on Drone Warfare, using a form of networked journalism to report on this type of warfare. They compile the report using links to news reports, statements, documents and press releases as well as information from terrorist propaganda as well as leaked US intelligence reports and WikiLeaks diplomatic cables. The Bureau of Investigative Journalism (n.d.) states that sometimes information is not reported in open media and that news can be lost in the mass of other news from countries such as Pakistan and Afghanistan, and they acknowledge that the CIA does not release information. The undertaking of drone warfare can be a complex procedure. Gregory (2011: 199) writes that for deliberate targeting, where targets are typically developed over 36 to 40 hours, "legal advisers review target folders containing imagery and other intelligence, collateral damage estimates and the weaponeering solutions proposed to mitigate those effects and monitor the continued development of the target". Gaining access to interview those involved in the process is difficult, if not impossible, because of the secrecy involved, and as technology takes over the process, finding a human source to question or to confront becomes challenging.

The way to cover this war is either to tell the story of the victims of drone attacks or to report the media of the opposition, civilians or NGOs involved, or else it falls out of the current remit of conflict reporting and becomes a story about procurement or political coverage as a domestic investigation in the home country of those controlling the drones. As seen, coverage of this form of war is best undertaken by investigative journalists or human rights groups which have funding and time to uncover information. For journalists reporting conflict on the ground, the news value of conflict is lessened and the ability to link military forces to conflict visually or at close hand disappears, along with the immediacy of holding power to account. With the basic storytelling content unavailable, the ability of the journalist to perform a fundamental role becomes more difficult and the risk of the story not being told becomes greater.

Compared to the reporting of traditional warfare, the journalism of asymmetrical warfare is more complicated, fraught with greater uncertainty and presents more risk to the war correspondent. After 2003 irregular warfare characterised the conflict in Iraq. With the absence of clear front lines, the difficulty of identifying and locating the combatants, the capacity to fight wars from a distance, 'push-button warfare' and the growing centrality of the media to the prosecution of war, journalists have had to reassess their role and practices. This has been undertaken at a time of enormous challenges to newspapers, news agencies and other news providers. Changes in technology generated new news sources of information about war and conflict which are more readily accessible to audiences and, in the process, undermined traditional business models of Western media. The practice of war reporting became more insecure. "The traditional functions of bearing witness, holding to account, opinion leadership and shaming are no longer provided solely by the news media" (Picard, 2014: 505). War correspondents have to compete with other sources and other ways of telling the story of war, which presents a challenge to the more traditional form of conflict reporting. As civilians become more involved in war and telling the story of war, the restricted system that pervaded traditional news generation is being replaced by a more open and fluid "ecosystem" which generates news from a broader range of sources and in different, more public ways. Post-war Iraq highlighted the changes that were taking place. Western reporters, unable to move freely outside the Green Zone in Baghdad, came to rely on local reporters and the internet to report the conflict. Their reporting increasingly depended on second-hand accounts of events. Personal safety was a major consideration, but perhaps the greater risk was associated with journalistic investigation and accuracy, fact-checking and responsibility to sources and those they relied on to access them.

7

RISK AND REPORTING NEW FORMS OF WAR AND CONFLICT

Identifying what is 'war' is more complex today than it has ever been. Recognising who is fighting is not simple, and knowing what weapons they are using is not obvious. Milena Michalski and James Gow argue that war is no longer just a Clausewitzian trinity (government, armed forces and people at home); it is now a "multifaceted, multivalent phenomenon" (2008: 14). Contemporary warfare involves the home front, each aspect of the opponent's triangle of political leaders, armed forces, people at home, and global audiences. Soldiers are not only warriors but also peacekeepers, police and diplomats (Hajjar, 2014). There are no set-piece battles, and much of the action of war takes place where it cannot be seen or where there is little access. The role of war correspondent is to 'make sense' of war, conflict and crises, to cut through the 'fog of war', which as the great war strategist Clausewitz noted, often ensures that not even the people fighting are aware of what is happening when it happens. The fog of war has become an impenetrable blanket. War and the nature of its reporting for some scholars have a new level of asymmetry. The 'asymmetric'[1] wars of Iraq and Afghanistan have moved on and correspondents now have to contend with 'new-generation warfare'. Rod Thornton (2015: 41) states, "at its most basic level, the aim [of this new form of warfare] is to generate a situation where it is unclear whether a state of war exists – and if it does, who is a combatant and who is not". At the heart of the new generation of conflicts is control of information and images, which has pre-eminence in military operations. The conduct of war in the Crimea, Ukraine, Libya and Syria has engaged and subverted the nature of war reporting and journalism in general.

The role of the journalist, the tools they are using and the nature of journalism, as we noted in earlier chapters, has been changing since the end of the Cold War. The traditional news media now compete with other forms of media. Rune Ottosen (2007) emphasises that large sections of young people have turned their backs on traditional news media; now they are seeking "cultural and visual impulses in entertainment and new digital media such as computer games, films, and interactivity in the blogosphere" (Nohrstedt and Ottosen, 2014: 81). News organisations and journalists now have to reconsider the audience and tread a fine line between traditional news values and the entertainment values of "market-driven journalism" (Cohen, 2010). The desire to generate higher circulation, more hits or better ratings is seen to exert a disproportionate influence on editorial decision-making (see Chapter 2). Losing the audience is a problem, especially in the context of demands for what the head of digital news at ITV listed as "pandas and skateboarding dogs or buses exploding across London Bridge and things like that" (Kalogeropoulos and Nielsen, 2017: 10) in "must-watch" videos. War reporting is becoming a spectacle, and audiences are in search of entertainment as much as information.

It is not only the type of media, but the type of reality they seek to represent that is different. It is a reality confirmed not just by the visual and the emotions, but one influenced by the medium on which it appears. Digital media is increasingly accessed through devices such as personal smartphones, in many ways dominated by platform companies like Facebook and Google, and has a growing interest in "participation", "interactivity" and "immediacy" (Usher, 2014). All of this has led to a new and challenging world for journalists. Technology is evolving daily, and if the journalist is going to keep her audience, she will have to forge tighter connections with them (McCollough *et al.*, 2017). The relationship between journalists and citizens is developing to produce a new form of journalism. For Adrienne Russell (2011: 1), "networked journalism is journalism that sees publics acting as creators, investigators, reactors, (re)makers, and (re)distributors of news and where all variety of media, amateurs and professional, corporate and independent products and interests intersect at a new level".

In this networked world, news and information are becoming the major resource of power (Castells, 1996), and the users of this networked media compete to access and own it. This struggle for a master narrative has led to transformations in the nature of war-fighting and the computerisation of war (Brunner and Cavelty, 2009). This chapter looks at the impact of contemporary conflict on reporting; the risks to the journalist caught up in this maelstrom of the increased speed and complexity of the news cycle, the reporting of terror and the role of verification in what has come to be labelled as 'hybrid war'.

Hybrid warfare

The term 'hybrid war' was first used to describe the strategy used by Hezbollah to prosecute the 2006 Lebanon War (Van Puyvelde, 2015). It emphasises the unequal capabilities of the adversaries, both state and non-state, and the combination of elements of regular conventional warfare with elements of irregular warfare, terrorism and criminality (Murray and Mansoor, 2012). It embraces the 'full spectrum' of modern warfare and, according to US Army Special Command (2014: 3), "involves a state or state-like actor's use of all available diplomatic, informational, military, and economic means to destabilize an adversary". It also is overt and covert, using information operations, espionage, agitation of the domestic population, criminal disorder, cultivation of fifth columns and insertion of unmarked soldiers. An example of this form of war is in the Ukraine where a 'new-generation war' is being fought by Russia (Berzins, 2014). Whether what is happening represents a major transformation of war is a matter of debate. Alexander Lanoszka (2016: 178) claims it is "a strategy rather than a new form of war" in which regular warfare is used as minimally as possible. He writes that different methods of domination are used to "undermine the target's territorial integrity, subvert its internal political cohesion and disrupt it economy". For Damien Van Puyvelde (2015), war has always been defined by a mixture of regular and irregular, conventional and unconventional tactics to exploit opponents' weaknesses. Technology has simply expanded war in a new direction.

To understand the nature of hybrid war, it is important to stress the close relationship between war reporting and war propaganda. Stig Nohrstedt (2001: 177) tells us that "war reporting is a discourse anchored in propaganda". The war of perceptions and battle for control of the mind continues, and the news media have always been used as a tool for propaganda in times of war. Whether they cooperate or are used against their will is a matter of debate. James Der Derian (2001) highlights the mutuality of the relationship between the news media and the military during conflict. He writes that the military needs the media to ensure support for their campaigns and the media needs the military because war coverage ensures high ratings and sales. Both need society to pay attention to them, and this is done by telling a good story, in exchange for which society is engaged, informed and entertained. Traditionally, propaganda and information campaigns have been seen as an 'adjunct' to military operations, but gradually over the post-Second World War period, and more rapidly since the US defeat in Vietnam, information and propaganda has taken "primacy" with conventional forces in a "supporting role" (NATO Stratcom COE, 2014: 6). Using journalists and the media has been part of an information strategy in which a variety of tools have been deployed to construct narratives of conflicts. As mentioned in previous chapters, information warfare is prosecuted not only by military superpowers but also by non-state actors, whose proficiency in using new media has been noted. The extent and the effectiveness of using the media in war propaganda have varied throughout history, but the advent of the digital world marked what has been described as the 'mediatisation' of war. Today the media are more influential than ever. As Maltby (2012: 108) writes: "War is no longer an activity that takes place outside of the media. Rather, the media have become progressively integrated into the planning and organisation of war as a weapon of persuasion and a legitimation tool."

There are different views on the impact of digital media on our understanding of war and conflict. From the opening up of a greater diversity of views and opinions to the enhanced capacity of government and military to manage the information environment, interpretation of the application of the new media to war and conflict has varied. Hoskins and O'Loughlin (2015) set out different stages in the mediatisation of war, identifying a new paradigm of war and media operations which they call "arrested war" to cover recent developments. In this state, they argue, "professional media and military institutions have arrested the once-chaotic social media dynamics and more effectively harnessed them for their own ends through new understandings, strategies and experiments" (Hoskins and O'Loughlin, 2015: 1320). They assert that the mainstream media is more sure of their basic functions and their centrality in the reporting of war. Journalists are now more confident in their ability to act as gatekeepers and set the agenda for the reporting of war. The confusion and complexity caused by the digital revolution have been arrested, and user-generated content and its chaotic dynamics 'out there' have been absorbed and appropriated. This is echoed in Brian McNair's (2006) argument that we have moved from control to chaos and back again as digital platforms allow a range of actors to promote their ideological causes and national interests. Journalists, according to Hoskins and O'Loughlin (2015: 1321), "seem more confident" and have more faith in the quality and integrity of the product. Arguably, it is not as simple as this. In the new complex world of increasing media logic, adapted and used by terrorists and others as a form of psychological warfare (Nacos, 2016), it is perhaps the military and terrorists who have engaged with and harnessed the media to their own ends, while journalists as foot soldiers in the media have to understand what news is and what is war. Reporting conflict becomes a rhetorical tool to justify or recruit for one side, and 'news' reporting becomes manipulated for bellicose ends. The distancing of the correspondent from the event, the availability of pictures from the Internet and combatants' increasing use of information as a battle tactic are perhaps furthering the risk that journalists are used by militant groups, activists or state-sponsored propaganda operations.

In 1948 the US government passed the Smith–Mundt Act, a Cold War measure to regulate US public diplomacy or propaganda which prohibits domestic distribution of propaganda information intended for foreign audiences. This meant that the US public should not be lied to by its government. However, with the advent of digital media, checking the origin of stories broadcast from a country such as Iraq, where they are picked up on the Web, it becomes more difficult to identify whether the stories broadcast are genuine or part of media operations campaigns constructed by various militaries or activists in the field. As Elgin Brunner and Myriam Cavelty (2009: 641) write, "postmodern notions of conflict deliberately blur boundaries between war and peace, between military and civilian systems and spaces and between information and influence/manipulation". They argue that this expansion of the battlefield into human perception threatens to result in "even more civilian involvement in conflicts" (Brunner and Cavelty, 2009: 642), which is arguably what is happening in Syria, the Yemen and Libya. Contemporary wars are difficult to see in terms that separate military engagements and civilian populations (Kaldor, 2003, 2006).

Whatever it is called, the character of contemporary conflict is changing the circumstances of the war reporter. Few contemporary wars end with decisive outcomes; more often fighting simply ceases (Kreutz, 2010). Moreover, war can be fought on different fronts: the military, the diplomatic, the media and the legal (Yarchi, 2014). As war becomes more fluid and less defined, a basic question for the war correspondent arises – what is it that the journalist is reporting? Reporters such as Anne Applebaum (2014) argue that "it's a new world we are now entering, and we need new tools to cope with it". Her concern is with Russian tactics in the Ukraine, which have nothing to do with the traditional application of military forces but more to do with "thugs, criminals and lies" allied with "slick modern media" and "sophisticated information campaigns". Others have drawn attention to the use of similar tactics by the US and other Western-led operations (see Brown, 2003; Kumar, 2006). They all highlight the increasing use of non-military means to attain objectives, including the advent of cyberwar, which demands a wider range of reporting and researching skills. How do you hold to account aggressors who cannot be identified or located and report on a war that cannot be witnessed? Is the hacking of politicians' emails by another country, opposed to their party, considered politics, or is it war? Are foreign forces helping police or engaged in humanitarian intervention in Iraq or Afghanistan waging war? Clausewitz writes that war is the extension of politics by any other means, but today where one begins and the other ends is more difficult to unravel, and many war correspondents are failing to keep up with the developments let alone understand them (Lee, 2015).

Complicating this is also the counter-insurgency strategy adopted by the US and other militaries. Counter-insurgency involves protecting the civilian population and building government institutions that serve them. An important aspect of war by the US and other NATO countries is foreign internal defence, which is the support of the host (or invaded) country to build up and strengthen the country's security involving training and support activities. The British and American armies trained parts of the Iraqi and Afghan security forces. The disintegration of the Iraqi Army in 2014 in the face of ISIS forces seemed to point to its spectacular failure. In her book on the increasingly blurred lines between war and peace, former lawyer Rosa Brooks (2017) points out that US soldiers are now involved in public health programmes, agricultural reform, small business developments and training in the rule of law. This was also the case in South Iraq after the 2003 invasion where British soldiers advised on date planting, building schools and inter-tribal negotiations. Attempts to get a commission for a programme on these activities received little or no interest as they were not perceived as 'war-fighting', even though they involved soldiers, and the activities were part of a COIN[2] strategy to win hearts and minds.

The 'weaponisation' of the media has increased exponentially the physical risks to journalists, as well as the risks to journalism. As some of the tools of journalism become the tools of war, the professional strictures of the journalist become much more important. The traditional journalistic role of bearing witness to war is being undermined with increasing use of social media, and this has introduced both new risks for journalists and new ways to report conflict. Western nations do not now tend to go to war against other nations directly or for territorial reasons, and globalisation has seen the increase in other ideologies and entities fighting wars. For Matheson and Allan (2009: 121), in Mary Kaldor's concept of "network war", non-state actors are organised less by the national identity of formal institutions than by shared "politically extreme narratives", where control of the narratives "becomes a central tool" of war.

> The growth of communications technology will increase our enemies' ability to influence, not only all those on the battlefield, but also our own society directly. We must therefore win the battle for information, as well as the battle on the ground.
>
> *(HM Government, 2010: 16)*

They all need to justify why they go to war on a global scale, and the proliferation of media organisations and technologies are now implements and theatres where journalists, combatants and civilians struggle for voices and the power to be heard and to manipulate.

Fuelling fear

The citizen is central to the logic of modern conflict, and fear and insecurity are tools in the mobilisation of people for political ends. They are most often used in and through the media. The manufacture of fear by governments and the media as a prelude to war has been noted by many writers (see Der Derian, 2001; Hoskins and O'Loughlin, 2009; Knightley, 2012; Altheide, 2013). Norman Fairclough (2006) argues that the reaction to ISIS and much of the conflict reporting after 9/11 could be interpreted in terms of an attempt to induce fear to legitimise policies and actions against the perpetrators. This is enhanced by "news journalism's penchant for spectacular, dramatic and threatening news events with accompanying visual images" (Nohrstedt and Ottensen, 2014: 75). Stig Nohrstedt and Rune Ottosen (2008) emphasise the culture of fear in shaping contemporary war reporting, arguing that the risk society has given way to what they describe as the "threat society". They describe a transnational culture of fear, driven not by uncertain risks with unforeseeable consequences, but by certain threats with predictable negative consequences. The widespread desire for knowledge about the threats and dangers is not being met by a media increasingly dominated by visual communication. Whether engendered by domestic politics or the political economy of news organisations, their practices or the desire to tell a good story, the representation of war is moving into something different – a reality constructed by those who tell the good war story.

Paul Virilio (1989) argues that the most ancient battlefield is the immaterial battlefield of perception, or the story of the battle that people perceive rather than the one that actually happened. Wars have always been about information and the way the tale is told, but in a world in which the media and information are the key feature of war, the necessity for victory becomes a matter of "information superiority" (Joint Chiefs of Staff, 2006). In part, this superiority is seen to be achieved through the conduct of Information Operations, which are defined as

> the integrated employment of electronic warfare (EW), computer network operations (CNO), psychological operations (PSYOP), military deception (MILDEC), and operations security (OPSEC), in concert with specified supporting and related capabilities, to influence, disrupt, corrupt, or usurp adversarial human and automated decision making while protecting our own.
>
> *(Joint Chiefs of Staff, 2006: ix)*

This form of warfare presents new and old risks to journalists. Particular skills are required to report on computer network operations and cyber technology; investigative skills are need to counter deception; and government and military demands for security in the face of seeming increased terror threats raise barriers to fact-checking. Despite and because of the apparent increase in openness of information that the ubiquity of social media has given rise to, the greatest risk offered by this form of warfare is that the media is now consciously being used as a weapon of war.

Hybrid information war

Much of the writing about hybrid war involves examination of the tactics that Russia used in its campaign in the Ukraine. In 2014 anti-government demonstrations known as Euromaiden led to the resignation of the pro-Russian President Yanukovych and Russia's annexation of the Ukrainian territory of Crimea after a controversial referendum was held where 97 per cent of the population apparently wanted to join the Russian Federation. This "indigenously led" decision by the people of the Crimea was, according to Lanoszka (2016: 180), heavily facilitated by the spreading of false information and fake news, an important tactic of hybrid war. Information superiority has become a necessity in contemporary warfare (Chekinov and Bogdanov, 2013; Thomas, 2016; Iasiello, 2017). NATO's Supreme Allied Commander Europe (SACEUR), General Philip Breedlove, noted that Russia waged "the most amazing information warfare blitzkrieg we have ever seen in the history of information warfare" (quoted in Vandiver, 2014). At a conference on countering violent extremism in London in 2015, Valentyn Petrov, the head of information for the National Security and Defence Council of Ukraine, stated that Russia's long-term strategy for war in the Ukraine was evident from the mid 1990s. They had control over Ukraine's mobiles, telecoms, media, social media, lobby groups and NGOs as well as critical segments of IT security; and 70 per cent of antiviral software was developed in Russia. Ulises Mejias and Nickolai Vokuev (2017: 1029) place emphasis on this aspect of the information war:

> The use of social media generally weakened the power of civil society by allowing for the rampant spread of disinformation ... and the fact that social

media campaigns can be co-opted and redistributed via mass media channels to amplify their effect is cause to fear similar applications in other parts of the world.

Veracity is not necessary. In an editorial in The Guardian (2015), Margarita Simonyan, the editor-in-chief of the Putin-leaning Russia Today satellite television station and website, describes Russian media output: "There is no objectivity – only approximations of the truth by as many different voices as possible". It is also becoming more difficult for journalists to identify whether who and what they are seeing is 'war'. Those involved in the invasion of the Eastern Ukraine are

> led not by officers in uniform but by men from Russian military intelligence and special operations forces, some wearing camouflage without insignia, some communicating with "activists" by telephone. They are supplied with Russian logistics and a few Russian automatic weapons, but not tanks or planes. There is no "shock and awe" bombing campaign, just systematic, organized attacks on police stations, city councils, airports.
>
> *(Applebaum, 2014)*

The general outrage over the 'little green men', as these soldiers were referred to, is perhaps naïve as British Special Forces have been involved in the support of Kosovo insurgents in NATO's war in Yugoslavia and in Libya, and Turkish, Arab and Western states all have or have had special forces in Syria (Ehrhart, 2017).

Hybrid warfare operates in a "grey zone" (Erhart, 2017) where some actions are political and some economic, as in the support of protest movements and dissidents and cyberattacks conducted by civilians. Such actions blur or eliminate existing boundaries in definition of war and, hence, pose a problem of deciding what and how to report. This 'new type' of warfare is associated with non-state actors, failing states and the long war against terrorism.

Terrorism

It is not just Western armies that have adopted the tactics of information and image warfare using the media as weapons of war. There are examples of insurgent videos from Chechnya in the 1990s, and in November 2012 Israel became the first nation to initiate hostilities by social media, launching Operation Pillar of Defence with a YouTube video of the assassination of Hamas leader Ahmed al-Jabari. The media wants drama, excitement and shock to keep viewers watching, and combatants can offer this in spades. In the competition for the audience's attention, the risk for journalists is that they have to keep up with this demand.

For the terrorist organisations, publicity is the necessary means to their political ends, and although the Internet allows terrorists to communicate directly to their audiences, the mainstream media is at the moment their "number one source of information and therefore a major target of terrorist propaganda" (Nacos, 2016:

362). Among top news searches in 2014, ISIS ranked behind only Ebola in terms of popularity according to Google Trends (Fryer-Briggs, 2015). Most media organisations are heavily reliant on web clicks, and ISIS knew what stories would garner the most clicks. If media organisations are reliant on clicks, the risk to journalism is that it is the kind of stories that produce them and the way these stories are told that become news, drowning out the political and less sensational information.

Zarqawi's Al-Qaeda in Iraq (AQI) group took the information war to new levels (Rogers, 2006). One of its first productions was a film in 2003 which showed the US bombing of Baghdad with graphic footage of civilian victims. *The Washington Post* critiqued the 46-minute documentary *All Religion Will be for Allah*, which had

> a specially designed Web page with dozens of links to the video so users could choose which version to download. ... Viewers could choose Windows Media or RealPlayer. They could even download 'All Religions Will be for Allah' to play on a cell phone.
>
> *(Rogers, 2006: 272)*

Learning from AQI, ISIS has been spectacularly successful in their information operations, utilising the media to broadcast their message and win hearts and minds. "IS has developed a multidimensional, multilingual Info Ops campaign, spread across a variety of platforms, that has become increasingly sophisticated" (Ridland, 2015: 31). Haroro Ingram (2015: 743) writes that in ISIS' insurgency campaign, "Information Operations plays a central strategic role in shaping how contested populations perceive a conflict, evaluate competing politico-military apparatuses (i.e. competitive systems of control) and make decisions about who to support".

ISIS' Wilayat information offices used online publications such as *Dabiq* magazine; they produced professional documentaries and videos such as *The Flames of War* (2014); and they produced communiqués that focused on local issues and events, using billboards, radio posters and public events to disseminate messages. Members also use thousands of Twitter accounts, mobile phones and social media forums like Diaspora and Facebook to send text, photo and video messages. When ISIS marched into Mosul in 2014, members produced up to 44,000 tweets a day, causing an image the group had tweeted to pop up among the first results when one searched Twitter for 'Baghdad' (Farwell, 2014: 51). "Such is the speed with which the group produces its publications that many of its articles read like news stories analysing current events" (Ingram, 2014: 5). This speed, availability and widespread dissemination make the coverage easy and appealing to access and disseminate for mainstream media and Internet users alike. A senior producer from a Syrian opposition radio station commented, "they know the fears and images that the Western media is hungry for, so Daesh give it and the media spreads it" (Ingram, 2015: 746). Their media packages also come from areas where there are few Western journalists and lots of news 'events', so they become integral to coverage from those war zones. According to Brigitte Nacos (2016: 370), the media has given the terrorists what they wanted; "attention, publication of their causes and grievances, and respect and legitimacy in some circles". The Syrian conflict has become the most socially mediated in history (Lynch *et al.*, 2014). One aspect of this, argues Fisher (2015), is that the US has been drawn into a war online with jihadists in what Robert Hannigan, Director of the UK government's intelligence and security organisation GCHQ, calls 'netwar'. Hannigan (2014) writes that large social media and web platforms have "become the command-and-control networks of choice for terrorists". In the same way that an online network is difficult for the military to see, locate and attack as it is not based in one physical location, it is also difficult for a journalist to film or report on. This liquid form of war – like the new liquid journalism – presents risks of delineation, definition and description for both journalists and audiences.

Speed and liveness

The seduction and delineation of content from the military and militias offer a risk to journalists as they must identify what is performance, what is war and whether they are being manipulated. However, they must also contend with its great appeal in terms of its liveness and the speed and availability with which content can be delivered. The coverage of the Boston Marathon bombing in April 2013 was much criticised for the broadcasting of unchecked facts and the mistakes made by the media "overwhelmed by the sheer volume of information being thrown at them by online reports and social media" (Martinson, 2015). Two years later, in 2015, the coverage of the Charlie Hebdo massacre aroused similar criticism. The risks had not been learned. The reporting on the situation as it unfolded led to the French broadcast regulator formally censuring several TV and radio networks for serious breaches in the coverage of the attacks (Chrisafis, 2015). The warnings were for the identification of the two gunmen despite, official requests not to do so, and to BFMTV, a rolling news channel, for reporting that someone was hiding in a supermarket while the perpetrators were actually in the supermarket looking for victims.

The demands for exclusive stories to be reported as they are happening, from places where the professional journalist cannot be a witness, is increasing the risk of possible manipulation, swelling the proliferation of inaccurate visuals and a growth of fake news. An early warning came from Dale Van Atta (1998: 66), who argues that "the media is still an integral part of achieving the terrorist's aim and therefore must be as judicious and responsible as possible in its reportage". As indicated above and evidenced in the US elections, it is not just terrorists who are manipulating the media. An understanding of this risk has led most mainstream news organisations to set up fact-checking departments. Liam Stack from *The New York Times* reflects the view of many of the mainstream news organisations when he states that his paper "approaches social media from a place of doubt" (Browne *et al.*, 2015: 1344).

Studies of the coverage of the Arab Spring in 2011 have brought to light many examples of instances where the media has been taken in by manipulation and fake stories. The story of "'A Gay Girl in Damascus' highlights how journalists and readers can be seduced by the mirage of the 'authentic voice' online" (Bennett, 2011: 188) as well as illustrating the failure of journalistic fact-checking and verification practices. The 'gay girl' who blogged about her personal life as a gay woman and her involvement in political protests against the Assad regime was in fact Tom MacMaster, a 40-year-old American studying at Edinburgh University. Adi Kuntsman and Rebecca Stein (2011) draw attention to the "myopia around the digital media", arguing that any digital enquiry should be accompanied by suspicion. Since their call for greater recognition that online material be subject to "considerable negotiation and contention", there have been increasing instances of the intrusion of false stories and pictures and the systematic generation of 'fake news'.

Fake news is not new; people have been peddling satire, lies and parody as news since before the birth of the modern newspaper (see Burkhardt, 2017). Disinformation has been a feature of political marketing, public relations and persuasion industries throughout the 20th century (see Miller and Dinan, 2008). However, the advent of new technology, the growing commercial problems of traditional news organisations and the rising dissatisfaction, particularly amongst young people, with traditional news sources has given the phenomenon more currency. The distinctive feature of fake news today is that it is widely circulated online, and as digital communication has proliferated, the scale of fake news has widened. What constitutes fake news is far from clear (Wardle, 2017), and its consequences for the practice of journalism are only now being given sufficient attention. The spread of false information clearly has implications for journalism. Some have examined how satirical programmes have held mainstream journalism to account (Berkowitz and Schwartz, 2016), how there has been a blurring of the boundaries between fact and fiction (Tandoc *et al.*, 2013) and how there has been a greater emphasis on "personally and emotionally targeted news" (Bakir and McStay, 2018). For war reporting, perhaps the most significant implications are the challenge for verification and the impact on credibility and trust. Kuntsman and Stein (2011) describe the "digital suspicion" that surrounds the frequently hybrid nature of the material that appears online. It is not so much that material is falsified, but that it is a mixture of different genres. For example, material posted on YouTube often elides documentary, home movie, political testimony and dramatic form, rendering it virtually useless in evidentiary terms. Fact-checking and accuracy have always been major attributes that separate journalists from non-professionals, and these are becoming more important as the journalist retreats from the field as primary witness and, instead, gathers information from those who are able to be involved in the event or close enough to take pictures or film it. The world of fake news, the perceived lack of 'facts' and 'evidence', undermines the capacity of reporters to verify what is happening. Autonomy and trust are eroded as war correspondents find it ever more difficult to fulfil their role as fact-checkers. Fact-checking is made more difficult when war is outsourced to non-military actors.

Outsourced war

A feature of the expansion of modern battlefield warfare is the rising use of civilian contractors to fight the new wars. The US Army has grown by over 100,000 civilians working in military roles (Kelty and Segal, 2007). In an article in *The Washington Post*, Thomas Gibbons-Neff (2016) reports that the ratio of civilian employees to US military personnel has more than doubled in the past two years. A story illustrating this was told by private US military contractor Sean McFate, who wrote about his role in thwarting the assassination of the Burundi president. His mission was to keep secret the fact that it was a US-led effort; he claims that private military contractors like himself are now conducting intelligence analysis, raising foreign armies and "trigger-pulling" (McFate, 2016). According to McFate, 75 per cent of US forces in Afghanistan are contracted, and he believes that US combat forces would be impotent without them. The chain of command leading to those fighting the battle has become increasingly obscured. "The US government ... often resorts to the CIA that itself has externalized many activities to private military and security companies (PMSCs), thus freeing civilian authorities from the bureaucratic procedures entailed by the mobilization of the armed forces" (Malesevich and Olsson, 2016: 720).

Many of these forces are even invisible to government members who do not have security clearance and unseen by reporters monitoring official military sources as they are sub-hired. McFate (2016) cites the example of the British military company ArmoGroup, which "sub-contracted two Afghan military companies that it called 'Mr. White' and 'Mr. Pink' to provide a guard force". A US Senate investigation found evidence that they were linked "to murder, kidnapping, bribery and anti-coalition activities" (McFate, 2016). International communications firms such as the Rendon Group and the Lincoln group, for example, were used by the US military to provide information operations during the Iraq War. Similar to finding sources to question about the use of drones, it is becoming more difficult for journalists to access private organisations which are covered by the blanket of state security. This is also extending to armies being trained and funded by the US. Recently, reports from the Special Inspector General for Afghanistan Reconstruction about the situation in Afghanistan which had been available online and sent to Congress in the US became classified (Rogers, 2017). This means that evidence of the "high casualty and attrition rate, low morale and poor administrative support systems" are no longer available to journalists (Hegseth, 2017). Paul Rogers (2017) refers to this as another example of the move towards remote warfare, noting, "a secret war is far less likely to be unpopular, the powers that be calculate. If the people don't know, they can't cause awkward problems."

Private military companies are not subject to Freedom of Information Act requests as they can cite the need to protect proprietary information (McFate, 2016). Reporting on such organisations is perhaps more the task of investigative journalism than that of war reporters. For example, the Private Security Company Violent Incident Dataset was created by Scott Fitzsimmons in 2012 to collect information from a range of sources, including the US State Department's Diplomatic Service. In 2015 he undertook a study of the 1,852 known violent incidents during the Iraq War and examined the behaviour of 12 private security companies (PSCs). He found that with the exception of Blackwater, all the firms' employees adhered to the *jus in bello* principle of proportionality in the rules of war, which governs the conduct of war, and even Blackwater adhered to a majority of the ethical standards examined under the principle. As well as PSCs, the rising use of Special Forces is another feature of 21st-century warfare; and as with the PSCs, this presents the journalist with increasing difficulties of access.

Special Forces

The UK government maintains a 'no comment' policy over all Special Forces operations. This means that large areas of modern warfare are hidden until books are published well after the end of operations, and even these are subject to stringent censorship. Mark Urban (2010), for example, records that in their six years of deployment in Iraq the Special Air Service, the SAS, the SBS (the Special Boat Service) and a number of other elite units had killed or captured 3,500 people. In individual operations, the SAS seized the leader of the Mehdi Army, killed a senior Al-Qaeda prison escapee named Omar al-Faruq and captured two key members of a secret branch of the Iranian Revolutionary Guards, which 15 days later led to the Iranians seizing 15 British Royal Navy seamen and marines. The Ministry of Defence will not comment on these actions, and any references to them have to be cut from reports in face of threats of contravention of the Official Secrets Act.[3] SAS members also sign strict confidentiality clauses about not speaking to the media.

As they become more involved in wars, a major side of conflict becomes inaccessible to journalists. It is not just the Special Forces, the SAS and SBS which are off limits; it seems that this is also the case for much larger numbers in the Special Forces Support Group, the Special Reconnaissance Regiment, those Army Air Corps and RAF units that support them or even regular troops temporarily seconded to work with them. In answer to a written question from Caroline Lucas to Secretary of Defence Michael Fallon, he stated: "When under the operational command of the Director of Special Forces, units of the Armed Forces attached to the Special Forces Support Group are subject to the same disclosure policy as other elements of the Special Forces" (Fallon, 2017).

In 2015 the UK committed to double Special Forces funding to £2 billion (HM Government, 2015). From 2001 to 2010 the numbers of US Special Operations Forces deployed overseas had quadrupled, and new plans seem to suggest that about 12,000 will remain deployed around the world (Knowles and Watson, 2017: 18). In June 2016 it was reported that British Special Forces were fighting against ISIS in Syria, but the MoD would not comment on this. As we have stated, the government never comments on Special Forces operations, but as Richard Norton Taylor (2014) notes, "their operations in Iraq and Afghanistan were trumpeted in the media, with the unofficial blessing of the Ministry of Defence, when they succeeded". The media's inability to confirm whether actions have taken place or find out details makes it difficult to verify stories, and when they do report, the media tends to use "hyperbolic and nonsensical language" (Knowles and Watson, 2017: 28).

In 2003 the only Australian forces on the ground were a 500 strong Special Forces task group, so no access was given to the Australian media to embed. John Tulloh, head of international coverage at ABC, found the Australian Defence Forces "unnecessarily secretive, obstructive and unhelpful on occasions, including proposing a form of censorship" (quoted in Anderson and Trembath, 2011: 363). In a television programme, Peter Leahy, now Director of the National Security Institute at the University of Canberra, revealed that he was extremely worried about the relationship between government, military and media. "It's not only broken, but I think dysfunctional and volatile" (Leahy, 2011). The US is more open in reporting actions of their Special Forces, but their missions, like those of the UK, are classified. The Pentagon did announce that 200 special operations troops had been sent to Syria in 2015, and they do reveal numbers of full-time troops sent abroad, which amounted to over 5,000 in Iraq in early 2017 and 500 in Syria. However, they do not reveal security personnel and troops sent on six-month contracts, estimated to be over a thousand, or the thousands of civilians contracted to the US military (Hennigan, 2017).

There is obviously an issue of operational security to consider, but as Knowles and Watson (2017) point out, the lack of public knowledge about what British (and other nations') forces are doing and the accountability gap that allows remote warfare to take place largely unscrutinised have the potential to fuel popular feelings of distrust in government war-making when information about the UK's secretive involvement in these conflicts invariably does surface. This is not a direct risk to journalism, but as one of the roles of journalism in its democratic function is to act as a watchdog, the increasing inaccessibility to war has wider repercussions. If part of war strategy is to gain support amongst your own population for the war (Clausewitz, 1976), a policy which increases distrust of the government's war-fighting capability will be counterproductive. The lack of open debate about the numbers of deployed troops gives rise to concern over questions of overall strategy regarding Syria and Iraq. There is also evidence from the US which reveals that long-term deployments are having a negative impact on the special forces and that the opacity of the British government potentially endangers "UK personnel, UK democracy and the effectiveness of UK operations abroad" (Watson, 2017). The anonymity and secrecy of the Special Operations Forces and the employment of mercenary groups represent a growing feature of military action and the deployment of manpower in hybrid warfare.

Freelance war reporter and blogger David Axe (2013) describes the growth of "shadow wars" in which reporters struggle to identify who is fighting and why. In recent years, US involvement in armed conflict "had never been so obscured" (Axe, 2013: 189). Special operations, proxy wars and drone warfare have resulted in fewer Americans involved in any direct fighting. Spurred by its reluctance to expend American lives, "wars were being fought many degrees removed from their origins" as "ever more sophisticated drones … flew from secret bases on secret missions over distant battlefields and did most of America's state sponsored killing by remote control" (Axe, 2013: 190). The clandestine nature of much of hybrid war is also associated with the growth of surveillance. The targeting of journalists as part of war-fighting takes a variety of forms, psychological, physical and political. The capacity of technology to help identify their locations is central to the discussion of war correspondents' personal safety. On arriving in Iraq, among the first things correspondents must do is store any smartphones safely and purchase small Nokia handsets with local SIM cards. Smartphones can reveal where you are and where you have been, and from this, anyone can map your social contacts by revealing where you meet others and how much contact you have with them. Snowden revealed that the National Security Agency could listen in to conversations even if the phone was turned off. Phones can be tapped and apps and social platforms interfered with. Governments can use updates and photos from Facebook to locate people and activities in much the same way. The growing surveillance of correspondents is not just a concern to journalists reporting on conflict; it is an issue that most journalists must now face, and this is reflected in the growing number of reports and handbooks published by media activist groups. The Centre for Investigative Journalism has published a handbook on Information Security for Journalists (Carlo and Kamphuis, 2014), and Reporters Without Borders (2017) released a report on the censorship and surveillance of journalists, stating that "there is growing concern about Facebook's active cooperation with certain governments, its deletion of journalistic content and its opaque content 'moderation' policies". According to *Times* correspondent Iona Craig (201:10), her experience in the Yemen highlighted that "encrypted email is now a basic requirement and simple counter surveillance measures are essential tools" of the job.

Attempts to control and manipulate data on reporters have today reached a "frenzy" (Craig, 2014: 12). Visible Technologies, a software firm that specialises in monitoring social media, has received funding from In-Q-Tel, the CIA's venture capital firm, and many Western intelligence services have start-up budgets to develop technologies that will enable even deeper mining of Internet user data (Stratfor, 2011). Since August 2016, WhatsApp users now have to opt out of sharing data with Facebook. However, even heavily encrypted communications may be subject to surveillance if the device of either end user is compromised. In a study of the 2014 Umbrella Movement, associated with the 2014 Hong Kong protests, Valerie Belair-Gagnon and her colleagues (2016) discovered that chat apps were the "most important digital tools for journalists to interact with their sources and audiences". They provided a safe, private and encrypted alternative to open, public social media platforms. Driven mainly by issues of privacy and surveillance, journalists used the chat sites to interact through secure channels with activists and protestors at risk of surveillance. Journalists' capacity to use chat apps was influenced by technical and linguistics considerations. Reporters often have to find a digital fixer to enable them to communicate or join a relevant site to get information and contacts, and there are language barriers to conducting personal chats or accessing group discussion. Indeed, availing oneself of online information is heavily influenced by linguistic considerations, which are often overlooked. The increasing fear of digital surveillance and the challenge of using new technology have led some correspondents to revert to the traditional tools of journalism, with all the dangers that implies in contemporary conflicts. For Craig (2014), mitigating the risks of government surveillance requires correspondents "to ignore technology and go back to the old ways of avoiding surveillance" by meeting people face-to-face.

As the possibility for increased surveillance and subterfuge becomes more apparent, the ability and capacity of war correspondents to effectively do their job becomes more difficult. As the number of foreign correspondents decreases, newsrooms cut costs and there is greater reliance on material taken from the huge outpouring of stories and images on the Web and social media, the authority of the journalist as an eyewitness has perhaps been lost. Witnessing has become a collaboration of technology and interpretation by the correspondent. In the past, reporters interviewed witnesses or themselves witnessed or filmed an event, but now they more often than not use the material witnessed by others. This comes with huge risks to accuracy and the threat of manipulation, particularly as large parts of war are now fought under the cover of state security by PSCs and Special Forces, which are mainly inaccessible to journalists and therefore unaccountable. Weapons of the information war are being turned on the journalists, making it more dangerous to operate in war zones, to look after one's personal safety and protect one's sources from identification and to prevent one's material becoming known to hostile organisations. The correspondent's basic modus operandi is beginning to look dated or ineffective. For example, the notion of objectivity appears out of place in the world of hybrid warfare. An enquiry in to the BBC reporting of the Israel–Palestine conflict found that the Corporation's requirements for balance and impartiality had become a "straightjacket that prevented it from properly relaying the 'dual narrative' of both sides" (Gibson, 2006). The report notes the "failure to convey adequately the disparity in the Israeli and Palestinian experience, reflecting the fact that one side is in control and the other lives under occupation". It also states that "given this asymmetry, the BBC's concern with balance gave an impression of equality between the two sides which was fundamentally, if unintentionally, misleading".

Notes

1   War which is fought "between one side which is militarily weak, yet determined and indigenous, and another side which is militarily powerful yet complacent and inattentive" (Cornish and Dorman, 2015: 357).
2   COIN or counter-insurgency is the civil-military support of a government's fight against insurgents. "It aims at the defeat of insurgency movement by the combination of military,

political, economic, administrative and informational activities leading to a secure environment, sustainable development and the strengthening of the host nation's ability to govern" (Ehrhart, 2017: 267).

3 This happened in the BBC2 series *Fighting the War* (2003) when references to SAS manoeuvres on the outskirts of Basra before the advance into the city had to be removed, even though the programme was broadcast in June 2003.

8

RISK AND THE REPORTING OF DEATH, DYING AND THE CASUALTIES OF WAR

War is about death and killing. That this is war's purpose is an often neglected aspect of the academic study of the media's coverage of war and conflict. Joanne Bourke, in *An Intimate History of Killing*, reminds us that "sanctioned blood-letting" is the "characteristic act of men at war" (1999: 1). Yet killing and death is a problematic matter in the reporting and representation of warfare. It is evident in the Western print and broadcast media coverage of the Gulf and Afghan wars that there has been a reluctance to illustrate death. Zelizer (2005) states journalists and audiences have no problem about how to use words when describing or reading about death, but showing death presents difficulties. Guidelines exist, for example, about portrayal of blood in TV news: according to a BBC memo, "blood and disturbing pictures must be excluded; we are here to show news not gore" (quoted in Seaton, 2005: 19). There are a variety of challenges about how to portray death: about "our dead versus their dead; about civilian versus military dead; about showing the faces of the dead; about class, race and the dead; about identifying the dead before their next of kin are notified" (Zelizer, 2005: 27). These are also physical and mental risks attached to actually taking photographs of death and dying. Digital media is changing the images used to portray conflict, influenced by their ease of use and the range of participants who contribute to their dissemination. However, images are not just used to illustrate, but also to "document experience, mobilise and recruit, sway public opinion, contest the legitimacy of authorities, secure legal evidence and appeal for humanitarian relief" (Blaagaard *et al.*, 2017: 1111). More and stronger images of warfare are today becoming available, and they hang around in hyperspace long after transmission, extending the time in which they can be viewed. The "sight of dead and dying is much more familiar than it was a generation ago" (Seaton, 2005: 220). More significant for the risks correspondents face on the battlefield, images have become an integral part of the propaganda component of waging war; atrocities, suffering and victims have become the justification for going to war. The risks that images of death and dying present to war correspondents are not just about how they are obtained but how they might be interpreted.

The power of the image

Images are intrinsic to news, for the press, television and social media. War has played an important role in the transformation of the news media by the visual, largely characterised by image and spectacle (see De Luca and Peeples, 2002). Integral to contemporary war is its visual articulation (Robinson and Schulzke, 2016). The greater importance of getting a picture has led to growing risks of photographing war. Adrian Wells of Sky News acknowledged in 2006 that "some of the images coming out of the Lebanon conflict were stronger than we have seen for a number of years, such as Fergal Keane's reports showing pictures of young children crushed by rubble being carried out" (quoted in Beckett, 2006). The risk attached to taking the pictures is associated not only with the strength of the images but also the meanings made of them. A photograph is not just a picture of the reality that was happening when the camera took the picture; it also represents "peripheral, symbolic and associative aspects" of the event (Zelizer, 2005: 31). The meaning invoked is more than just what is shown; "photographs signify more than the sum of their surface parts" (Brothers, 1997: 15).

The image represents far more than what is photographed. A photograph, still or moving, is a record of an event, but as documentary maker Errol Morris (2004) writes, pictures make us think about motivation, intent, how we interpret an experience and how we understand the motives of others. In this way, images give meaning to wars and the events illustrated, sometimes by the words that accompany the image. "Photographers are seeking answers to not only formal problems of visualization but also ideological problems: ways of seeing war and state violence and ways of seeing U.S. foreign policy" (Kennedy, 2016: 162). If war is the extension of politics, then the pictures of war are where the politics plays out to the public. A visual frame never simply exhibits the realities of war; rather, it actively participates in producing and enforcing what will count as reality (Butler, 2009). This is especially so for pictures of death.

Pictures of death and the casualties of war have a purpose. Accompanying the risk of filming or taking pictures of death on the battlefield is the issue of where and how they are used. Michael Griffin (2010: 8) emphasises that "war is a high-stakes enterprise; public perceptions and public support are never left to chance", and images of death and dying are usually seen as playing a significant role in this respect. They have since the early days of war photography been assumed to "sway public perceptions and attitudes, potentially reinforcing or eroding public support for war" (Griffin, 2010: 8). Deploying such images is an essential ingredient of the information wars that surround conflict. Atrocity stories are a long-standing technique of war propagandists (Taylor, 2003). Since the Crusades images of death, dying and suffering have played their part in the promotion of atrocity stories. In recent years such images have become central to mobilising public support for war. Pictures of deaths from Sarajevo played a significant role in garnering support in the West for intervention against the Serbs during the war in Bosnia, where showing death to engender "the full nature and extent of horror" came with a narrative of eliciting support for the victims (Campbell, 2004: 62). Images from ISIS videos are used to illustrate the evilness of ISIS and to legitimise US air strikes in Syria (Friis, 2015). Images of executions and beheadings are one way in which news brings home to publics distant from the war zone the horror of war. They are also used to distinguish between the civilised West and the barbaric East, between friend and foe, good and evil. Pictures of dead soldiers come with considerable ideological baggage, steeped in the legacy of the Vietnam War when many perceived the graphic pictures of dead US soldiers to have changed public support for the war. The expansive literature on military casualties and support for war is not matched by the study of public reactions to civilian casualties, especially foreign civilian casualties (Johns and Davies, 2017). The emphasis on visual imagery to get nations to go to war or to bring about the withdrawal of armed forces should be placed in the evolving context of the conflict. During conflict, the nation's view of war changes and the official justification for military action varies, and reporters have to be continually aware of the reception and use of their pictures. If they are not, they risk either not being able to place their work or having their pictures used for intentions other than they would hope for.

Photographs have to fit the news agenda determined by the editorial approach of the news organisation (see Chapter 3). H. R. McMaster (2014), commander of the Third US Armoured Cavalry Regiment in Tal Afar in Iraq in 2005, tells the story of an Italian photographer who accompanied American and Iraqi soldiers on their operations in the field against Al-Qaeda. He took many personal risks to take photos of soldiers in close combat, sending them to a national US weekly magazine. Rather than choosing one of his many combat photographs, the editor selected a file photograph of a lone US soldier in a courtyard, taken from above, for the cover of the magazine. "The image evoked a sense of confusion, isolation and disorientation – the soldier as hapless victim of circumstance rather than a warrior who possesses a degree of agency over his condition" (McMaster, 2014: 197). The photographer was not happy, but according to McMaster, the editor's decision was consistent with the thinking of the 'post-heroic' age in which Western militaries no longer depend on heroic motivation. The editor had a different story to tell about the war, the military and the nature and purpose of the sacrifice portrayed.

The complexity of determining the meaning of an image adds to the problem confronting the journalist in the field, the person who takes the picture. The reading of an image by a viewer/reader might be entirely different from that of the person who took the photo. The reading of images depends heavily on the culture from which people come. The globalisation of the media presents enhanced risks in terms of the use and reception of images of death and dying in war. The viewer's "ideological, ethical, religious standpoints, his psychological attitudes, his tastes, his value systems ... constitute a patrimony of knowledge which interacts with the image and determines the selection of codes with which the image is read" (Eco, quoted in Brothers, 1997: 20). A photographer taking a picture of the dead for his or her national audience might find that it is not acceptable to an international audience or vice versa, or that it is capable of a different interpretation. Non-US media are more willing to show graphic images (Himelboim and Limor, 2008; Robertson, 2004), and in Iraq in 2003 it was politically expedient not to broadcast such images, particularly of US soldiers killed in action, to the domestic public. A documentary on the reporting of the war found confusion, inconsistency and contradiction in the handling by TV stations across Europe, North America and the Middle East of images of dead American soldiers that were released by the Iraqi authorities. Filmed by Iraqi TV, they were aired initially by Al Jazeera and then shown with warnings about their distressing nature or with the faces and/or bodies of the fallen soldiers pixelated out (2003). Besides one fuzzy still photograph, US TV news channels did not broadcast these images.

Different parties to a conflict can use a photograph for purposes unintended by the person who took the picture. As the image and the narrative become more important in waging asymmetrical war, the use of the photograph is more open to abuse. "Imagefare" is "the use or misuse of images as a guiding principle or a substitute for traditional military means to achieve political objectives" (Ayalon et al., 2016: 265). The "weaponization of images" has generated considerable debate about the use of pictures and photographs of war in the news media (Roger, 2013). The representation, portrayal and context of death is central to this debate, but the extent to which the increased focus on information as a battle arena presents greater risks for those taking pictures on the battlefield has been neglected.

Not showing death

The reporting of death in covering war and conflict is unavoidable. For the news media its representation is essential: "death – and especially hard, undeserved, brutal and often unexpected, that is 'bad', death – is a key feature of news" (Seaton, 2005: 183). The journalist reporting from a war wants to show the reality of war, death, dying, destruction and devastation. Doing this is not simple. The correspondent has to negotiate the balance between the public's right to know about the horrors of war and respecting the dignity of the dead (Morse, 2014). The risk is in upsetting this balance. Despite the newsworthiness of death and dying, their actual display is unusual. Many studies have found that Western media hide images of death (Aday, 2005; Campbell, 2004; Griffin, 2004; King and Lester, 2005), presenting an anaesthetised and sanitised version of war that does not reveal the 'true' horror of what happens on the battlefield. B. William Silcock and his colleagues (2008) examined 2,500 war images from US television news, newspapers, news magazines and online news sites during the first five weeks of the US-led invasion of Iraq in 2003 and found that only 10 per cent showed injury or death. One reason for this often identified in the scholarly literature is the ideological framing that the media uses to construct and support political and military agendas to mobilise public support, which excludes showing the deaths of Western troops (see Zelizer, 2004). Images of death are not seen as supportive of the military endeavour. In 2003 showing the deaths of Iraqi citizens would counter the story that Allied troops were fighting for humanitarian purposes; in 1991 it would undermine their claims to be prosecuting a "clean war". Many in the military, government and news media still hold the view that images of death and dying can sway public support for the prosecution of war. In 2013 Barack Obama gave a speech to the US Naval Academy in which he said that "in our digital age, a single image from the battlefield of troops falling short of their standards can go viral and endanger our forces and undermine our efforts to achieve security and peace" (quoted in Shear, 2013). From the beginning of the 2003 Iraq War, the US administration banned the images of flag-draped coffins flown back to Dover Air Force Base. A military contractor, Tami Silicio, who took a photo of the coffins loaded into a plane in Kuwait, was fired by her employer after the picture was published in *The Seattle Times* in April 2004. The administration's critics argued the ban highlighted the efforts of the US government and military to manipulate public opinion. Hiding images of death and dying is not always in the interest of governments. In the context of the reporting of terrorist atrocities in Israel, Tal Morse (2014) found ministers and legislators in favour of releasing ghastly images as they believed it would build public support for government policy. The differing attitudes are to some extent explained by conflicting understandings of the impact of such images.

Most journalists believe that vivid and dramatic pictures are crucial to the impact of television (Shaw, 1992), but whether, by themselves, they persuade people of something is debatable. Many deploy common sense to refute the impact of such pictures. *New York Times* war correspondent Charles Mohr, drawing on his experience of the London Blitz, refutes the notion that graphic pictures swayed American public opinion during the Vietnam War on the grounds that "most wars literally, not merely photographically, go through people's living rooms" without influencing support for war (cited in Mercer *et al.*, 1987: 225). Some studies suggest that visuals can have an impact on public opinion (for example, Perlmutter, 1999; Fahmy *et al.*, 2006; Pfau *et al.*, 2006). This is not conceptualised as the result of just seeing or viewing a picture but in terms of the "interaction with individuals' existing understanding of the world" (Domke *et al.*, 2002: 132). Such an interaction is complex, involving history, culture and emotion. In recent years this has be explored in relation to the "CNN effect" (see Livingston, 1997; Robinson, 2005). The broadcast of images of atrocities and suffering is said to have led to changes in government policy. Susan Sontag (2001: 263) points out that the converse is possible; in a world hyper-saturated by images, "we become inured ... more callous, a little less able to feel and respond as we should". She argues that in spite of the images of ethnic cleansing transmitted from Bosnia, people were apathetic because American and European leaders announced the conflict was an unsolvable problem. There is "little hard evidence about the persuasive power of photographs in general, let alone news photographs of war casualties" (Pfau *et al.*, 2006: 150), and "claims about the persuasive power of visual images far outstrip actual evidence of such influence" (Domke *et al.*, 2002: 137).

The censorship and control of images of death and dying is often justified on grounds of taste, decency and the feelings of the general public. The Bush administration in 2003 believed it was protecting families and their right to privacy by banning images of body bags and coffins. Gory and horrific images may "dishonour the dead and distress families" (Morse, 2014: 100). As civilians have been more in the firing line, particularly with the advance of the global war on terror, news organisations, particularly broadcasters, have tightened their guidelines on the reporting of casualties. Editors have sought to introduce more care in how they represent death and dying. In most media systems, it is accepted that images of the dead should not be published before next of kin are informed. There are, however, differences of opinion as to how these images should appear on publication. Folker Hanusch (2012: 655) has shown "significant differences in graphic images" across 15 countries "both in terms of the amount of images and the degree of visibility of death". He attributes the differences to socio-cultural factors, such as different religious traditions and societal levels of violence. Tal Morse (2014), in his study of the reporting of a terrorist atrocity by Israeli media, draws attention to the issues that news media everywhere must address. He refers to standards that stress the "need to be respectful" when images are published and to "not go beyond the need to satisfy the public interest" (Morse, 2014: 104). In practical terms this means, for example, preference for "longshot images ... over close-ups" (Morse, 2014: 104). However, as Morse highlights, the standards for covering death in Israel have not always been followed, as sometimes "the newspaper published images of uncovered corpses, identifiable corpses or images that positioned the readers close to the corpse" (2014: 107). He also found that there is a distinction between showing images of Israelis and non-Israelis, with more dignity and respect in death reserved for the former. This reflects a hierarchy in death based on national affiliations and distinctions, between 'them' and 'us'. At the height of the conflicts in Afghanistan and Iraq, civilians were often the forgotten casualties; for example, receiving "less attention from the same American media which give extensive and sympathetic coverage to the deaths, repatriation, and funerals of military casualties" (Johns and Davies, 2017: 1).

The phrase "the economy of 'taste and decency'" has been used in describing the considerations about what pictures to publish (Campbell, 2004: 70). This process is regulated in most media systems by guidelines that influence the context in which the images are viewed. The BBC, for example, has very clear guidelines on what it will publish.[1] These guidelines state:

> There are very few circumstances in which it is justified to broadcast the moment of death. It is always important to respect the privacy and dignity of the dead. We should never show them gratuitously. We should also avoid the

gratuitous use of close-ups of faces and serious injuries of those who are dead, suffering or in distress.

(BBC, n.d.: 7.4.39)

Clause 4 of the UK Editors Code of Practice (Independent Press Standards Organisation, n.d.) also states that care should be taken to avoid exacerbating peoples' grief or shock by publishing unnecessary or sensationalist details of an event and that the family should have been notified before identifying any deceased person.

There are restrictions on what images are broadcast. For example, a producer on the BBC2 series *Sarajevo: Street Under Siege* (1995) was prevented from using some footage of the deaths in the Market Place bombing, being satellited in to the TV Centre news room from other European and US media sources, by the executive producer. He thought the images were too graphic and would not be covered by the BBC Guidelines or editorial policy. The use of guidelines in reporting war casualties is subject to debate. Fahmy (2005), in her study of the attitudes of photojournalists and photo editors to the visual depiction of the Afghan War, found that limited consideration was given to organisational codes of ethics. Johnson and Fahmy (2010: 46) similarly assert that "few media codes offer guidelines for images of tragedy and violence and graphic images in the context of war or politically motivated violence". Some authors believe that reporters in the field are not given enough guidance regarding images of death (Keith *et al.*, 2006). Most agree that the codes are struggling to keep up with the technological changes taking place, although the problem of digital photo manipulation is increasingly addressed.

The BBC rule that the family of the dead have to be notified before images are shown is also a military stipulation for UK embedded journalists. This can prevent live news from showing deaths in combat. Some viewers and readers are squeamish about what they want to see, and it is not surprising that broadcasters take into account viewer preference for visual restraint and understatement (Petley, 2004: 169). More than 70 per cent of Americans surveyed by Pew Research Center in 2004 applauded the US media for its restraint in showing the charred, battered remains of four US contractors killed on 31 March, 2004, in Fallujah, Iraq; only 7 per cent said they would support the use of more explicit images (Silcock *et al.*, 2008: 37). However, Fahmy and Johnson (2007b) found that followers of Al Jazeera's Arabic-language website strongly supported the decision to run graphic images; more than nine out of ten viewers surveyed agreed. A later study showed that viewers of Al Jazeera's English-language site and its Arabic-language site overwhelmingly supported Al Jazeera's decision to run graphic images from the Iraq War (Johnson and Fahmy, 2010). Cultural and political context shape what is shown, but the researchers admit that the results may not be representative of all Al Jazeera users and certainly do not represent US and Western audiences as a whole (Johnson and Fahmy, 2010: 61). They do indicate the lack of agreement over what constitutes a graphic image, which can be the cause of discussion and differences between reporters and editors (Fahmy, 2005).

Adhering to industry standards and the informal social norms regarding taste and privacy shape what is shown. However, the production of images of death is dependent on sources' use of such material. In 2006 dissemination of filmed beheadings by Al-Qaida in Iraq declined. Paul Rogers (2006) states that a letter from Al-Zawahiri, leader of Al-Qaeda, to Abu Musab al-Zarqawi of AQI suggests that the beheading videos were bad publicity and counterproductive to Al-Qaeda's long-term strategy. The strategy was obviously later reversed by ISIS, which because of new technology was able to disseminate these images themselves. The ability to access combatants' own stories and images through blogs and video-sharing sites such as YouTube has "thrown into sharp relief the ways in which mainstream media and governments cover the reality of war" (Anden-Papadopoulos, 2009: 921). Not only is the traditional media competing for attention, but it is also becoming more difficult for editors and reporters to be gatekeepers to what is shown. The decline of the ability to act as a gatekeeper to the dissemination of images of death and dying has added a new dimension to the debate about what to show of death. Editors and their men and women in the field now have to address soldiers' visual representations of war, which are often motivated by sadism, morbid voyeurism and spectacle. This form of visual representation of war challenges the moral intention to show the agony and suffering of others in order to procure a public response. Rather, it emphasises what is often hidden in war reporting: the fact that, for many involved, war is exciting. William Broyles, a former marine and editor of *Texas Monthly* and *Newsweek*, has explored some of the contradictions inherent in telling war stories (Broyles, 1984). He asserts that when combat soldiers are questioned about their war experiences, they generally say that they do not want to talk about it, implying that they "hated it so much, it was so terrible". Not so, Broyles argues: "most men who have been to war would have to admit, if they are honest, that somewhere inside themselves they loved it too". This also applies to many war correspondents who believe that physical risk and personal danger "is not hell. It is fun" (quoted in Evans, 2003: 38). Balancing the pain and suffering against the 'glamour' and excitement is made more difficult by the plethora of images now available to the global media audience. Deciding what to capture on camera, however, is reliant on one basic requirement – being there.

Being there

Distinctions in the representation of death are often explained in terms of cultural proximity. Cultural distance tolerates gruesome photographs of victims (Hanusch, 2008: Sontag, 2003). The more readers, listeners and viewers can identify with the victims or the more they can empathise with the type of death, the less likely it is to be represented in photographs or images. However, certain cultures place more emphasis on representing the 'humanness' of the victims of war. Reporting by Al Jazeera's English service of conflict in Gaza has sought to establish a connection between its viewers and the people caught up in the fighting by providing the names, faces, personal histories and family backgrounds of the dead and dying (see Morse, 2018). The globalisation of the media means that audiences across the world have access to this coverage, making it more difficult to assert a sanitised or restrained representation of death and dying. It is argued that the values of cosmopolitanism demand greater sensitivity to the misfortune and suffering of others and that people's vulnerability should be represented in the news media (see Chouliaraki, 2013). For correspondents, the pressure is that you have to get closer to the action, understanding and, if possible, sharing the experiences of those who are suffering, with all the risk that this involves.

There are other more pragmatic reasons to explain the lack of pictures of death in war. Journalists are rarely present when the killing takes place. The logistics of war often mean that the journalist is not actually present at 'the moment of death'. In many cases, they are prevented from being there. During the 1986 invasion of Grenada, reporters were banned from the island, and those who tried to land on the island were arrested and imprisoned on US ships offshore (Block and Mungham, 1989). Journalists similarly were prohibited from covering the invasion of Panama in 1989. In 1991 when the US and Allied forces removed Saddam Hussein's forces from Kuwait, evidence of death and destruction was sometimes covered up. War correspondent Leon Daniel witnessed no bodies of Iraqi dead after an engagement in February between the US First Infantry Division and Iraqi forces in which thousands of Iraqi soldiers died; their bodies had been buried by ploughs mounted on Abrams tanks (Sloyan, 2003). The US military had hidden the deaths before the journalists arrived.

The absences of images of the injured or dead in the first 24 hours of the 2003 Iraq War was not because of bias (Exoo, 2010) or the reluctance of the news media to show them. It was because most US photographers and videographers were not in Baghdad, the target of the 'shock and awe' bombing (Silcock et al., 2008). In 2003 Pew Research Center conducted a study of embedded journalists' coverage, concluding that "not a single story examined showed pictures of people being hit by fired weapons" (Exoo, 2010: 115). This is probably because the embedded journalists accompanied the British and American military, the people who fired the weapons. Filming where the bombs landed, with the Iraqis on the receiving end, was a trifle more dangerous. Throughout the invasion, only a small number of the embedded US journalists actually saw action. Analysis is required of the type of media present with units to assess whether there were cameras with the units that saw the action. Feinstein (2006) states that not one of the 85 journalists who took part in his study regarded the first phase of the Iraq War as their most dangerous assignment. It was only in April 2004 after the attack on Fallujah, where journalists could no longer travel unaccompanied, that the situation became much more lethal and they perhaps felt closer to death.

Although the BBC's documentary crew was with the Black Watch, one of the British regiments that led the drive into Basra, they were not allowed to travel with the Warrior troop carriers or the units that would have encountered any opposition from Iraqi military. This was the same for journalists embedded with tank regiments such as the Scots Dragoon Guards, that also saw action in the drive into

Basra. No journalist could travel in a Challenger. There is no room inside a tank for any object that is unnecessary to its functioning, and it is forbidden to film or take pictures of the inside. Pictures of any deaths accompanying these units would not be possible unless the cameraman travelled with medics in an accompanying Warrior or a camera was strapped to the gun barrel (as the documentary crew did when the Scots Dragoon Guards' Challengers took out TV masts in Basra). Much of the killing of Iraqis was done from the air or from distant artillery, so getting footage of dead civilians was generally difficult. By the time journalists arrived at the location, the dead had often been cleared away by families or the military. The media might claim to be keeping up with the action, but much of what happened militarily was told to the journalist or TV crew when the forces returned to the particular unit's headquarters, where the journalist was more probably based.

Of the 68 journalists embedded with the US Marines, there were 9 photographers, 4 of whom were with 15th Marine Expeditionary Unit (marineparents. org), which secured Umm Qasr and Az Zubayr and helped 'rescue' Jessica Lynch, but the majority of reporters were from newspapers, magazines and radio.[2] The Marines then moved to Nasriyah and were not in the move to Baghdad. Chip Read, a US journalist embedded with the Marines for the invasion, travelled with the Marines but reported via satellite phone. He writes that when he crossed the border into Iraq, he was the only reporter "for miles" (Reid, 2004). Fifteen journalists from TV stations were also embedded with the Marines, including David Bowden of Sky News, who reported on the Iraqi "resistance" at Umm Qasr (Fuchs, 2003). They filmed shots fired at a building, but then tanks and an air strike were called in (Fuchs, 2003) and it became logistically more difficult to film action. It became easier for many journalists to turn the camera on themselves and reflect on their own war stories (Fuchs, 2003) as well as filming convoys, Iraqi civilians and material damage, rather than "human losses" (Griffin, 2010: 31), as these were more frequent occurrences than battles. The risk to all reporters is that they might not be where the action is, but even if they are and can film what is happening, they have to consider the reaction of both the home audiences and the media organisations that transmit or publish their material.

What to show

The decision about what death to show is thus a composite choice, influenced by the photographer, the news media organisation and the audience. It has huge implications on what is shown, but for all parties, death is monumental and thus carries a greater risk than other types of images, both for the reporter and organisation, who might be accused of trivialising or exploiting death, and for the audience, who might be offended or extremely upset by images of death. Showing death gives meaning to conflict, but it is challenging not just in its implications but also in how to convey its monumentality. Vivian Sobchack (2004: 287) writes that "being can be represented, nonbeing is not visible. It lies over the threshold of visibility and representation." The image of a dead body is just a body that is still, so how do you convey the enormity of the fact that the life that the body held is now no more, that it is a non-being? Death is a traumatic event. Trauma is an experience "which simultaneously demands urgent representation but shatters all potential frames of comprehension and reference" (Guerin and Hallas, 2007: 3). Conveying its meaning is very problematic because no one alive has experienced it; thus, one cannot understand it as one can understand grief, rage or love. "The most effective cinematic signifier of death in our present culture is violent action inscribed on the visible lived-body" (Sobchack, 2004: 288), which is why the media are much more likely to show photos of those about to die rather than photos of dead bodies (Zelizer, 2010). It is easier to convey the enormity of death by showing a dying body rather than the corpse as you see a transition in a being from life to death, not just a body. The 'moment of death' and its significance can also be captured by the response of others to the dead, and this is often done in documentary making. For example, Michael Moore, to great effect in his documentary *Fahrenheit 9/11*, did not use images of the Twin Towers – just the reaction of onlookers to the events.

A reporter has to convey the meaning of death in the picture and be aware of the ethical risk in showing that death.

> The filmmaker watches the dying, we watch the filmmaker watching and judge the nature and quality of his or her interest … the very act of vision which makes the representation of death possible is itself subject to moral scrutiny.
>
> *(Sobchack, 2004: 291)*

As a witness to the death, the film-maker has to justify the showing of death; hence the strict guidelines laid down by news organisations. Jessica Auchter (2017) contends that the showing of death is political, and as mentioned above, pictures of death are shown for a purpose. The photographer has to weigh up justifications for showing the body or not, including assessment of the purpose for showing it. At a distance from the event, the purpose of not showing death might seem obvious. Death, especially by gunfire, is not pretty. Auchter (2017) writes that Osama bin Laden's body was not shown after he was killed, and both she and Tiffany Jenkins (2011) believe it was a strategic act to strengthen the security narrative in the US. However, according to the SEAL who has written about the raid to kill Osama, he was killed by a gunshot that split his head in two, and then the rest of the team fired more than 100 bullets into the body (Szoldra, 2017). What was left would have been a mess that could probably not have been identified as Osama, or even a body. If, as Chouliraki (2015) writes, images can define who it is worth grieving about, showing an undefinable pulp with no identity achieves little. The lack of visuals is thus perhaps less about conspiracy than cock-up. This opens up issues about the savagery of killing and death, which is difficult to convey and less easy to comprehend unless you have seen it without the mediation of a cameraperson.

Decisions have to be made about showing the body, but once a decision has been taken to do so, further choices must be made: whether the picture shows a close-up of the face or body or a wide shot; or whether or not to blur the image or hide the face. Seeing death first-hand in war is not the same as reading about it or looking at it in the cinema. Death is a humiliation; the person has lost control of their body and cannot resist the invasion of privacy, so showing death in close-up arguably degrades the humanity of the victim. When the intent is to humiliate, close-ups are often shown, as in the pictures of Gadaffi and Saddam Hussein. The dead body of Alan Hennings, the contractor killed by ISIS, was not shown in the mainstream British media as his death was not to be celebrated. Dead children, such as the iconic shot of the 3-year-old refugee, Alan Kurdi, who died on 2 September, 2015, are shown when they are whole and resemble sleeping children. The distortion of sleep becomes a condemnation of the disparity between the ideal and reality, but they are recognisable and not usually shown in close up having been mortared or horribly disfigured by the death. Even the portrayal in an Israeli newspaper of a Palestinian child, Diya Tamaizi, who was shot by a Jewish sniper was shown seemingly "peaceful and calm" (Morse, 2013: 149) although there are blood stains on the white sheet that wraps him. John Baglow (2007: 230) writes that no culture fails to engage its dead in one way or another; the living have to observe the obligations of their culture and society to the corpse, and not respecting those obligations carry risks of condemnation and exclusion. In Jewish tradition, for example, it is customary to cover a dead body and not display it in public (Lamm, 1969).

The squeamishness and ethics of showing humiliating death is also a risk that the reporters in theatre must consider for themselves. For the documentary film-maker in Iraq, there was the worry about what the reporter's family would see if she had been killed and what image would be shown on television or, more likely, captured by mobile phone footage. Personal feelings dictate coverage. If a film-maker reasons that they would not like close-up bits of them to be broadcast in various states of desiccation, it is unlikely they could do this to others, whether they be Western or Iraqi corpses. Documentary does not have the same obligation to be objective that news has, but the motivation for showing images of the dead should still be considered as a risk to ethical values and a question of the representation of power. Deborah Scranton displayed stills of dead Iraqis to show Sergeant Steve Pink's point of view in *The War Tapes* (2006), arguably to mobilise anti-war sentiment. *Severe Clear* (2009) likewise used soldiers' footage, shot on mini-DV by Marine First Lieutenant Mike Scotti when his company was deployed to Baghdad. Shmulik Duvdevani (2013) argues that the personal accounts of the soldiers in the midst of battle might give an alternative view of the conflict, the view of the regular soldier as opposed the official viewpoint; but such a perspective positions the soldiers as victims, garnering sympathy for their situation but never addressing their own accountability in war. These images provide close-up and personal accounts of conflict but often obscure the context in which they take place (Blaagaard *et al.*, 2017). There is also, as stated, the problem that the soldier filming from one end of the gun or tank barrel cannot see or photograph what is happening at the other end, and as a result, death is not seen.

Another army that films deaths carried out by its own troops, often at close hand, is ISIS. The growing global circulation of images through digital media has enabled the increasingly explicit pictures of death to be disseminated on a large scale. Susan Tait (2009) argues that the ethical space round the imagery of death is being reconfigured, and the beheadings uploaded by insurgents were being watched not "by a sense of duty to witness atrocity" but for entertainment, much as people would watch a horror film. Some of the graphic images of dead Iraqis uploaded by Coalition soldiers on sites such as nowthatsfuckedup.com – closed down in 2005 – were not interpolated to bear witness to atrocity but, she argues, to bear "false witness"; that is, to identify with revenge killings in response to the loss of comrades (Tait, 2009: 348). Tait believes that these pictures and the comments that accompany them are "offensive" and "disregard any rights the deceased or their families may have over their representation" (2009: 348). The images of the dead and body parts become pornography.

Social media corporations tried to remove beheading videos as quickly as possible, but images from the videos circulated widely and soon entered the traditional media. Although only ten per cent of ISIS' visuals are videos (Kraidy, 2017a) and execution videos are only a fraction of all military visuals (Milton, 2016), it is these that people remember. Their purpose had a strategic dimension as well as being a symbolic act. They had a range of objectives such as, arguably, to hamper foreign investment, to discredit transitional states, to recruit supporters and to weaken the resolve of their opponents (Kydd and Walter, 2006). The Islamic State publication *Ayyuha al-E'lamy Anta Mujahidon* (Oh Media Worker, You Are a Mujahid) highlights the importance of the media and of images by comparing militant media to "arrows, bullets and bombs". It quotes the leader of Islamic State in Iraq, Abu Hmza al-Muhajer, saying that "the military front and … the confrontation with the demonic media … media rockets exceed in their ferocity and danger the flames of bombs dropped from airplanes" (Kraidy, 2017b). There can be little doubt that these images revealed the horror of war, but for reporters and photojournalists, where does one go now to represent conflicts like these?

In a world saturated by images of death and dying, how do war reporters show the horror of war and picture the dreadful way that man kills man yet avoid the risk of feeding the pornography or propaganda of such images. 'War pornography' has a political consequence. It lacks empathy, builds fear and contributes to the idea that the world is a dangerous place and must be confronted by more force (Muller and Measor, 2011). ISIS perhaps did something new on a global scale, which was to horrify and shock the audience with images of brutality and extreme violence. The risk is that the reporter may continue in this vein of invoking spectacle, sensation and horror. Ashley Gilbertson (2011), an Australian photographer who received the Robert Capa Gold Medal for his pictures from Fallujah in 2004, writes that after ten years of the Iraq and Afghan war, "these pictures start to meld into one. We have a responsibility to find a new way to look at these stories". In

2014 he published a collection of photographs showing the intact bedrooms of service members killed in Iraq and Afghanistan. Patricia Zimmermann (2000) examines how documentary film-makers, who she considers as having been marginalised by government controls in the 1980s, sought to question the global media's images of war. She writes that spectacle silences and advocates the use of language to fill this silence left by the image, whereas testimonies can both witness events and challenge the notion of victimhood.

The increasing use of images of death from contemporary conflicts in Iraq, Libya and Syria are a result of the change wrought by social media. As the audience moves from being readers, listeners and viewers to becoming increasingly 'active' as producers, bystanders and journalists share eyewitness footage, which is added to by others for a variety of motives (Bruns and Hanusch, 2017: 1123). The dissemination and reproduction of these images and the increasing commodification of user-produced images also mean that those images which receive public attention are "algorithmically privileged over those that remain noticed" (Bruns and Hanusch, 2017: 1129), and as Poell and van Dijck (2015) argue, the images that are favoured are the more spectacular and violent. The ethical risk is not only one of wanting to use this material or to compete for it on commercial grounds, but also the pressure and temptation to digitally alter the image to do the same. In her study of the changing work practices of photojournalists, Jenni Maenpaa (2014) found that to prevent this invidious practice, photojournalists used a rule called the 'darkroom principal' as a measure of what was permissible for photographers in the manipulation of their images. This stipulates that all possible and relevant adjustments "be made before or at the moment of releasing the shutter on the camera and not afterwards on a computer" (Maenpaa, 2014: 96). The strict adherence to professional ethics separates the professional from the amateur or citizen journalist and is becoming more vital to all of those in the media as the opportunities for digital manipulation and wider utilisation of user-generated content increase.

Body counts

Taking pictures of the dead offers risk, but also counting the dead, the "fatality metric of war" (Hyndman, 2007: 38), is a highly contentious exercise which can present risks for the unwary journalist. Journalists can have problems with statistics because of a dislike of mathematics and because of the varying and competing origins of their statistical data. Generating reliable data on casualties of war is "notoriously complex" (Roberts, 2010: 116), something that is accentuated by the cynical use of body counts during the Vietnam War to show US military progress. The complexity, confusion and lack of clarity during the Vietnam War led to military success measured quantitatively – weapons captured, villagers relocated, areas searched, areas cleared and enemies killed (Knightley, 2003a: 418). Numerical inflation came from the reporting process, which encouraged military units up the chain of command to exaggerate their figures. The lesson learned from Vietnam was not to release "casualty ratio data", and during the early years of counter-insurgency war in Iraq, US military leaders did not do this (Boettcher and Cobb, 2006). However, in 2004 reports of "limited" US casualties and "significant" insurgents killed began to emerge, resembling the military briefings of the Vietnam years (Boettcher and Cobb, 2006: 831), the so-called "five-o'clock follies" which overestimated enemy casualties and overstated the relationship between enemy casualties and US military success (832). The change of policy is explained by the difficulties of measuring success in asymmetrical warfare and the hope that "the high ratio of Iraqi deaths to U.S. deaths will reduce the negative impact of American losses" (Boettcher and Cobb, 2006: 833).

Responding to the news media's need for statistics is perhaps another reason. A recent survey in the UK found that statistics were regularly referenced in news coverage (Cushion et al., 2016). In the wake of the 2003 war, the number of Iraqis killed in the fighting became a matter of controversy, particularly surrounding the number of civilians killed. Claims were made that challenged official estimates, of which there were few. The Iraq Body Count (IBC; iraqbodycount.org/database/), a London-based NGO, puts civilian deaths from violence in Iraq from 2003 to February 2017 at up to 200,433, but states that an analysis of the WikiLeaks Iraq War Logs "may add 10,000 civilian deaths". Other studies comprised numbers on 'excess' deaths which could be attributable to the war and violence in Iraq, such as those due to the collapse of infrastructure, hospital closures or other indirect causes. These included studies by British medical journal *The Lancet* in 2004 and 2006 and a study done in 2013 by researchers from universities in the US, Canada and Iraq. The 2013 study counted 461,000 deaths compared to the 112,000 deaths revealed by Iraq Body Count (BBC, 2013). The IBC is accused of underestimating the body count because of its focus on Baghdad and the methods by which it collected information. However, much criticism is also levelled at the reporting of the figures: journalists are condemned for not having a sufficient understanding of statistics or time to interrogate the numbers (Bienaime, 2015).

At the centre of the difficulty of counting deaths and casualties is the problem of identification of the bodies and the causes of death. Is a dead body that of a civilian or a combatant? Was the injury an 'excess' of war or can it be from another cause, and therefore should it be reported? Following the first Gulf war and Iraq's invasion of Kuwait, the UN Security Council imposed economic sanctions against Iraq. In 1995 a UN Food and Agriculture Organisation study found that as many as 576,000 Iraqi children may have died since the end of the war because of the sanctions imposed (Crossette, 1995). The effect of sanctions was rarely mentioned in media reports leading up to the Iraq War in 2003, nor were its effects acknowledged as context for the coverage of the insurgency after 2003. This had consequences not only for the reporting on the Iraq War and occupation but also perhaps for the expectations of the Western military and public. The country was hugely damaged by past wars and sanctions, which challenged the idea that the West could fix this situation immediately. For example, when filming in the hospital in Sadr City, a doctor told the documentary crew that there were no dentist chairs in Iraq. The stool cylinder of the chair had been considered to be a rocket launcher and so was banned under sanctions. This is a small example of the effects of the sanctions, but the rapid disillusionment with the Coalition government fed the insurgency, and if the causes were not understood, partly as a result of lack of information about sanctions in the press, the risks of not counting, not understanding and not fully reporting led to further death and suffering.

Although journalists have a key role in interpreting data, historically they have shown a "vast misunderstanding, underestimation and ignorance of the nature of statistics" (Nguyen and Lugo-Ocando, 2016: 3). Attempts to redress poor reporting have been made in the effort to conduct "precision journalism", including citing the source of figures used in news reports. However, these efforts have begun to flounder in the age of social media. Witnessing death and dying has a quantitative aspect and there has been unprecedented growth of data on casualties, particularly from whistle-blower websites such as WikiLeaks, in recent years. WikiLeaks, for example, released nearly 80,000 individual official reports on events in Afghanistan between 2004 and 2009, each including counts of killed and wounded people, local administrative reports and description of incidents (Rusch et al., 2013). This data generated stories as well as assessments of fatalities. Making sense of the material was fraught with problems (see Rusch et al., 2013; O'Loughlin et al., 2010), and for those reporting war, the increased flow of data such as this presents analytical and interpretative challenges. This is illustrated by the coverage of drone warfare, which has failed to effectively interpret the statistics provided by the US government to justify the 'success' of the policy (Ahmad, 2016). In the absence of eyewitness accounts of the effects of drone strikes, the casualty figures as well as information on the nature of the casualties has come from official sources, usually unnamed. While lack of access and scarcity of information have made it difficult for correspondents to report drone strikes, there has also been a failure to scrutinise the figures and examine the underlying assumptions behind the production of drone statistics. Reliance on the numbers game and lack of confidence and knowledge to challenge the rigour of the methods used to compile data have led to the reporting of these strikes as being more accurate, more effective, cheaper and less risky than conventional warfare. The number of civilian deaths caused by drone strikes is under-reported. Obtaining reliable figures is not easy, and human rights organisations have struggled to put together an accurate death toll. The danger of accessing events on the ground and the unquestioning acceptance of the figures and how they are calculated have masked the reality of the number of civilians killed and the effectiveness of drone warfare.

Reporting death in conflict is inherently risky for a journalist. She not only has to report on or picture the dead when the dying takes place in a distant location where many people don't want it to be reported, but she also has to give it context and the correct signification. She must respect the media organisation's guidelines and the humanity of the corpse but also convey the meaning and monumentality of the death to a diverse audience, many of whom do not want to face the horrors of war and mortality. She must also be wary of the possible manipulation and use to which the dead are put as well as considering her own safety and psyche in the reporting of such events. Death is part of war, but as societies to a greater or lesser extent find death difficult to confront, there are risks in how it is reported by correspondents. These risks are accentuated as the new technologies of fighting and recording make death in war not only more distant but more personal.

Notes

1 For discussion of UK codes on visual representation of death, dying and suffering, see Taylor (1998).
2 Further study on which media were with which military units is being undertaken.

9

GENDER, RISK AND WAR REPORTING

The increased risk of reporting war is associated with the 'feminisation of news' and the growing number of women covering war. Women reporters face a specific and distinct set of risks which have only now been recognised by news organisations and journalists' unions. These include sexual assault and harassment, which is why gender-specific security training is becoming more common (see CPJ, 2016b). Specific cases have underlined the risks female war correspondents face in their work. The treatment of CBS news correspondent Lara Logan, who was physically and sexually assaulted in Egypt's Tahrir Square, and *New York Times* photographer Lynsey Addario, who suffered sexual violence when held hostage in Libya, highlight the routine abuse women correspondents have faced (see McAfee, 2011; Addario, 2015). A survey conducted by the International News Safety Institute (INSI), "Women Reporting War", found a high number of the women war reporters interviewed had suffered physical attack or intimidation (82%), and more than half of respondents reported sexual harassment (55%), with a significant number stating they had experienced sexual abuse (7%) (INSI, 2005). Obviously wider issues such as the law, culture and women's rights impact on women reporting war – and this is not the place to consider these issues in depth – but the increasing intimidation of female journalists is a feature of the reporting of conflict. This chapter considers how women contribute to war reporting in a world of risk, how risk impacts on women and specific dangers for women in reporting conflict. It does so by highlighting questions of access, exploring the consequences of the real or apparent risk to women and examining whether the exclusion of women's voices is a risk to the diversity of ideas that is fundamental to a free press.

Two points are emphasised at the outset. First, it cannot be contested that men continue to do the majority of war and conflict reporting (UNESCO, 2015) and that even where women have had a long history of involvement in journalism, men are still in authority and in control of newsrooms and news organisations and, overall, receive more pay (Byerly, 2013; Franks, 2013; Melki and Mallat, 2016). The increasing number of women reporting war must be placed in the context of the overall increase in the number of both male and female war journalists (Palmer and Melki, 2016), and most women journalists are and remain answerable to a male editor. Second, the debate about women reporting war has centred around the question as to whether gender makes a difference to the way in which war and conflict is reported. This is tied to a subsidiary question about whether woman journalists are more at risk than their male counterparts in the war zone. Several women reporters and a number of scholarly studies have sought to distinguish between the ways in which men and women report war. Women war reporters "are different in so many ways" (Feinstein and Sinyor, 2009). According to Cindy Kinnard of CBS News, women war correspondents "possess a missionary zeal while covering the battlefield – a desire to expose the horrors of war as opposed to detailing the weapons, strategy and deployment" (quoted in Kinnard and Murphy, 2005: 130). The Women and War project on US TV news coverage of three contemporary conflicts found that women consistently file more victim-based stories than men (Kinnard and Murphy, 2005: 137). The suggestion that men want to write about tanks and women want to write about refugees is disputed. The BBC's Orla Guerin says, "I just don't think that is the case. A good journalist will follow the story" (quoted in Ray, 2003). It is the propensity to report victims, human rights and refugees that makes war reporting today more dangerous for both women and men. However, many still believe there is a set of innate characteristics that lead women to approach the work of war reporting differently, which makes war reporting riskier for women.

News organisations and media unions may be increasingly aware of the nature of the risks women correspondents face in the war zone, but editors' attitudes to their female workers do not always reflect this. Despite many more women covering the war in Bosnia, one British newspaper editor insisted that there were stories to which he would not allow women to be assigned, arguing that "there are some things women shouldn't see" (Delano, 2003: 275). If the editors who assign correspondents are men, the specific concerns about violence towards women, particularly rape, will remain a major determinant in assigning women war reporters (see Susman, 2012). If differences are flagged up in the way in which women report war and the risks they face in the war zone, it might provide editors and news organisations with an excuse not to send women to conflict zones. Adriana Gomez Licon (2012: 133) believes that "editors have sometimes stopped me from covering stories … instead of making it safe for me to go". Women correspondents' reluctance to report abuse and assault is often identified in terms of retribution from the home office. The 2005 INSI survey found that women often do not report violence, abuse and harassment or even talk about it for fear it would have consequences for their ability to be sent on future assignments (Matloff, 2007). Egyptian TV anchor Shahira Amin (2012: 35) voices these worries: "I think a lot of female journalists would choose not to raise these issues because of the fear that they might not get sent out". Jenny Nordberg, a Swedish correspondent, was sexually assaulted in Pakistan but did not tell her editors for "fear of losing assignments" (quoted in Wolfe, 2011). She did not "want them to think of me as a girl. Especially when I am trying to be equal to, and better than, the boys". The absence of a female editor may have been crucial: "I may have told a female editor though, had I had one". Sexual violence is a threat to men as well as women reporters, but the focus is on cases in which women's vulnerability is emphasised, a product of a set of general attitudes to women reporting war (see Høiby, 2016).

Attitudes to women reporting war

The history of war reporting shows that the military and the media have been reluctant to accredit or assign women to report war. For a female journalist or producer, assumptions and behaviour driven by attitudes towards gender are encountered both from colleagues and from those she is filming or reporting on, and from all nationalities and cultures. In the Second World War, Field Marshal Montgomery banned women war correspondents from travelling with and covering British forces on D-Day (Chambers et al., 2004: 204). Margaret Bourke-White was initially refused accreditation on the grounds that there were no female toilets, a familiar refrain throughout history. It is therefore an irony that Martha Gellhorn smuggled herself onto a hospital ship to get to Normandy and locked herself in a toilet to become the first woman to report on the D-Day invasion. Gellhorn wrote in a letter to the military authorities, "I have too frequently received the impression that women war correspondents were an irritating nuisance. I wish to point out that none of us would have our jobs unless we knew how to do them and this curious condescending treatment is as ridiculous as it is undignified" (quoted in Doucet, 2014).[1] She was banned for her subterfuge. All 558 of the reporters, radio journalists and photographers accredited to cover the D-Day landings by the British government were men (Blake, 2010). However, during the Second World War, female journalists became more prominent on the battlefield, with American women better represented than their British and European counterparts. Increased presence was not accompanied by a significant change in male attitudes. Women reporters were subject to a litany of accusations which would be repeated in most post-war conflicts. They were reproached for using their sex to access stories and their appearance to gain assignments as well as for their failings as wives and mothers.

The open nature of the war in Vietnam meant that journalists did not have to be accredited to a military unit or gain military permission to travel, so many women found their own means of travel to cover the conflict. Nevertheless, the US military supplied credentials to 467 women, nearly half of whom were Vietnamese (Elwood-Akers, 1988). In this respect, the military authorities might be seen as more conciliatory than the male editors who assign journalists to a story. "I don't believe women should cover wars", UPI foreign editor Bill Landry told Tracy Wood (2002). Moreover, fellow male correspondents dismiss their female colleagues as "girl reporters" (Becker, 2017). According to Peter Arnett (1994: 220), the Vietnam press corps was a male bastion that women entered only at the risk of being humiliated and patronized; the prevailing view was that the war was being fought by men against men and that women had no place there.

Supreme Commander General William Westmoreland attempted to ban women from overnight stays with troops on the battlefield as they might prove an "unacceptable distraction" (Hoffman, n.d.). This attitude did not permeate down the chain of command, and women reporters were generally accepted by the ordinary soldiers, not least because of the discomfort they brought to the officer class. Despite the reluctance of editors to send women to the conflict zone, the nature of this war, with no set front line and easy access, meant that a determined woman could find her way to the war. While these women reporters established the role of women as war correspondents, their contribution to the reporting of Vietnam is largely unacknowledged and their experience of the war was a "dispiriting ordeal, one that demanded measures of persistence, tact and abundant patience" (Hoffmann, n.d.).

The women journalists who covered the war in Vietnam began the long march by female journalists not to be seen as an aberration but an accepted, if not always acceptable, part of the reporting of war. The number of women covering conflict post Vietnam continued to be low. By 1970 only 6 per cent of foreign correspondents were women (McAfee, 2011), and negative attitudes towards women correspondents continued to persist. A confidential BBC report in 1973, for example, revealed a wide range of hostility towards women in the Corporation. On the possibility of hiring women reporters, it noted that women would be "unable to work in the cold and wet" and "are not able to make overnight stays on location with a man as wives would not like it" (Franks, 2013: 3). The Ministry of Defence in Britain did not allow women journalists on ships or in the war zone during the Falklands War in 1982 (Chambers et al., 2004: 13). Gradually the ratio of women to men in the profession changed. More women war reporters appeared, and their presence in Bosnia is seen by some as one of the "defining moments in journalism" for their exposé of the systematic use of rape as a weapon of warfare (Poggiolo, 1997). Chechnya was also covered by a large number of women reporters. According to the Freedom Forum, in 1998 during the first war in Chechnya nearly half of the accredited reporters were women (Freedom Forum, 1998: 307). Perhaps the most celebrated was Anna Politkovskaya, who won the Courage Award in 2000 for her coverage of war in Chechnya, making more than 40 trips to what she called "a living hell" and refusing to be muzzled by the Russian government. In Iraq in 2003 nearly 50 per cent of the US press corps was female (Steiner, 2017). Hilary Andersson, who was in Iraq in 2003 with the BBC, writes that it was a "good war for women war reporters" (2003: 20). She notes that there was an equal division in the number of female and male reporters based with the British Divisional Headquarters in southern Iraq (Andersson, 2003: 21). In the Israel–Gaza conflict in November 2012, freelance war correspondent Phoebe Greenwood observed that the majority of the correspondents reporting on the ground, representing media from all over the world, were women, stating also that "this high number of female correspondents in a conflict zone is as a result of gender-equality finally filtering down – making it totally normal for women to report from the frontline" (Barnett, 2012). Marina Prentoulis and her colleagues (2005) argue that women front-line correspondents are actually less subjected to gender prejudice today because they face the same physical and psychological hazards as men. Their work is routinely described as "sharing in the high risks of war" with men, and as a result, risk appears as an agent of equalisation among news workers (see Chambers et al., 2004).

Women reporting war today are no longer 'novelties' or 'oddities' but a familiar sight in the world's war zones. Viewers are used to female reporters in flak jackets reporting from the battlefield. Many younger women reporters refer to the "undeniable impact" of role models such as Christine Amanpour and Kate Adie (Day, 2004: 23). Adie is a notable female journalist who achieved prominence for her coverage of the Iranian Embassy siege in London in 1980 and went on to cover the conflict in Libya in 1986 and the Tiananmen Square killings in China in 1989, eventually being appointed the BBC's Chief Foreign Correspondent. Her frequent appearance on British TV screens in the 1980s and 1990s made her part of "our cultural consciousness" (Day, 2004: 23). Her rise to prominence was accompanied by casual sexism. She drew attention to how her appearance was commented on more than her male colleagues. The emphasis on the appearance of female correspondents is seen as a result of the growing commercialism of the news media. Andersson (2003) believes the high profile of women war correspondents on-screen is attributable to "the wow factor". There is an "entrenched belief at a high level of media management that audiences want to see and hear women on screen" (Andersson, 2003: 20). Adie complains that news organisations are interested in employing women for their looks, not their skills (Peachey, 2001). It is argued that executives believe that "pretty faces leaven the sight of body bags and that audiences may even enjoy seeing women doing what was the epitome of maleness" (Steiner, 2017). The employment of more women is good for ratings – the increase in women in war zones is part of what some scholars describe as a market-oriented "feminisation" of the news media (see Franks, 2013).

The focus on the looks of women war reporters is a challenge in the field. US reporter Ashleigh Banfield describes the dangers of being blonde and how she dyed her hair darker as a security measure before going to cover the war on terrorism in Pakistan (Chambers et al., 2004: 214). Appearance is used to criticise women war reporters at home. Lara Logan's assault in Tahrir Square must be contextualised by the sexist discourse on her work as a war correspondent. In 2001 a British colleague attributed his access to Afghani fighters to the 'physical charms' of his colleague "the delectable Lara Logan" (quoted in Chambers et al., 2014: 197). Joe Hagan's (2014) account in *New York* magazine of Lara Logan's rise to fame and fall from grace not only documents her fearlessness and dedication but also refers to how she used her 'good looks' to become CBS' chief foreign correspondent and to cultivate military sources. She is also accused of dressing inappropriately in Afghanistan, and her failings as a war correspondent are attributed by Hagan to her "telegenic sexual charisma" as much as her "almost insatiable stomach for risk". Logan's misreporting of the assassination of the American ambassador in Libya in 2012 was not explored in terms of the flawed reporting environment or her journalistic integrity, but her appearance – a risk for all women war correspondents.

Political economy of women war reporters

The choice of which journalist or director to send to a war zone depends on many things: experience, character, connections and cost. The last factor is increasingly offered as an explanation for the growth in women war correspondents. The changing market for news has been a major factor in determining the employment and resourcing practices of news organisations in their coverage of war (see Chapter 3). The problems of the media industries, the structure of the new global economy, the changing nature of the job market and the drive to freelance work have compelled far more journalists out of staff jobs. Cutbacks, retrenchment and reorganisation have significantly impacted on who is deployed to report war, conflict and crisis. The growing practice of employing freelance journalists is behind the increase in the number of women journalists. This is partly because of the suitability of the new tools of digital journalism and its work patterns to the lifestyle and work practices of many women. It is also because freelancers tend to be paid less. The head of the Russian organisation of investigative journalists, Galina Sidorova (2012), attributes the high proportion of women in journalism to high risk and low pay. It has been estimated that 80 per cent of Russian journalists are female (Franks, 2013). In the UK a survey of 700 news professionals found that 55 per cent of the industry is male but that two-thirds of those who joined the profession since 2013 are female (Thurman et al., 2016). By 2012 female students outnumbered men by at least two to one on many of the most well-established journalism programmes. (Franks, 2013: 3). This finding is echoed by studies elsewhere – for example, in the Lebanon on average four females enrol in journalism programmes for every male student (Melki, 2009). Female presence, however, tends to disappear up the chain of command in newsrooms (Franks, 2013). In the Lebanese news industry, despite the large number of women training to enter the profession, men outnumber women by a ratio of more than two to one (Byerly, 2011). In her study for the International Women's Media Foundation, Carolyn Byerly (2011) found that at the start of the second decade of the 21st century, 73 per cent of the top management jobs were occupied by men. There is, however, little evidence to show that women editors make "significantly different decisions" (Steiner, 2017). Amongst reporters the gap is diminishing, but although more women are coming into journalism and covering conflict, the current state of the news media means men still dominate the decision-making structures and it is an insecure place for women to work.

The precarious nature of freelance reporting is seen as having a disproportionate impact on female war reporters. Freelance journalism is increasingly seen as women's work. There are twice as many women freelance journalists than male freelancers in Canada (Steiner, 2017), and it was estimated in 2004 that three out of four freelancers in the US are female (Massey and Elmore, 2011: 676). Rates of remuneration for freelancers are lower and freelance rates have been in free fall. A Reuters study of British journalists found that 83 per cent of journalists in their mid to late twenties earn less than £29,000, just above the average wage, and that 27 per cent of them are engaged in other paid work (Thurman *et al.*, 2016: 7). This applies not just to Britain; everywhere freelance reporters are suffering "declining incomes, layoffs and competition" (Steiner, 2017). The growing culture of fear amongst journalists is the result of precarious employment, the anxiety of losing your job or not getting a job. The fear that gender plays an important role in being employed to cover conflict reinforces this fear for women journalists. Surveys, however, have tended to find that women are "happier" working for themselves (Massey and Elmore, 2011). It allows them to escape the sexism of the male-dominated newsroom culture and the pressure of long, irregular hours and tight deadlines that characterise full-time work in journalism. It also enables them to better manage their professional and family commitments – but this comes at the price of a riskier working environment.

Women war correspondents at home

Freelance work might favour women journalists because of the need to manage family commitments, but it is family issues which often prevent women from covering war. Jad Melki and Sarah Mallat (2016) highlight the decision by many women to voluntarily remain in junior positions to devote more attention to their families. A journalist who had worked for over 30 years at an Arabic daily newspaper told them, "I didn't want to cover the war anymore. There were car bombs everywhere, and I wasn't willing to orphan my children" (quoted in Melki and Mallat, 2016: 63). *The Guardian*'s Maggie O'Kane spoke of the fear of losing her children as well as "an intuitive sense of having had enough of playing the odds with her life", which ultimately led her to realise that she should no longer be going to war (quoted in Fulton, 2007). Janine Di Giovanni had the same issues:

> I have a son. I don't take the same kind of risks now since I had him. And when I'm away I miss him. And it's very different for men [reporting from war zones]. People argue with me about this, but fathers have a different relationship to their children than mothers. I mean, we give birth.
>
> *(Quoted in Leigh, 2013)*

Regardless of the attitudes of women and men to family commitments, female journalists receive far more criticism than their male counterparts for what is perceived to be 'neglecting' their normative domestic responsibilities (Chambers *et al.*, 2004). Deborah Patta, who has covered stories on Boko Haram and Al Shabaab and has two children, says,

People are saying to me, "How can you do that when you have children? Do you really think you should take that kind of risk?" Almost the implication being that you're reckless as a mother. Men don't get asked that.

(Quoted in Torregrosa, 2015)

The treatment of *Sunday Express* reporter Yvonne Ridley typifies attitudes to women war correspondents with children. In 2001 she spent her daughter's ninth birthday in the custody of the Taliban in an Afghan jail and was accused as a single mother of acting immorally and recklessly in leaving her child (Steiner, 2016).

Managing risk for women with children is a great challenge, but surveys have found that women war reporters tend to be single and without children (see Feinstein and Sinyor, 2009). Susanne Franks (2013) found that the places where women were doing better in journalism are the news organisations which had well-regulated workplaces and high levels of encouragement for mothers to work. The decline in staff jobs due to pressure from the exigencies of the job market might mean that the future for women with children who cover conflict will be more insecure. Women working as freelancers do not escape the gender-related problems and biases of the news media industry. The crucial point is that male perceptions of women's vulnerability are influential in shaping women war reporters' risk culture. A survey of journalists covering war carried out by Cardiff University staff found that more men than women believed it was more dangerous to be a female war reporter (Harris *et al.*, 2016) that women need more protection in reporting war, that family considerations impact on women reporters more than men, that men are more likely to be assigned to report conflict and that women are more at risk covering war – these are the attitudes of men, especially those in positions of authority.

Blending in

War reporting is traditionally construed as a "masculine space" in which women must negotiate a specific set of gendered practices (Palmer and Melki, 2016). Mark Pedelty (1997: 49) identified the ritual performances which dominated the culture of the press corps in El Salvador, which men used as a means of "escaping the stultifying disciplines of corporate press institutions". These performances took the form of "drinking sessions, conspicuous adventures in prostitution, ritual drug use, and other liminal performances" which took place "beyond the glare of editorial sanction and routine" (Pedalty, 1997: 54). While these might help male journalists to alleviate their frustrations, they have implications for women and the way in which they do the job. Anthony Feinstein and Mark Sinyor (2009) found that women war journalists do not differ from their male counterparts in many respects, including the capacity to drink. They describe this gender parity as "remarkable", but since women in general do not drink the same amounts as men, this attribute shows that the women war correspondents want to be seen as equals and will seek to blend in with their male counterparts (Feinstein and Sinyor, 2009: 25).

Lindsay Palmer and Jad Melki (2016) describe how female war reporters must navigate the conflict zone through the strategy of "shape shifting", switching gender performances depending on the environment and the audience. This enables them to carry out their work more effectively and more safely. Working in the same way as their male counterparts, seeking to act and behave like male reporters to blend in, is one way of adapting to the war zone. Pedelty's study documents how female reporters accept the rituals of group identity and "act like them" yet have to work much harder (1997: 60). Kate Adie believes that female reporters should be assertive and take charge of their own careers: "You don't not go, and you don't have people telling you, 'Oh we won't send a woman.' You merely say, 'We will go in, and I will make sure I have as much ability to report as anyone else'" (quoted in Palmer and Melki, 2016: 8). There are, however, other approaches. Some female reporters respond by "foregrounding their feminine accessibility and intuition", while a third strategy of coping is by performing "an exaggerated version of feminine weakness or tacitly accept sexist treatment ... to help circumvent obstructions" (Palmer and Melki, 2016: 1). For women who seek to blend in, working in the same way as men, there is perhaps the worry of being seen not to 'behave like men'. The photojournalist Lynsey Addario (2015: 11–12) writes about being in a car in Libya that was coming under fire from snipers; although she knew her male colleagues "would never have accused [her] of being wimpy or unprofessional, [she] was all too aware of being the only woman in the car". Addario said that she is "always conscious of my gender" and the need for "not drawing attention to myself" whether it is being "appropriately dressed" with Afghan men or being able to "keep up" with US soldiers (quoted in Cooke, 2015). To an extent it could also be argued that the traits identified as masculine – being competitive, self-sufficient and dedicated – are the qualities that all journalists must have in any situation. If you do not have the confidence to ask difficult questions or the ability to ask direct questions and be clearly understood, you are not going to be a very good journalist, wherever or whatever you are reporting on. Managing risk for female war reporters is about adjusting to a male-dominated environment, and there is more than one way of doing this. More women reporting war lessens some of the problems women face in adapting to the circumstances in the field, but the lack of females in positions of authority in news organisations emphasises that women reporters are more at risk and in need of protection than their male counterparts.

When gender becomes an issue

Studies into the intimidation and harassment of women journalists who report conflict indicate that the risk of abuse is from co-workers as well as those the journalist reports on. A recent survey by the IFJ found that 45 per cent of the violence and abuse was outside the workplace, from sources, politicians, people in the streets, readers or listeners, but 38 per cent came from a boss, supervisor, or co-worker (IFJ, 2017a). There were similar findings from a 2014 survey reported by the INSI and the International Womens Media Foundation (IWMF (Barton and Storm, 2014). Intimidation and harassment occur on the home front as much as in the field. These are obviously related and part of a general pattern of gender discrimination. Risk is a product of "human hands and minds" (Beck, 2009: 25), and it is not just the tools and practices deployed by journalists in war zones that put them at risk; it is also obviously what goes on in their minds. Responses to acts of sexual violence reflect the general set of attitudes that pervades news organisations and the profession towards managing risk in relation to female war reporters. When Laura Logan was attacked in Tahir Square in Egypt in 2011, Reporters Sans Frontiers urged news organisations not to send women to Egypt: "It is unfortunate that we have come to this but, given the violence of these assaults, there is no other solution" (Sherwood, 2011). There was an immediate hostile reaction to this and the statement was amended to read: "it is more dangerous for a woman than a man to cover the demonstrations in Tahrir Square. That is the reality and the media must face it" (Harris *et al.*, 2016: 903). The perception is that the risk and danger of reporting conflict is assigned to gender rather than profession. Location, culture and assignment contribute to risk as much as gender, but as Tina Susman, *Los Angeles Times* bureau chief in Baghdad during 2007–09, states, "when a female is assaulted the questions immediately arise as to why a woman was there in the first place, and whether it is wise to have a woman reporting from a dangerous place" (2012: 25).

In terms of the notion that it is riskier to assign a woman than a man, Lindsey Hilsum voices a concern felt by many women journalists when she says that "it's one step away from saying it's our fault, for Christ's sake". She accepts that "it's dangerous, and there are particular risks for women, but it's not more dangerous as a result. It would be a mistake to let that thinking dominate when preparing for what might happen" (quoted in Neilan, 2012). A feature of the risk society, according to Beck, is the emphasis placed on individuals to make decisions about their lives as pre-existing social forms such as fixed gender roles break down (Elliott, 2002: 298). However, for the individual women war correspondent, the management of the dangers and hazards they face is located not only in terms of decisions made on the ground but also in the context of attitudes to being female. Being female becomes a factor in attributing the blame when women correspondents get into difficulties.

It is not possible to say with certainty that women journalists are targeted because they are women or because they are journalists. Referring to the 2014 IWMF/INSI study mentioned above, Pirmasari (2016: 79) states that sexual violence is "frequently used to silence and intimidate women journalists", and women reporters are "additionally exposed to attacks because their work challenges gender stereotypes". This reflects the situation in society. A study in the UK by the TUC and Everyday Sexism Project (2016) found that 52 per cent of women had experienced unwanted behaviour at work, including groping, sexual advances and inappropriate jokes. In November 2017 a group of female journalists founded a group, The Second Source, to tackle harassment in the UK media (Andersson,

2017). The increase in violence against women reporters has risen along with the increase for all journalists. Many women who report on conflict are wary about assigning a certainty to motive in attacks on female journalists. Caroline Wyatt (2012: 8) from the BBC states that the danger in Afghanistan wasn't to do with being female but with "being foreign, and by local standards, rich". In the Cardiff survey (Harris *et al.*, 2016), when asked whether it was more dangerous to be a female or a male journalist, half of the recipients responded that female journalists were in more danger; however, nearly two-thirds thought that it was the job itself that was the most dangerous factor. However, more than half of the respondents (63%) thought there were advantages as well as disadvantages in being a female journalist.

Advantages

The advantages of assigning a woman to cover war and conflict are often to do with matters of access. For example, in the Middle East women journalists can enter homes and speak to women, an undertaking that men cannot do. For a full picture of war, the voices of women and families are a vital component, and without access to them, a proper understanding cannot be given. It is not just reporting on the effects of war that might be lost. As war is changing from large-scale set battles and national conflicts to insurgency and local wars, women are not only fighting, but many are involved in raising funds and encouraging men to go to war.[2] A recent report in *Science Advances* states that in networks such as ISIS, women are key players in both high-profile online and offline settings (Manrique *et al.*, 2016). The extent to which ISIS uses female bombers to attack civilian targets is a matter of discussion (Bloom and Winter, 2015), but if such groups are increasingly using women behind the scenes, it might be an advantage to be a woman journalist when trying to access them. As well as being able to access other women, women are also perceived to be less threatening and thus can often get an interview or story, whereas a man might become part of the story or be refused. Sometimes playing up the 'only a woman' label can be a good strategy to get access to stories where men might pose a threat or be an obvious intrusion.

Maggie O'Kane remarks that when she was in Bosnia, being a woman gave her good cover. She said,

> I am a woman. Nobody pays attention to me. […] To the soldiers, I was just a pain in the ass; a funny red-haired creature; a dumb female. They didn't find me a threat. … If they think I'm a bimbo, that's just fine. They become less guarded and give me better quotes.
>
> *(quoted in Ricchiardi, 1994)*

CNN reporter Clarissa Ward believes it is preferable to be a female reporter in the Middle East (Steigrad, 2016). As a woman, she says, she can put on a headscarf and get through checkpoints: "nobody looks twice at me whereas my male counterparts, Western counterparts may have a tougher time getting through"; she also is able to access the 50 per cent of the population that her male colleagues cannot. Alice Martins, a photojournalist who has reported from Syria, has also stated that as a woman, she can cross checkpoints without being stopped. "These guys are scary", she said, "but they try to avoid women" (quoted in Traub, 2014). However, even she has stopped reporting from Syria as the situation there became so dangerous.

In a conflict zone when wearing a flak jacket and helmet, it can be difficult for observers at a distance to spot whether the reporter is male or female; but as many Western reporters wear bright blue jackets and helmets, it is at least clear they are from the media. Lyse Doucet (2012), a BBC reporter who has covered many conflicts, describes how Western female reporters become a type of 'third gender'. Likewise, Bay Fang, the chief correspondent in Iraq during 2003–04 for *US News & World Report* magazine, states, "For the most part, we were seen as a third gender ... we were just a curiosity" (2012: 33). Clarissa Ward has talked about the difficulties of setting up interviews as a woman correspondent and being a victim of sexism, but on the whole she found that men would talk to a Western woman, even some men who would not usually talk to a local woman (Steigrad, 2016). She concluded that Western female journalists

> enjoy this kind of weird honorary male status almost where I can sit in the kitchen with the women and I can sit in the front room with the men, unlike, perhaps, their own women. You're like the third sex.
>
> *(Quoted in Steigrad, 2016)*

This is echoed in the interviews with women war correspondents undertaken by Kristin Orgeret (2016a). Some of the female journalists said they were often seen as both man and woman. For example,

> In the Middle East I am seen as something in between a man and a woman, and that is clearly a professional advantage. I can both speak to the men and I can enter the female areas where not men are allowed.
>
> *(Quoted in Orgeret, 2016a: 170)*

Many of the advantages women war reporters are perceived to enjoy relate primarily to white, Western women who have "capitalised upon their differences in order to bring a wider dimension to their reporting" (Franks, 2013: 30). According to Milly Buonanno (2012: 809), the conditions to do this "lie in the sexism and the patriarchal cultures in force in those societies and territories where armed conflict has broken out in recent years". For many Arab women correspondents, the increased access in conservative societies is related to "traditional patriarchal values" such as sense of duty in protecting women and the view women are less threatening than men (Melki and Mallat, 2016: 67). Constructing women war reporters as the "third gender" "overtly stereotype Arab women as oppressed and Arab men as oppressors" (Edney-Browne, 2015).

There may be people being reported on in war zones who see the journalist before the gender, but that does not necessarily minimise the risk. Orgeret (2016b: 106) refers to the need, particularly in conservative cultures, to develop "situational awareness". She notes that some types of conversation are considered inappropriate and certain types of eye contact could be construed as flirting. Some reporters describe techniques such as carrying two business cards or wearing fake wedding rings to ward off unwanted attention. This is most apparent in negotiating with their primary sources of information.

Sources and women war reporters

Female war reporters may be able to access sources that male reporters cannot, but relationships with sources are generally more problematic for women correspondents. Official sources have traditionally exerted a disproportionate influence over the sourcing of war and conflict news, and these sources are collectively dominated by men (see Ottosen, 2010). This has had an impact on the working practices of women reporters. This impact is not straightforward, but operating in an environment in which the "overwhelming majority of editorially-sanctioned sources are males, specifically those in positions of power", presents challenges which male correspondents do not face (Pedelty, 1997: 59). In a study in Israel, nearly one-third of the women journalists surveyed reported that they had been harassed, mainly verbally, by sources (Steiner, 2017). Female correspondents covering conflicts in Central America in the late 1980s found that "sources don't take you seriously"; "women have to work harder to get sources here and to be taken seriously" (quoted in Pedelty, 1997: 59). BBC East Africa Correspondent Cathy Jenkins (1999) writes about her experience of accessing Ethiopia during the country's war with Eritrea in the 1990s. She was accused of bias; rumours were circulated she had been sacked and that she was being paid by the Eritrean government to write their propaganda. Unlike rumours about her male colleagues, she was reported to be "having an affair with an Eritrean government official" (Jenkins, 1999).

Female war correspondents have complained about discrimination, derogatory attitudes and sexual harassment by certain male sources (Pedelty, 1997; Lachover, 2005). Not being taken seriously and having to work harder to get sources are familiar concerns for women war reporters (see Pedelty, 1997; Robbins, 1991). Carla Robbins (1991) of US News & World Report describes the physical obstacles to working in Saudi Arabia during the 1991 Gulf War, such as the absence of women's toilets in government buildings. Despite these handicaps, she found the "most disturbing prejudice" was experienced at the hands of her own colleagues (Robbins, 1991: 39). The psychosexual difficulties for female correspondents of working with male sources have been commented on in various contexts (see Cogan, 2013). Newsgathering can be a "flirty business", and the notion of "sex for access" is popularised by shows such as *House of Cards*. Einat Lachover (2005), in her study of the relationship between female reporters and male sources in Israel, found that women were functioning within a framework of gendered relations which they had to negotiate. Women were sometimes treated as sexual objects and faced verbal harassment and derogatory attitudes, and flirting was the currency of their interaction with their male sources. However, the Israeli women reporters interviewed did not see themselves as passive objects; creating sexual tension and flirting was seen as part of professional practice. These women saw navigation between "creating sexual tension and placing strict boundaries on it" as part of what they have to do. Sometimes they were encouraged by editors, but some reporters stressed the feminine advantages that accompany dealing with male sources. Other women identified with their male sources, often adopting male characteristics, appearances or behaviour, blurring their femininity in becoming one of the boys. There are a variety of ways in which the gendered framework is negotiated by women reporters, but the process of negotiation is part of the risk culture that they must operate within.

Blending in with military sources has been more difficult for women reporters, but in recent years with the influx on women into the armed forces, particularly on front-line duty, attitudes have changed. While a general directive prohibiting women from accessing the battlefield, such as that considered by General Westmoreland in Vietnam, is unthinkable, there is still a variety of informal ways in which women reporters are restricted in how they operate (Braiker, 2003). Fewer women were embedded with front-line units in Iraq in 2003. One reporter was told that the aircraft carriers were for the "girls and fat people". Some women referred to the 'ma'am factor', highlighting the extreme to which soldiers would go to show respect and courtesy to women, making it more difficult to build up an effective working relationship. The BBC series *Fighting the War*, made during the invasion of Iraq in 2003, had seven documentary crews embedded with various military units. Two of the crews had female directors, one with the Scottish infantry regiment the Black Watch which was on the front line, and one with the Royal Logistics Corps (RLC). After the move into Basra, the director and crew moved from the RLC to embed with the Royal Military Police in Basra. Experiences differed depending on the regiment that the crews were embedded with (Lewis *et al.*, 2006), but for the crew with the Black Watch regiment, what was very clear from the beginning was that the last thing they wanted was a television crew messing up their war-fighting. For the director with the Black Watch, this hostility was directed at the journalist, not at the gender; although what was said out of earshot cannot be commented on. It was only one military liaison officer in the regiment who said that women should not be on the front line.

Digital harassment

The digital world offers both opportunities and challenges to women war reporters and bloggers. Managing risk could been seen as more feasible in an environment in which face-to-face communication is less necessary. However, a considerable amount of harassment and intimidation is perpetrated through social media and the Internet, and in general women journalists face more online harassment than men. Studies have found that female journalists experience approximately three times as many abusive comments online as their male counterparts (Orgeret, 2016a). Binns (2017) found that women were more likely than men to report often receiving insults or threats, and they had stronger emotional reactions to abuse. The level of threat is a growing phenomenon (Henrichsen et al., 2015: 43), and for many female journalists, online threats of rape and sexual violence are part of daily working life (OSCE, 2016).

The gendered nature of the online abuse has been identified by several studies (see Barton and Storm, 2014; OSCE, 2016). The "online attacks tend to degrade the journalist as a woman rather than address the content of the article" (Orgeret, 2016b: 110). Following the assault on Lara Logan in Tahrir Square in early 2011, NPR had to remove countless offensive messages from their message boards attacking her as a woman (Daily Mail, 2011). Certain conflicts, such as that between Israel and Palestine, generate considerable personal abuse. Technology has facilitated this type of hate mail by making it easier to leave comments or to tweet anonymously. Such abuse aims to silence, humiliate and make it more difficult to comment and report. Many editors are slow to respond; burdened down by their workloads, women journalists tend to see it as part of the job. But with news organisations encouraging their employees to comment on Facebook and partici-pate in Twitter chats, they are beginning to realise the need for some filtering system (Bouchart, 2015). Vice News has blocked the posting of anonymous comments, for example. For women reporters "inundated with threats of murder, rape, physical violence and graphic imagery via email, commenting sections and across all social media platforms", safety risks have been transferred from the offline to the online world (OSCE, 2016: 1). The fear, discomfort and anger associated with online abuse is often compounded by the loneliness of the online experience. Digital safety for women reporters is now recognised as a major issue and a threat to freedom of expression as more women are more reluctant to speak up online (Henrichsen et al., 2015; OSCE, 2016). For war reporting, it threatens the loss of a female perspective on war and represents a risk to diverse and representative journalism.

Gendered war journalism

The question of whether women report on conflict differently from men under-pins much of the discussion of women reporters at war and the decision to send a male or a female journalist to a conflict. Di Giovanni thinks that women do write differently. "I know this may be sexist, but I do think women report war differ-ently", she says. "I don't know anything about weapons. Macho male journalists sit around talking about 62mm mortars and AK-47s and Kalashnikovs" (quoted in Ricchiardi, 1994). She also thinks that women make better listeners (di Giovanni, 2013), and Marie Colvin agrees, drawing on her own experience of talking for hours to a civilian whose baby was killed, something she believed a male journalist would not have done (Chambers *et al.*, 2004: 213). Caroline Wyatt (2012: 8), a defence correspondent for the BBC in Afghanistan, argues that women bring a different perspective to war: "a little less focus on the bombs and bullets, and more on what the end of the Taliban's rule in the north would mean for the families we met, and for their future". There is little in the way of conclusive evidence to support the view that gender has a significant impact on the attitudes and values of journalists; newsroom and community environments, family background and training have a greater influence (see Chambers *et al.*, 2004: chapter 5). Nevertheless, there is considerable anecdotal support for the view that the presence of women reporters in modern conflict has "disrupted the ... traditional masculine reporting styles", shifting the emphasis from "bullets and bombs" to "civilian sufferings" (Chambers *et al.*, 2004: 11).

Anthony Delano (2003: 275) argues that the reporting from the Balkans wars "betokened a weakening of ... the hegemonic masculinity that had hitherto governed news values". A female perspective is seen as one that allows for "greater engagement with the lives of the victims of war rather than its technical and strategic aspects" (McLaughlin 2002: 172–3), which was evident in the reporting from women correspondents such as Maggie O'Kane, Janine de Giovanni and Kim Willsher during the Balkans wars. They "frequently focused on the plight of non-combatant victims and the effect of war on individual participants, rather than on battlefield tactics and weaponry" (Delano, 2003: 275). *The Guardian*'s Maggie O'Kane was one of the first to break the story of Serb concentration camps in central Bosnia, to give voice to the Muslim victims of the Serb policy of mass rape and to report on profiteering and prostitution amongst UN Protection Force soldiers in Sarajevo. Her style of reporting is described as "direct, personal, moral and angry" (O'Tuathail, 1996: 174). For O'Kane (2005: 92), this focus is to do with a change in journalism, with a more "personal take" being applied to political reporting. Her desire to tell the victims' stories, especially those of women and children, led her to make courageous efforts to get to the key sites of the war. The favourable reception of this style might have influenced other journalists and editors to emulate her efforts and reporting. She was in the vanguard of practicing the 'journalism of attachment' that replaces the masculine aloofness of objective journalism with a more caring, feminine sense of moral outrage.

For many of the same reasons that she is wary about stating that women are at more risk than men in conflict zones, Lindsay Hilsum believes there is less distinction between male and female reporting in war.

> I think you'd be hard pressed to find a consistent distinction between men's and women's reporting of wars and revolutions. But I would say that when a man does the weepy, human side, he is regarded as empathetic and sensitive, but a woman may be perceived as "not coping" if she shows emotion. So, women broadcasters have to be very careful not to play into peoples' stereotypes.
>
> *(Quoted in Cooper, 2011: 242)*

This can perhaps be seen in John Simpson's criticism of a report by his BBC colleague Kate Adie from China after the student killings at Tiananmen Square, when she and her crew were caught in the crossfire. Chief Diplomatic Correspondent for the BBC John Simpson said at the time that her report was "horribly emotional"; However, he later altered his opinion:

> Kate went to the hospital and she gave you a real feeling of the awfulness of it. You felt how frightened she was, as indeed most of us were and I thought she gave a damn sight better account by seeing the aftermath than the real thing.
>
> (Quoted in Sebba, 1994: 269)

This shift away from 'objective' reporting containing an embedded masculine bias (Allan, 2004) to a feminised interest in the 'human story' is part of the general story about the changing culture of journalism, as well as a challenge to the rationality of experts (Beck, 1992). Women reporters in the Balkans were strong advocates of bringing "emotion, passion and commitment to a story" (Chambers *et al.*, 2004: 209). The emergence of a more emotive journalism is fuelled by the rise of citizen journalists, many of whom have been female. During the Arab Spring, citizen journalists and social media informed and influenced traditional media by the "contestation of knowledge with competing knowledge claims" (Cottle and Rai, 2006: 165). The shift towards a more involved journalism was noticeable during the events of the Arab Spring. Heavy policing of journalism in countries like Egypt and Libya led many journalists being excluded from the traditional media and becoming online activists. Hossam el-Hamalawy, a prominent Egyptian blogger and citizen journalist, stated in 2009 that "in a dictatorship, independent journalism by default becomes a form of activism, and the spread of information is essentially an act of agitation" (quoted in Radsch, 2012: 11). Women in the Middle East active on social media such as the Libyan Hana El Hebshi[3] and the American-Egyptian Shima'a Helmy[4] were able to inform and set the agenda for media interest and coverage. The Egyptian-American activist Mona Eltahawy stated: "The power of women is in their stories. They are not theories, they are real lives that, thanks to social networks, we are able to share and exchange" (quoted in Radsch, 2012: 31). Digital journalism might be opening new arenas for women to write about conflict, perhaps more safely and without the discrimination of the newsroom and editors and encouraging a more human interest style of writing, but it is also furthering a more committed journalism. Reporting on the conflicts in Gaza and Syria highlights an increased emphasis on emotion, commitment and passion. Any evaluation of gendered war reporting needs to distinguish between women and between conflicts in different parts of the world. The war in the Lebanon in 2006 put Arab women war reporters on the front line for the first time (Miles, 2006), and many experienced the same problems as their Western counterparts (see The New Arab, 2015). But their reporting on the suffering of those caught up in the wars in the Middle East does not differentiate them from their male colleagues.

Risk is a problem for male and female war reporters – it does not discriminate on the grounds of gender. However, managing risk is a completely different problem for female war reporters. Threats to their personal safety come in a variety of different forms, and the camaraderie that bonds men together in warfare cannot always be assumed in relation to women and their male colleagues. Sexual harassment, discrimination and intimidation are part of the world of the woman war correspondent. Dealing with patriarchal attitudes and perceptions is central to women's world of risk. Beck (1997: 30) writes that "risks always depend on decisions"; that is, they presuppose decisions. If a decision is made that women are at more risk than men, the probability of editors not sending women to cover conflict, or women not choosing to report war, becomes greater. Recognition of the specific nature of risk to women war reporters has risen with the changing economic circumstances of the news industry. Freelance reporting is often described as 'women's work', and to ensure news organisations retain their women workers in war zones, more attention has to be paid to the provision of proper training in safety as well as insurance and childcare. Security training has been described by women journalists as highly "masculine" and often fails to acknowledge the particular challenges female reporters face in war zones (Orgeret, 2016b: 111). They are vulnerable to different kinds of risk and must negotiate risk in different ways from their male colleagues, which shapes the way they do their job and can influence how they write their copy and how they represent war and conflict.

Notes

1 In 2003 a BBC documentary crew embedded on a British ship for the series *Fighting the War* (2003) was, for 'security measures', locked in the wardroom when the invasion was announced. The crew was male and female, and Janet Harris thinks this is an illustration of the unchanging attitude of the military towards journalists in general. They are all a nuisance, regardless of their sex.

2 In her book on killing in war, Joanna Bourke (1999) writes that during war women as well as men are aroused by bloodletting and that women's encouragement of men to commit violent acts in war has added to men's satisfaction in killing.

3 Hana El Hebshi was awarded the International Woman of Courage award by the US government for "reaching out to the international media to share the realities of living under the previous regime" (US Department of State, 2012).

4 Shima'a Helmy, an anonymous Egyptian blogger, wrote on her blog, "I was concerned with how non-Arabic-speaking media were portraying our story. I contacted as many foreign journalists as I could—speaking to them and helping them out" (quoted in Radsch, 2012: 15).

REFERENCES

Abbott, K. (2009) 'Working together: NGOs and journalists can create stronger international reporting', *NiemanLab*, 9 November. www.niemanlab.org/2009/11/kimberly-abbott-working-together-ngos-and-journalists-can-create-stronger-international-reporting/

Aday, S. (2005) 'The real war will never get on television: An analysis of casualty imagery in American television coverage of the Iraq War', in Seib, P. (ed.), *Media and Conflict in the Twenty-First Century*, pp. 141–156. New York: Palgrave Macmillan.

Addario, L. (2015) *It's What I do: A Photographer's Life of Love and War*. New York: Penguin.

Adie, K. (1998) 'Reporting war: Dispatches from the front', in *Reporters and the Reported: The 1998 Vauxhall Lectures*. Cardiff: Centre for Journalism Studies, Cardiff University.

Adie, K. (2002) *The Kindness of Strangers*. London: Hodder.

Adie, K. (2015) Interview with BBC Wales, *Sunday Supplement*, 2 August.

Ahmad, M. (2016) 'The magical realism of body counts: How media credulity and flawed statistics sustain a controversial policy', *Journalism*, 17(1): 18–34.

Al-Adnan, H. (2016) 'Inside Syria's war', *Index on Censorship*, 45(2): 28–31.

Alagiah, G. (1999) 'New light on a dark continent', *The Guardian*, 3 May.

Ale, B. (2009) *Risk: An Introduction. The Concepts of Risk, Danger and Chance*. Abingdon: Routledge.

Allan, S. (2002) *Media, Risk and Science*. Milton Keynes, UK: Open University Press.

Allan, S. (2004) *News Culture*. Milton Keynes, UK: Open University Press.

Allan, S. (2006) *Online News*. New York: Open University Press.

Allan, S. (2011) 'Amateur photography in wartime', in Anden-Papadopoulos, K. and Pantti, M. (eds), *Amateur Images and Global News*, pp. 41–60. Bristol, UK: Intellect.

Allan, S. (2013) *Citizen Witnessing: Revisioning Journalism in Times of Crisis*. Cambridge: Polity Press.

Allan, S., Sonwalkar, P. and Carter, C. (2007) 'Bearing witness: Citizen journalism and human rights issues', *Globalisation, Societies and Education*, 5(3): 373–389.

Allbritton, C. (2003) 'Blogging from Iraq', *Nieman Reports*, 57(3): 82–85.

Altheide, D. (2013) 'Media logic, social control and fear', *Communication Theory*, 23(3): 223–238.

Amanpour, C. (1996) 'Television's role in foreign policy', *The Quill*, 84(3): 16–17.

Amin, S. (2012) Shahira Amin, in Storm, H. and Williams, H. (eds), *No Woman's Land: On the Frontlines with Female Reporters*. pp. 29–31, London: International News Safety Institute.

Anand, P. (1993) *Foundations of Rational Choice under Risk*. Oxford: OUP.

Anden-Papadopoulos, K. (2009) 'Body horror on the Internet: US soldiers recording war in Iraq and Afghanistan', *Media, Culture & Society*, 31(6): 921–938.

Anden-Papadopoulos, K. and Panatti, M. (2013) 'Professional ideology of journalists and citizen eyewitness images', *Journalism*, 14(7): 960–977.

Anderson, D. (2011) *History of the Hanged: Britain's Dirty war in Kenya and the End of Empire*. London: Hachette.

Anderson, F. (2009) 'Mosquitoes dancing on the surface of the pond', *Journalism Practice*, 3(4): 404–420.

Anderson, F. and Trembath, G. (2011) *Witnesses to War: The History of Australian Conflict Reporting*. Melbourne: Melbourne University Press.

Andersson, H. (2003) 'The wow factor', *British Journalism Review*, 14(2): 20–24.

Andersson, J. (2017) 'For too long, female journalists have been subject to sexual harassment, assault and discrimination. We're here to make sure that never happens again', *Independent*, 3 November.

Andrews, J. Cutler (1955) *The North Reports the Civil War*. Pittsburgh, PA: University of Pittsburgh Press.

Applebaum, A. (2014) Putin's new kind of war, *The Slate*, 16 April. www.slate.com/arti cles/news_and_politics/foreigners/2014/04/vladimir_putin_s_new_war_in_ukraine_the_ kremlin_is_reinventing_how_russia.html

Armoudian, M. (2017) *Reporting from the Danger Zone: Frontline Journalists, their Jobs and an Increasingly Perilous Future*. London: Routledge.

Arnett, P. (1994) *Live from the Battlefield: From Vietnam to Baghdad, 35 Years in the World's War Zones*. New York: Simon and Schuster.

Aronson, J. (1990) *The Press and the Cold War*. New York: Monthly Review Press.

Ashmead-Bartlett, E. (1913) *With the Turks in Thrace*. New York: George H. Doran Company.

Auchter, J. (2017) 'Visible dead bodies and the technologies of erasure in the war on terror', in Hellmich, C. and Purse, L. (eds), *Disappearing War: Interdisciplinary Perspectives on Cinema and Erasure in the Post-9/11 World*, pp. 111–130. Edinburgh: Edinburgh University Press.

Axe, D. (2013) *Shadow Wars: Chasing Conflict in an Era of Peace*. Washington, DC: Potomac Books, Inc.

Ayalon, A., Popovich, E. and Yarchi, M. (2016) 'From warfare to imagefare: How states should manage asymmetric conflicts with extensive media coverage', *Terrorism and Political Violence*, 28(2): 254–273.

Ayers, C. (2005) *War Reporting for Cowards*. London: John Murray.

Baglow, J. (2007) 'The rights of the corpse', *Mortality*, 12(3): 223–239.

Bahador, B. (2007) *The CNN Effect in Action: How the News Media Pushed the West to War in Kosovo*. New York: Palgrave Macmillan.

Bajoria, J. and McMahon, R. (2013) 'The dilemma of humanitarian intervention', *Council on Foreign Relations*. www.cfr.org/humanitarian-intervention/dilemma-humanitarian-inter vnetion/p16524

Baker (2014)

Bakir, V. and McStay, A. (2018) 'Fake news and the economy of emotions', *Digital Journalism*, 6(2): 154–175.

Balguy-Gallois, A. (2004) 'The protection of journalists and news media personnel in armed conflict', *International Review of the Red Cross*, 86(853): 37–67.

Bamford, J. (2016) 'Every move you make', *Foreign Policy*, 7 September. http://foreignp olicy.com/2016/09/07/every-move-you-make-obama-nsa-security-surveillance-spying-intelligence-snowden/

Baraniuk, C. (2016) 'Citizen journalism is playing a crucial role in Aleppo – but it comes at a cost', *Wired*, 2 November. www.wired.co.uk/article/syrian-citizen-journalists

Barnett, E. (2012) 'The unique advantages of female war reporters in Muslim countries', *The Telegraph*, 21 November.

Barton, A. and Storm, H. (2014) *Violence and Harassment Against Women in the News Media: A Global Picture.* Washington, DC and London: International Women's Media Foundation and International News Safety Institute.

BBC (2013) Iraq study estimates war-related deaths at 461,000. 16 October. https://www.bbc.co.uk/news/world-middle-east-24547256

BBC (n.d.) Editorial guidelines. www.bbc.co.uk/editorialguidelines/guidelines/privacy/reporting-death

Beaumont, P. (2010) *The Secret Life of War: Journeys Through Modern Conflict.* London: Vintage.

Beck, U. (1991) *Ecological Enlightenment: Essays on the Politics of the Risk Society.* Amherst, NY: Prometheus Books.

Beck, U. (1992) *Risk Society: Towards a New Modernity.* London: Sage.

Beck, U. (1997) *The Reinvention of Politics.* Cambridge: Polity.

Beck, U. (1998) Politics of risk society, in Franklin, J. (ed.), *The Politics of Risk Society*, pp. 9–22, Cambridge: Polity Press.

Beck, U. (2000) *World Risk Society.* Cambridge: Polity.

Beck, U. (2006) 'Living in the world risk society', *Economy and Society*, 35(3): 329–345.

Beck, U. (2009) *World at Risk.* Cambridge: Polity.

Becker, E. (2015) 'Journalists don't always testify at tribunals. Here's why I did', *The Washington Post*, 6 March.

Becker, E. (2017) 'The women who covered Vietnam', *The New York Times*, 17 November.

Beckett, C. (2006) *Killing Journalism?*London: POLIS: Journalism and Society at the LSE. www.lse.ac.uk/media%40lse/POLIS/Files/killingjournal.pdf

Belair-Gagnon, V., Agur, C. and Frisch, N. (2016) 'How foreign correspondents use chat apps to cover political unrest', *Columbia Journalism Review.* www.cjr.org/tow_center_reports/foreign_correspondents_chat_apps_unrest.php

Bell, E. and Owen, T. (2017) *Journalism After Snowden: The Future of the Free Press in the Surveillance State.* New York: Columbia University Press.

Bell, M. (1995) *In Harm's Way: Bosnia: A War Reporter's Story.* London: Hamish Hamilton.

Bell, M. (1997) 'TV news: How far should we go', *British Journalism Review*, 8(1): 7–16.

Bell, M. (1998) 'The journalism of attachment', in Kieran, M. (ed.), *Media Ethics*, pp. 15–22. London: Routledge.

Bell, M. (2008) 'The death of news', *Media, War and Conflict*, 1(2): 221–231.

Bell, M. (2012a) *In Harm's Way: A War Reporter's Story*, revised edition. London: Icon Books.

Bell, M. (2012b) 'Why they want to silence the voice that brings us truth', *The Times*, 23 February.

Bell, M. (2017) *War and the Death of News.* London: Oneworld.

Bennett, D. (2011) 'A "gay girl in Damascus", the mirage of the "authentic voice" – and the future of journalism', in Keeble, R. and Mair, J. (eds), *Mirage in the Desert? Reporting the Arab Spring*, pp. 187–195. Bury St Edmunds, UK: Abramis.

Bennett, D. (2013) 'Exploring the impact of an evolving war and terror blogosphere on traditional media coverage of conflict', *Media, War & Conflict*, 6(1) 37–53.

Berkowitz, D. and Schwartz, D. A. (2016) Miley, CNN and The Onion, *Journalism Practice*, 10(1): 1–17.

Bernstein, N. (2002) 'Should war reporters testify, too? A recent court decision helps clarify the issue but does not end the debate', *The New York Times*, 14 December.

Berzins, J. (2014) *Russia's New Generation Warfare in Ukraine: Implications for Latvian Defense Policy*, Policy Paper No. 2. Riga: National Defence Academy of Latvia.

Bienaime, P. (2015) 'Are journalists lowballing the number of Iraqi war dead?', *Columbia Journalism Review*, 7 July. https://www.cjr.org/criticism/iraq_body_count.php

Binns, A. (2017) 'Fair game? Journalists' experiences of online abuse', *Journal of Applied Journalism & Media Studies*, 6(2): 183–206.

Blaagaard, B., Mortensen, M. and Neumayer, C. (2017) 'Digital images and globalized conflict', *Media, Culture & Society*, 39(8): 1111–1121.

Blake, S. (2010) 'Women war correspondents', *The Telegraph*, 12 July.

Block, M. and Mungham, G. (1989) 'The military, the media and the invasion of Grenada', *Contemporary Crises*, 13(2): 91–127.

Bloom, M. and Winter, C. (2015) 'The women of ISIL', *Politico*, 12 July. https://www.politico.eu/article/the-women-of-isil-female-suicide-bomber-terrorism/

Bloor, M. (1995) *The Sociology of HIV Transmission*. London: Sage.

Boettcher, W. and Cobb, M. (2006) 'Echoes of Vietnam? Casualty framing and public perceptions of success and failure in Iraq', *Journal of Conflict Resolution*, 50(6): 831–885.

Borri, F. (2013) 'Woman's work: The twisted reality of an Italian freelancer in Syria', *Columbia Journalism Review*. https://archives.cjr.org/feature/womans_work.php?page=all

Bouchart, M. (2015) 'Tackling online harassment of women journalism', *Global Editors Network*. https://www.globaleditorsnetwork.org/press-room/news/2015/12/digital-safety-for-women-in-journalism/

Bourdieu, P. (1984) *Distinction: A Social Critique of the Judgement of Taste*. Cambridge, MA: Harvard University Press.

Bourke, J. (1999) *An Intimate History of Killing: Face-to-face Killing in 20th Century Warfare*. London and New York: Granta Press.

Bowen, J. (2006) *War Stories*. London: Pocket Books.

Boyd-Barrett, O. (2004) 'Understanding: The second casualty', in Allan, S. and Zelizer, B. (eds), *Reporting War: Journalism in Wartime*, pp. 25–42. London: Routledge.

Bradshaw, P. (2008) 'When journalists blog: How it changes what they do', *Nieman Reports*, 62(4): 50–52.

Braiker, B. (2003) 'Fembeds' reflect on covering war. What was it like to be a female reporter embedded with U.S. troops during the war on Iraq?', *MSNBC*, 16 May. www.msnbc.com/news/914570.asp?0cv=KB20&cp1=1

Braman, S. (2003) *Communication Researchers and Policy Making*. Boston, MA: MIT Press.

Brandenburg, B. (2007) 'Security at the source: Embedding journalists as a superior strategy to military censorship', *Journalism Studies*, 8(6): 948–963.

Brock, P. (2006) *Media Cleansing: Dirty Reporting, Journalism and Tragedy in Yugoslavia*. Los Angeles: GM Books.

Broersma, M. (2007) 'Form, style and journalistic strategies: An introduction', in Broersma, M. (ed.), *Form and Style in Journalism: European Newspapers and the Representation of News 1880–2005*, pp. ix–xxix. Leuven: Peeters.

Brooks, R. (2017) *How Everything Became War and the Military Became Everything*. New York: Simon & Schuster.

Brothers, C. (1997) *War and Photography: A Cultural History*. New York: Routledge.

Brown, R. (2003) 'Spinning the war', in Thussu, D. and Freedman, D. (eds), *War and the Media*, pp. 87–100. London: Sage.

Browne, M. (1997) 'Notes from the trenches', *The New York Times*, 8 June.

Browne, M., Stack, L. and Ziyadah, M. (2015) 'Streets to screens: Conflict, social media and the news', *Information, Communication & Society*, 18(11): 1339–1347.

Broyles, W. (1984) 'Why men love war', *Esquire*, November.

Brunner, E. and Cavelty, M. (2009) 'The formation of information by the US military: Articulation and enactment of infomanic threat imaginaries on the immaterial battlefield of perception', *Cambridge Review of International Affairs*, 22(4): 629–646.

Bruns, A. (2009) *Gatewatching: Collaborative Online News Production*. New York: Peter Lang.

Bruns, A. and Hanusch, F. (2017) 'Conflict imagery in a connective environment: Audio-visual content on Twitter following the 2015/2016 terror attacks in Paris and Brussels', *Media, Culture & Society*, 29(8): 1122–1141.

Buchanan, E. (2016) 'Dogs of war: Who are the British mercenaries roaming Africa accused of "war crimes"', *International Business Times*, 6 February. https://www.ibtimes.co.uk/hold-saturday-8am-dogs-of-war-who-are-british-mercenaries-roaming-africa-accused-war-crimes-1542030

Bullard, F. (1914) *Famous War Correspondents*. Boston: Little, Brown and Company.

Buonanno, M. (2012) 'Women war correspondents: Does gender make a difference on the front line?'in *Congreso International de Comunicacion y Genero Sevilla* 5, 6, & 7 de Marzo, pp. 800–816. Seville: Editorial Mad.

Bureau of Investigative Journalism (n.d.) 'Drone warfare'. https://www.thebureauinvestigates.com/projects/drone-war

Burkhardt, J. (2017) 'Combating fake news in the digital age', *Library Technology Reports*, 53 (8): 1–19.

Busch, P. (2012) 'The future of war teporting', *The RUSI Journal*, 157(3), 60–67.

Butler, J. (2009) *Frames of War*. London: Verso.

Byerly, C. (2011) *Global Report on the Status of Women in the New Media*. Washington, DC: International Women's Media Foundation.

Byerly, C. (2013) 'Factors affecting the status of women journalists: A structural analysis', in Byerly, C. (ed.), *The Palgrave International Handbook of Women and Journalism*, pp. 11–26. New York: Palgrave Macmillan.

Cameron, J. (1967) *Points of Departure*. London: Grafton.

Campbell, D. (2004) 'Horrific blindness: Images of death in contemporary media', *Journal for Cultural Research*, 8(1): 55–74.

Campbell, K. (2001) 'Today's war reporting: It's digital, but dangerous', *Christian Science Monitor*, 4 December. https://www.csmonitor.com/2001/1204/p2s2-ussc.html

Campbell, W. (2006) *The Year that Defined American Journalism: 1897 and the Clash of Paradigms*. New York: Routledge.

Carlo, S. and Kamphuis, A. (2014) *Information Security for Journalists*. Commissioned by Centre for Investigative Journalism. Creative Commons Licence (CC BY-NC-SA 4.0).

Carr, D. (2014) 'At front lines: Bearing witness in real time', *The New York Times*, 27 July.

Carroll, J. (2005) 'Letter from Baghdad: What a way to make a living', *American Journalism Review*, February/March, 54–56.

Carruthers, S. (2000) *The Media at War: Communication and Conflict in the Twentieth Century*. Basingstoke: Palgrave.

Carruthers, S. (2011) *The Media at War: Communication and Conflict in the Twentieth Century*, 2nd edition. Basingstoke: Palgrave.

Castells, M. (1996) *The Rise of the Networked Society*. Oxford: Blackwell.

Chambers, D., Steiner, L. and Fleming, C. (2004) *Women and Journalism*. New York: Routledge.

Chekinov, S. G. and Bogdanov, S. A. (2013) The nature and content of a new-generation war, *Military Thought*, 4: 12–23.

Chilcot, J. (2016) *The Report of the Iraq Inquiry: Executive Summary*. London: HSMO.

Chouliaraki, L. (2010) 'Ordinary witnessing in post-television news: Towards a new moral imagination', *Critical Discourse Studies*, 7(3): 305–319.

Chouliaraki, L. (2013) 'Mediating vulnerability: Cosmopolitanism and the public sphere', *Media, Culture & Society*, 35(1): 105–112.

Chouliaraki, L. (2015) 'Digital witnessing in war journalism: The case of post-Arab Spring conflicts', *Popular Communication: The International Journal of Media and Culture*, 13(2): 105–119.

Chozicknov, A. (2012) 'For Syria's rebel movement, Skype is a useful and increasingly dangerous tool', *The New York Times*, 30 November.

Chrisafis, A. (2015) 'Paris shootings survivor sues French media for "putting his life in danger"', *The Guardian*, 19 August.

Clausen, L. (2003) *Global News Culture*. Copenhagen: Copenhagen Business School Press.

Clausewitz, C. 1976 *On War* Guildford: Princeton University Press.

Cockburn, A. (1988) *Corruptions of Empire*. London: Verso.

Cockburn, P. (2010) 'Embedded journalism: A distorted view of war', *Independent*, 23 November.

CoE (2017)

Cogan, K. (2013) 'House of cads: The psycho-sexual ordeal of reporting Washington', *The New Republic*, 23 February. https://newrepublic.com/article/112486/psycho-sexual-ordeal-reporting-washington

Cohen, E. (2010) 'Online journalism as market-driven journalism', *Journal of Broadcasting & Electronic Media*, 46(4): 532–548.

Coker, C. (2009) *War in an Age of Risk*. Cambridge: Polity Press.

Coll, S. (2014) 'The unblinking state: Drone war in Pakistan', *The New Yorker*, 24 November.

Collier, R. (1989) *The Warcos: The War Correspondents' View of World War Two*. London: Weidenfeld and Nicholson.

Colvin, M. (2012) 'Marie Colvin: Our mission is to report these horrors of war with accuracy and without prejudice', *The Guardian*, 22 February.

CPJ (Committee for the Protection of Journalists) (2016a) 'Fresh threats to journalists from Islamic State group'. https://cpj.org/2016/06/fresh-threats-to-journalists-from-islamic-state-gr.php

CPJ (Committee for the Protection of Journalists) (2016b) *Information Security for Journalists*. www.tcij.org/resources/handbooks/infosec

CPJ (Committee for the Protection of Journalists) (2018) 'Journalists killed between 1992 and 2018'. https://cpj.org/data/killed/?status=Killed&motiveConfirmed%5B%5D=Confirmed&type%5B%5D=Journalist&start_year=1992&end_year=2018&group_by=year

Conway, L. (2005) 'Iraq War documentaries fill a press vacuum', *Nieman Reports*, 59(1): 106–108.

Conway, M. (2009) *The Origins of Television News in America: The Visualizers of CBS in the 1940s*. London: Peter Lang.

Cooke, R. (2015) 'Interview: Lynsey Addario, "War journalists are not all addicted to adrenaline: It's a calling"', *The Observer*, 5 April.

Cooper, G. (2011) 'Why were women correspondents the face of coverage in the Libyan Revolution', in Mair, J. and Keeble, R. L. (eds), *Mirage in the Desert: Reporting the Arab Spring*. Bury St Edmunds: Abramis.

Cornish, P. and Dorman, A. (2015) 'Complex security and strategic latency: The UK Strategic Defence and Security Review 2015', *International Affairs*, 91(2): 351–370.

Cottle, S. (1998) 'Ulrich Beck, "risk society" and the media: A catastrophic view?', *European Journal of Communication*, 13(1): 5–32.

Cottle, S. (2006) *Mediatized Conflict: Development in Media and Conflict Studies*. Maidenhead, UK: Open University Press.

Cottle, S. (2013) 'Journalists witnessing disasters: From the calculus of death to the injunction of care', *Journalism Studies*, 14(2): 232–248.

Cottle (2017) 'Communication, human insecurity and the responsibility to protect'. In Robinson, P. ed. *The Routledge Handbook of Media and Security*. pp. 321–333. London: Routledge

Cottle, S. and Nolan, D. (2007) 'Global humanitarianism and the changing aid-media field: Everyone was dying for footage', *Journalism Studies*, 8(6): 862–878.

Cottle, S. and Nolan, D. (2009) 'How the media's codes and rules influence the ways NGOs work', *NiemanLab*, 16 November. www.niemanlab.org/2009/11/simon-cottle-and-david-nolan-how-the-medias-codes-and-rules-influence-the-ways-ngos-work/

Cottle, S. and Rai, M. (2006) 'Between display and deliberation: Analyzing TV news as communicative architecture', *Media, Culture and Society*, 28(2): 163–189.

Cottle, S., Sambrook, R. and Mosdell, N. (2016) *Reporting Dangerously: Journalist Killings, Intimidation and Security*. London: Palgrave Macmillan.

Cousins, M. and Macdonald, K. (2006) *Imagining Reality*. London: Faber & Faber.

Cozens, C. (2003) 'Burridge: War is not "infotainment"', *The Guardian*, 7 April.

Cozma, R. (2010) 'From Murrow to mediocrity?', *Journalism Studies*, 11(5), 667–682.

Craig, I. (2014) 'Back to the future: Trying to stay safe in war zones', *Index on Censorship*, 43 (4): 9–12.

Crane, B. (2014) 'The rise of the stringer: War reporting in the new media landscape', *The American Interest*, 3 May. https://www.the-american-interest.com/2014/05/03/war-reporting-in-the-new-media-landscape/

Crawford, A. (2010) 'Embedded – with the Taliban', in Keeble, R. and Mair, J. (eds), *Afghanistan, War and the Media: Deadlines and Frontlines*, pp. 33–41. Bury St Edmunds, UK: Arima.

Creech, B. (2015) 'Disciplines of truth: The "Arab Spring", American journalistic practice, and the production of public knowledge', *Journalism*, 16(8): 1010–1026.

Creech, B. (2017) 'Bearing the cost to witness: The political economy of risk in contemporary conflict and war reporting', *Media, Culture & Society*. doi:10.1177/0163443717715078

Crossette, B. (1995) 'Iraq sanctions kill children, UN reports', *The New York Times*, 1 December.

Culloty, E. (2014) *Embedded Online: Iraq War Documentaries in the Online Public Sphere*. PhD thesis, Dublin City University.

Curry, C. (2014) 'James Foley among many young close-knit freelance war reporters', *ABC News*, 22 August. abcnews.go.com/james-foley-among- many-young-close-knit-freelance-war –reporters/story?id=25084338

Cushion, S. and Lewis, J. (2010) *The Rise of 24-Hour News Television*. New York: Peter Lang.

Cushion, S., Lewis, J. and Callaghan, R. (2016) 'Data journalism, impartiality and statistical claims', *Journalism Practice*, 11(10) 1198–1215.

Daily Mail (2011) 'No one told her to go there: Now FEMALE pundit lays into Egypt sex attack victim Lara Logan ...', 18 February.

Dannatt, R. (2010) *Leading from the Front*. London: Random House.

Day, E. (2004) 'Why women love journalism', *British Journalism Review*, 15(2): 21–25.

Deacon, D. (2008) *British News Media and the Spanish Civil War: Tomorrow May Be Too Late*. Edinburgh: Edinburgh University Press.

De Burgh, H. (2000) *Investigative Journalism: Context and Practice*. London: Routledge.

de Jomini, Le Baron (1838) *Précis de l'Art de la Guerre: Des Principales Combinaisons de la Straté-gie, de la Grande Tactique et de la Politique Militaire*. Brussels: Meline, Cans et Copagnie.

Delano, A. (2003) 'Women journalists: What's the difference?', *Journalism Studies*, 4(2): 273–286.

De Luca, K. and Peeples, J. (2002) 'From public sphere to public screen: Democracy, activism, and the "Violence" of Seattle', *Critical Studies in Media Communication*, 19(2): 125–151.

Der Derian, J. (2001) *Virtuous War: Mapping the Military–Industrial–Media–Entertainment Complex*. Boulder, CO: Westview.

Desmond, R. (1984) *Tides of War: World News Reporting 1940–1945*. Iowa City, IA: University of Iowa Press.

Deuze, M. (2005) 'What is journalism? Professional identity and ideology of journalists reconsidered', *Journalism*, 6(4): 442–464.

Deuze, M. (2008) 'The changing context of news work: Liquid journalism and monitorial citizenship', *International Journal of Communication*, 2: 848–865.

Di Giovanni, J. (2006) 'When bearing witness overrides a reporter's fear', *Nieman Reports*, 60 (2): 61–63.

Dodson, G. (2010) 'Australian journalism and war: Professional discourse and the legitimation of the 2003 Iraq invasion', *Journalism Studies*, 11(1): 99–114.

Domke, D., Perlmutter, D. and Spratt, M. (2002) "The primes of our times", *Journalism*, 3 (2): 131–159.

Dorman, W. and Farhang, M. (1987) *The US Press and Iran: Foreign Policy and the Journalism of Deference*. Berkeley andLos Angeles: University of California Press.

Doucet, L. (2012) 'Lyse Doucet', in Storm, H. and Williams, H. (eds), *No Woman's Land: On the Frontlines with Female Reporters*. London: International News Safety Institute.

Doucet, L. (2014) 'The women reporters determined to cover World War Two', *BBC News Magazine*, 5 June. www.bbc.co.uk/news/magazine-27677889

Douglas, M. (1992) *Risk and Blame: Essays in Cultural Theory*. London andNew York: Routledge.

Dredge, S. (2014) 'Social media, journalism and wars: Authenticity has replaced authority', *The Guardian*, 5 September.

Duvdevani, S. (2013) 'How I shot the war – ideology and accountability in personal Israeli war documentaries', Studies in Documentary Film, 7(3): 279–294.

ECoHR (European Court of Human Rights) (2018). Fact Sheet-Protection of Journalistic sources. https://www.echr.coe.int/Documents/FS_Journalistic_sources_ENG.pdf

Edney-Browne, A. (2015) 'White women war reporters: Interrogating the 'third gender' category'. https://www.e-ir.info/2015/10/09/white-women-war-reporters-interrogating-the-third-gender-category/

Ehrhart, H. (2017) 'Postmodern warfare and the blurred boundaries between war and peace', *Defense & Security Analysis*, 33(3): 263–275.

Elkins, C. (2005) *Imperial Reckoning: The Untold Story of Britain's Gulag in Kenya*. New York: Henry Holt & Co.

Elliott, A. (2002) 'Beck's sociology of risk: A critical assessment', *Sociology*, 36(2): 293–315.

Elliott, P. (1977) 'Professional ideology and organisational change: The journalist since 1800', in Boyce, G., Curran, J. and Wingate, P. (eds), *Newspaper History: Studies in the Evolution of the British Press*, pp. 172–191. London: Constable.

Elmes, S. (2013) *Hello Again: Nine Decades of Radio Voices*. London: Random House.

Elwood-Akers, V. (1988) *Women War Correspondents in the Vietnam War, 1961–1975*. Metuchen, NJ: Scarecrow Press.

Engelhardt, T. (1994) 'The Gulf War as total television', in Jeffords, S. and Rabinovitz, L. (eds), *Seeing Through the Media: The Persian Gulf War*, pp. 81–96. New Brunswick, NJ: Rutgers University Press.

Erickson, J. (2013) 'Torture: Henri Alleg and the Algerian War', *Iowa Historical Review*, 4(1): 25–41.

Ericson, R., Baranek, P. and Chan, J. (1989) *Negotiating Control: A Study of News Sources*. Milton Keynes: Open University Press.

Ertel, M., Pech, E., Ullsperger, P., Von Dem Knesebeck, O. and Siegrist, J. (2005) 'Adverse psychosocial working conditions and subjective health in freelance media workers', *Work & Stress*, 19(3), 293–299.

Espinoza, N. and Peterson, M. (2012) 'Risk and mid-level moral principles', *Bioethics*, 26(1): 8–14.

Evans, H. (2003) *War Stories: Reporting in the Time of Conflict from Crimea to Iraq*. Boston, MA: Bunker Hill Publishing Inc.

Exoo, C. (2010) *The Pen and the Sword: Press, War and Terror in the 21st Century*. New Delhi: Sage.

Fahmy, S. (2005) 'Photojournalists' and photo editors' attitudes and perceptions: The visual coverage of 9/11 and the Afghan War', *Visual Communication Quarterly*, 12(3–4), 146–163.

Fahmy, S. and Johnson, T. (2005) 'How we performed: Embedded journalists' attitudes and perceptions towards covering the Iraq War', *Journalism & Mass Communication Quarterly*, 82(2): 301–317.

Fahmy, S. and Johnson, T. J. (2007a) 'Embedded versus unilateral perspectives on Iraq War', *Newspaper Research Journal*, 28(3): 98–114.

Fahmy, S. and Johnson, T. J. (2007b) 'Show the truth and let the audience decide: A web-based survey showing support for use of graphic imagery among viewers of Al-Jazeera', *Journal of Broadcasting & Electronic Media*, 51(2): 245–264.

Fahmy, S. and Kim, D. (2008) 'Picturing the Iraq War: Constructing the image of war in the British and US Press', *International Communication Gazette*, 70(6): 443–462.

Fahmy, S., Cho, S., Wanta, W. and Song, Y. (2006) 'Visual agenda-setting after 9/11: Individuals' emotions, image recall, and concern with terrorism', *Visual Communication Quarterly*, 13(1), 4–15.

Fainberg, M. (2017) *Curtain of Lies: The Battle over Truth in Stalinist Eastern Europe*. Oxford: Oxford University Press.

Fairclough, N. (2006) *Language and Globalisation*. London: Routledge.

Fallon, M. (2017) 'Armed forces: Written question – 65279', *UK Parliament*, 1 March. www.parliament.uk/business/publications/written-questions-answers-statements/writtenquestion/Commons/2017-02-23/65279

Fang, B. (2012) 'Bay Fang', in Storm, H. and Williams, H. (eds), *No Woman's Land: On the Frontlines with Female Reporters*, pp. 33–35. London: International News Safety Institute.

Fardon, R. (2013) 'Introduction: How cultures precipitate risk and resolution', in Fardon, R. (ed.), *Mary Douglas Cultures and Crises: Understanding Risk and Resolution*, pp. 1–8. London: Sage.

Farwell, J. P. (2014) 'The media strategy of ISIS', *Survival*, 56(6): 49–55.

Feinstein, A. (2006) *Journalists Under Fire: The Psychological Hazards of Covering War*. Baltimore: John Hopkins University Press.

Feinstein, A. (2013) 'Mexican journalists and journalists covering war: A comparison of psychological wellbeing', *Journal of Aggression, Conflict and Peace Research*, 5(2): 77–85.

Feinstein, A. and Sinyor, M. (2009) 'Women war correspondents: They are so different in so many ways', *Nieman Reports*, 63(4): 24–25.

Feinstein, A., Owen, J. and Blair, N. (2002) 'A hazardous profession: War, journalism and psychopathology', *American Journal of Psychiatry*, 159(9): 1570–1575.

Feinstein, A., Audet, B. and Waknine, E. (2014) 'Witnessing images of extreme violence: A psychological study of journalists in the newsroom', *Journal of the Royal Society of Medicine Open*, 5(8): 1–7.

Fenton, N. (2009) 'Has the Internet changed how NGOs work with established media? Not Enough', *NiemanLab*, 23 November. www.niemanlab.org/2009/11/natalie-fenton-has-the-internet-changed-how-ngos-work-with-established-media-not-enough/

Filkins, D. (2013) 'Photographers' oral history of the Iraq War', *The New York Times*, 14 March.

Finkelstein, D. (2010) 'Radio journalism', *Journalism Practice*, 4(1): 114–118.

Fisher, A. (2015) 'Swarmcast: How jihadist networks maintain a persistent online presence', *Perspectives on Terrorism*, 9(3). http://terrorismanalysts.com/pt/index.php/pot/article/view/426/html

Fisk, R. (2002) 'It is not my job to provide the evidence for a war crimes tribunal', *Independent*, 23 August.

Fisk, R. (2008) *The Age of the Warrior*. London: HarperCollins.

Fisk, R. (2012) 'Robert Fisk: The heroic myth and the uncomfortable truth of war reporting', *Independent*, 3 March.

Fitzpatrick, A. (2012) 'Social media becoming online battlefield in Syria', *Mashable UK*, 9 August. https://mashable.com/2012/08/09/social-media-syria/#1Ta.WBcL35q1

Forbes, A. (1895) *Memories of War and Peace*. New York: Charles Scribner's Sons.

Franks, S. (2013) *Women and Journalism*. London: I. B. Taurus.

Freedom Forum (1998) *Journalists in Danger: Recent Russian Wars*. Freedom Forum.

Freedom House (1998) 'Algeria: Freedom in the World 1998'. https://freedomhouse.org/report/freedom-world/1998/algeria

Friis, S. (2015) '"Beyond anything we have ever seen": Beheading videos and the visibility of violence in the war against ISIS', *International Affairs*, 91(4): 725–747.

Froneman, J. and Swanepoel, T. (2004) 'Embedded journalism – more than a conflict reporting issue', *Communicatio: South African Journal of Communication Theory and Research*, 30(2): 24–35.

Frosh, P. and Pinchevski, A. (2015) 'Media witnessing and the ripeness of time', *Cultural Studies*, 28(4): 594–610.

Fryer-Biggs, Z. (2014) 'Are the media feeding the ISIS monster?', *Newsweek*, 14 April. http://europe.newsweek.com/feeding-isis-monster-321982?rm=eu

Fuchs, C. (2003) 'The war show, it's clear, is all about winning: "Truth on the battlefield"', *The War Show*, 63, April. https://bad.eserver.org/issues/2003/63/fuchs

Fulton, R. (2007) 'Women writing war', *English Pen*, 17 October. www.englishpen.org/events/women-writing-war/

Furedi, F. (1997) *Culture of Fear: Risk Taking and the Morality of Low Expectation*. London: Cassell.

Furneaux, R. (1944) *The First War Correspondent: William Howard Russell of The Times*. London: Cassell and Company Ltd.

Gandy, O. H. (1982) *Beyond Agenda Setting: Information Subsidies and Public Policy*. Norwood, NJ: Ablex.

Gervais, T. (2010) 'Witness to war: The uses of photography in the illustrated press, 1855–1904', *Journal of Visual Culture*, 9(3): 370–384.

Gibbons-Neff, T. (2016) 'How Obama's Afghanistan plan is forcing the Army to replace soldiers with contractors', *The Washington Post*, 1 June.

Gibbs, P. (1923) *Adventures in Journalism*. London: William Heinemann Ltd.

Gibson, O. (2006) 'BBC's coverage of Israeli-Palestinian conflict "misleading"', *The Guardian*, 3 May.

Giddens, A. (1991) *Modernity and Self-identity: Self and Society in the Late Modern Age*. Stanford, CA: Stanford University Press.

Gilbertson, A. (2011) "The consequences of war: A photographer's perspective", *PBS*, 6 June. http://www.pbs.org/wnet/need-to-know/culture/the-consequences-of-war-a-pho tographers-perspective/9675/

Gillmor, D. (2003) 'Moving toward participatory journalism', *Nieman Reports*, 57(3): 79–80.

Glassner, B. (2009) *Culture of Fear: Why Americans Are Afraid of the Wrong Things*, revised edition. New York: Basic Books.

Gollmitzer, M. (2014) 'Precariously employed watchdogs?', *Journalism Practice*, 8(6): 826–841.

Gow, J. and Michalski, M. (2008) *War, Image and Legitimacy: Viewing Contemporary Conflict*. London andNew York: Routledge.

Greenslade, R. (2010) 'Colvin: Why we journalists must continue going to war despite the dangers', *The Guardian*, 12 November.

Greenwood, K. and Jenkins, J. (2015) 'Visual framing of the Syrian conflict in news and public affairs magazines', *Journalism Studies*, 16(2): 207–227.

Gregory, D. (2011) 'From a view to a kill: Drones and late modern war', *Theory, Culture & Society*, 28(7–8): 188–215.

Grey, S. (2009) 'A lack of cover', *The Guardian*, 15 June.

Griffin, M. (2004) 'Picturing America's "war on terrorism" in Afghanistan and Iraq', *Journalism*, 5(4): 380–397.

Griffin, M. (2010) 'Media images of war', *Media, War & Conflict*, 3(1): 7–41.

Guerin, F. and Hallas, R. (2007) *The Image and the Witness: Trauma, Memory and Visual Culture*. New York: Columbia University Press.

Gutman, R. (2003) 'Consequences occur when reporters testify', *Nieman Reports*, 57(1): 74–77.

Gynnild, A. (2005) 'Winner takes it all: Freelance journalism on the global communication market', *Nordicom Review*, 26(1): 111–120.

Hagan, J. (2014) 'Benghazi and the Bombshell', *New York* magazine, 4 May.

Hajjar, R. M. (2014) 'Emergent postmodern US military culture', *Armed Forces and Society* 40(1): 118–145.

Hall, S., Critcher, C., Jefferson, T. and Clarke, J. (1979) *Policing the Crisis*. London: Constable.

Hallin, D. (1986) *Vietnam: The Uncensored War*. Berkeley, CA: University of California Press.

Hallin, D. (1991) 'Living room wars: Vietnam vs. Desert Storm', *Media & Values*, www.medialit.org/reading-room/living-room-wars-vietnam-vs-desert-storm

Hamilton, J. H. and Jenner, E. (2004) 'Redefining foreign correspondence', *Journalism*, 5(3): 301–321.

Hammond, P. (2000) 'Reporting "humanitarian" warfare: Propaganda, moralism and NATO's Kosovo War', *Journalism Studies*, 1(3): 365–386.

Hammond, P. (2002) 'Moral combat: Advocacy journalists and the new humanitarianism', in Chandler, D. (ed.), *Rethinking Human Rights: Critical Approaches to International Politics*, pp. 176–195. London: Palgrave Macmillan.

Hanitzsch, T. (2007) 'Deconstructing journalism culture: Toward a universal theory', *Communication Theory*, 17(4), 367–385.

Hankinson, A. (1982) *Man of Wars: William Howard Russell of The Times*. London: Heinnemann.

Hannigan, R. (2014) 'The web is a terrorist's command-and-control network of choice', *Financial Times*, 3 November. http://on.ft.com/1qmo2QJ

Hanusch, F. (2008) 'Valuing those close to us', *Journalism Studies*, 9(3): 341–356.

Hanusch, F. (2012) 'The visibility of disaster deaths in news images: A comparison of newspapers from 15 countries', *International Communication Gazette*, 74(7): 655–672.

Harding Davis, R. (1910) *Moments in Hell: Notes of a War Correspondent*. New York: Charles Scribner's Sons.

Harries, G. and Wahl-Jorgensen, K. (2007) 'The culture of arts journalists: Elitists, saviors or manic depressives?', *Journalism*, 8(6): 619–639.

Harriman, E. (1987) *Hack*. London: Zed Press.

Harris, J., Modsell, N. and Griffiths, J. (2016) 'Gender, risk and journalism', *Journalism Practice*, 10(7): 902–916.

Hastings, M. (2000) *Going to the Wars*. London: Pan Books.

Hayward, D. (2010) 'Why embedded reporting is a necessary evil', in Keeble, R. and Mair, J. (eds), *Afghanistan, War and the Media: Deadlines and Frontlines*, pp. 49–55. Bury St Edmunds, UK: Arima.

Hegseth, P. (2017) 'Secrecy shrouds US development of Afghan security forces', *FDD's Long War Journal*, 4 November. https://www.longwarjournal.org/archives/2017/11/secrecy-shrouds-us-development-of-afghan-security-forces.php

Henderson, K. (1994) 'War reporters debate Gulf War press standards', *Christian Science Monitor*, 11 March. https://www.csmonitor.com/1994/0311/11161.html

Heng, Y. (2006a) 'The "transformation of war" debate: Through the looking glass of Ulrich Beck's world risk society', *International Relations*, 20(1): 69–91.

Heng, Y. (2006b) *War as Risk Management: Strategy and Conflict in the Age of Globalised Risks*. London: Routledge.

Hennigan, W. J. (2017) 'Trump administration stops disclosing troop deployments in Iraq and Syria', *Los Angeles Times*, 30 March.

Henrichsen, J. R., Betz, M. and Lisosky, J. M. (2015) *Building Digital Safety for Journalism*. A report prepared for UNESCO's Division for Freedom of Expression and Media Development. Paris: UNESCO.

Henwood, K., Pidgeon, N., Sarre, S., Simmons, P. and Smith, N. (2008) 'Risk, framing and everyday life: Epistemological and methodological reflections from three socio-cultural projects', *Health Risk and Society*, 10(5), 421–438.

Herman, E. and Chomsky, N. (1988) *The Political Economy of the Mass Media*. New York: Parthenon.

Hermida, A. (2009) 'The blogging BBC', *Journalism Practice*, 3(3): 268–284.

Hermida, A. and Thurman, N. (2008) 'A clash of cultures', *Journalism Practice*, 2(3): 343–356.

Hilsum, L. (2013) *War and Journalists: Why Do We Go?* Speech, St Bride's Church, Fleet Street, 12 November.

Himelboim, I. and Limor, Y. (2008) 'Media perception of freedom of the press: A comparative international analysis of 242 codes of ethics', *Journalism: Theory, Practice and Criticism*, 9(4): 235–265.

Hirashiki, T. (2017) *On the Frontlines of the Television War*. Oxford: Casemate Publishers.

HM Government (2003) 'Written answers to questions', 27 March. https://www.publications.parliament.uk/pa/cm200203/cmhansrd/vo030327/text/30327w01.htm

HM Government (2010) *Securing Britain in an Age of Uncertainty: The Strategic Defence and Security Review*. Cm 7948. London: The Stationery Office.

HM Government (2015) *National Security Strategy and Strategic Defence and Security Review 2015*. Cm 9161. London: The Stationery Office.

Hobson, J. (1901) *The Psychology of Jingoism*. London: Grant Richards.

Hoffmann, J. (n.d.) 'On their own: Female correspondents in Vietnam'. http://ww2.odu.edu/ao/instadv/quest/femalecorrespondents.html (accessed 18 February, 2017).

Høiby, M. (2016) 'Sexual violence against journalists in conflict zones: Gendered practices and cultures in the newsroom', in von de Lippe, B. and Ottosen, R. (eds), *Gendering War and Peace Reporting: Some Insights – Some Missing Links*, pp. 75–87. Gothemburg: Nordicom.

Hood, J. (2011) *War Correspondent: Reporting Under Fire Since 1850*. London: Anova.

Hoskins, A. and O'Loughlin, B. (2007) *Television and Terror: Conflicting Times and the Crisis of News Discourse*. London: Palgrave Macmillan.

Hoskins, A. and O'Loughlin, B. (2009) 'Media and the myth of radicalization', *Media, War & Conflict*, 2(2): 107–110.

Hoskins, A. and O'Loughlin, B. (2015) 'Arrested war: The third phase of mediatization', *Information, Communication & Society*, 18(11): 1320–1338.

Hoyer, S. and Pottker, H. (2005) *Diffusion of the News Paradigm 1850–2000*. Gothemburg: Nordicom.

Hume, M. (1997) *Whose War Is It Anyway? The Dangers of the Journalism of Attachment*. London: Informinc.

Huxford, G. (2016) 'The Korean War never happened: Forgetting a conflict in British society and culture', *Twentieth Century British History*, 27(2): 195–219.

Huxford, J. (2004) 'Surveillance, witnessing and spectatorship: The news and the "war of images"', in *Proceedings of the Media Ecology Association*, Volume 5. http://media-ecology.org/publications/MEA_proceedings/v5/Huxford05.pdf

Hyndman, J. (2007) 'Feminist geopolitics revisisted: Body counts in Iraq', *The Professional Geographer*, 59(1): 35–46.

Iasiello, E. J. (2017) 'Russia's improved information operations: From Georgia to Crimea', *Parameters*, 47(2): 51–63.

Ibrahim, F., Pawanteh, L., Peng, K. C., Kartini, F., Basri, H., Redzuan, B., Hassan, A., Amizah, W. and Mahmud, W. (2011) 'Journalists and news sources: Implications of professionalism in war reporting', *The Innovation Journal: The Public Sector Innovation Journal*, 16 (3): 1–12.

Independent Press Standards Organisation (n.d.) 'Editors' code of practice'. https://www.ipso.co.uk/editors-code-of-practice/

Ingram, H. (2014) 'Three traits of the Islamic State's information warfare', *The RUSI Journal*, 159(6): 4–11.

Ingram, H. (2015) 'The strategic logic of Islamic State information operations', *Australian Journal of International Affairs*, 69(6): 729–752.

INSI (International News Safety Institute) (2005) *Women Reporting War*. London: International News Safety Institute.

ICC (International Criminal Court) (2013) 'Rules of procedure and evidence', 2nd edition. https://www.icc-cpi.int/iccdocs/pids/legal-texts/rulesprocedureevidenceeng.pdf

ICTY (International Criminal Tribunal for the former Yugoslavia) (2002) 'The Prosecutor v. Radoslav Brdjanin & Momir Talic "Randal Case": Appeals Chamber defines a legal test for the issuance of subpoenas for war correspondents to testify at the tribunal', 11 December. www.icty.org/en/press/prosecutor-v-radoslav-brdjanin-momir-talic

IFJ (International Federation of Journalists) (2003) *Live News – A Survival Guide for Journalists*. Brussels: IFJ.

IFJ (International Federation of Journalists) (2017a) 'IFJ survey – one in two women journalists suffer gender-based violence at work'. www.ifj.org/nc/news-single-view/backpid/240/article/ifj-survey-one-in-two-women-journalists-suffer-gender-based-violence-at-work/

IFJ (International Federation of Journalists) (2017b) 'Safety – journalists and media staff killed list 2017'. ifj-safety.org/en/killings/killed

IFJ (International Federation of Journalists) and Statewatch (2005) *Journalism, Civil Liberties and the War on Terrorism*. Brussels: IFJ.

Jackson, J. (2017) 'BBC sets up team to debunk fake news', *The Guardian*, 12 January.

Janis, I. (1982) *Groupthink: Psychological Studies of Policy Decisions and Fiascoes*, 2nd edition. Boston, MA: Houghton Mifflin.

Jaramillo, D. (2009) *Ugly War, Pretty Package: How CNN and Fox News Made the Invasion of Iraq High Concept*. Bloomington, IN: Indiana University Press.

Jenkins, C. (1999) 'Africa eyewitness: Reporting the war in the Horn', *BBC News*, 1 March. http://news.bbc.co.uk/1/hi/world/africa/288239.stm

Johns, R. and Davies, G. (2017) 'Civilian casualties and public support for military action: Experimental evidence', *Journal of Conflict Resolution*, 1–31. https://doi.org/10.1177/0022002717729733

Johnson, T. and Fahmy, S. (2010) 'When blood becomes cheaper than a bottle of water: How viewers of Al-Jazeera's English-language website judge graphic images of conflict', *Media, War & Conflict*, 3(1): 43–66.

Johnson, T. and Kaye, B. (2010) 'Believing the blogs of war? How blog users compare on credibility and characteristics in 2003 and 2007', *Media, War & Conflict*, 3(3): 315–333.

Johnston, L. (2017) 'Looking after Ibrahim', *Journalism Practice*, 11(2–3), 195–212.

Joint Chiefs of Staff (2006) *JP 3–13, Joint Doctrine for Information Operations*. Washington, DC: Department of Defense.

Kaempf, S. (2017) 'UQxMED1024. Iraq 2003: Embedded Journalism', *YouTube*. www.youtube.com/watch?v=pvuNHijniQA&t=286s (accessed 10 October, 2017).

Kalcsics, M. (2011) *A Reporting Disaster? The Interdependence of Media and Aid Agencies in a Competitive Compassion Market*. Oxford: Reuters Institute for the Study of Journalism, University of Oxford.

Kaldor, M. (2003) *Global Civil Society: An Answer to War*. Cambridge: Polity Press.

Kaldor, M. (2006) *New and Old Wars: Organised Violence in a Global Age*. Cambridge: Polity Press.

Kalogeropoulos, A. and Nielsen, R. (2017) 'Investing in online video news', *Journalism Studies*. doi:10.1080/1461670X.2017.1331709 1–10

Kaye, B. and Johnson, T. (2004) 'Weblogs as a source of information about the 2003 Iraq War', in Berenger, R. (ed.), *Global Media Go to War: Role of News and Entertainment During the 2003 Iraq War*, pp. 291–301. Spokane, WA: Marquette Books.

Keane, F. (2005) *All of These People: A Memoir*. London: Harper Perennial.

Keeble, R. and Mair, J. (eds) (2010) *Afghanistan, War and the Media: Deadlines and Frontlines*. Bury St Edmunds: Arima.

Keighron, P. (2003) *Media minefield*. Broadcast 4 April.

Keith, S., Schwalbe, C. and Silcock, B. (2006) 'Images in ethics codes in an era of violence and tragedy', *Journal of Mass Media Ethics*, 21(4): 245–264.

Kellner, D. (2000) 'From Vietnam to the Gulf: Postmodern wars?', in Bibby, M. (ed.), *The Vietnam War and Postmodernity*, pp. 199–236. Boston, MA: University of Massachusetts Press.

Kellner, D. (2008) 'War correspondents, the military, and propaganda: Some critical reflections', *International Journal of Communication*, 2: 297–330.

Kelty, R. and Segal, D. (2007) 'The civilianization of the U.S. military: Army and navy case studies of the effects of civilian integration on military personnel', in Jäger, T. and Kümmel, G. (eds), *Private Military and Security Companies: Chances, Problems, Pitfalls and Prospects*, pp. 213–239. Wiesbaden: VS Verlag für Sozialwissenschaften.

Kennedy, L. (2016) *Afterimages: Photography and U.S. Foreign Policy*. Chicago: University of Chicago Press.

Kent, K. (2013) 'Propaganda, public opinion, and the second South African Boer war', *Inquiries Journal*, 5(10). www.inquiriesjournal.com/a?id=781

King, C. and Lester, P. (2005) 'Photographic coverage during the Persian Gulf and Iraqi wars in three US newspapers', *Journalism and Mass Communication Quarterly*, 82(3): 623–637.

Kinnard, C. and Murphy, S. (2005) 'Characteristics of war coverage by female correspondents', in Seib, P. (ed.), *Media and Conflict in the Twenty-First Century*, pp. 127–140. New York: Palgrave Macmillan.

Kitzinger, J. (1999) 'Researching risk and the media', *Health, Risk & Society*, 1(1): 55–69.

Kitzinger, J. and Reilly, J. (1997) "The rise and fall of risk reporting: Media coverage of human genetics research, "false memory syndrome" and "mad cow disease"', *The European Journal of Communication*, 12(3): 319–350.

Kleinman, A. and Kleinman, J. (1996) 'The appeal of experience; the dismay of images: Cultural appropriations of suffering in our times', *Daedalus*, 125(1): 1–23.

Knightley, P. (1983) Remarks to conference. Vietnam Reconsidered: Lessons of a War, University of Southern California, 6–9 February.

Knightley, P. (1991) 'Here is the patriotically censored news', *Index on Censorship*, 4(5): 4–5.

Knightley, P. (2001) 'The war on journalism', *The Guardian*, 26 November.

Knightley, P. (2003a) *The First Casualty: The War Correspondent as Hero, Propagandist, and Myth-Maker from the Crimea to Iraq*. London: Andre Deutsch.

Knightley, P. (2003b) 'Turning the tanks on the reporters', *The Guardian*, 15 June.

Knightley, P. (2012) 'When is a terror threat not a terror threat? Let's ask a man called Felix … All intelligence services rely on convincing the public there is a monster at large waiting to grab them', *Independent*, 11 May.

Knowles, E. and Watson, A. (2017) *All Quiet on the ISIS Front? British Secret Warfare in an Information Age*. London: Remote Control.

Korte, B. (2009) *Represented Reporters: Images of War Correspondents in Memoirs and Fiction*. London: Transaction Publishing.

Kraidy, M. (2017a) 'The projectilic image: Islamic State's digital visual warfare and global networked affect', *Media, Culture & Society*, 39(8).

Kraidy, M. (2017b) 'This is why the Islamic State shocks the world with its graphically violent imagery', *The Washington Post*, 9 February.

Kramp, L. and Weichert, S. (2014) 'Covering the world in despair: A survey of German crisis reporters', *Journal of War & Culture Studies*, 7(1): 18–35.

Krause, C. (2011) 'Reporting and the transformations of the journalistic field: US news media, 1890–2000', *Media, Culture & Society*, 33(1) 89–104.

Kreutz, J. (2010) 'How and when armed conflicts end: Introducing the UCDP Conflict Termination Dataset', *Journal of Peace Research*, 47(2): 243–250.

Kuby, E. (2012) 'A war of words over an image of war: The Fox Movietone scandal and the portrayal of French violence in Algeria, 1955–1956', *French Politics, Culture & Society*, 30 (1): 46–65.

Kuhn, M. (2005) 'Interactivity and Prioritizing the Human: A code of blogging ethics'. Paper presented to the Media Ethics Division of the Association for Education in Journalism and Mass Communication, San Antonio, Texas, 10–13 August.

Kumar, D. (2006) 'Media, war, and propaganda: Strategies of information management during the 2003 Iraq War', *Communication and Critical/Cultural Studies*, 3(1): 48–69.

Kuntsman, A. and Stein, R. (2011) 'Digital suspicion, politics, and the Middle East', *Critical Inquiry*. https://criticalinquiry.uchicago.edu/digital_suspicion_politics_and_the_middle_east/

Kurlansky, M. (2002) *A Chosen Few: The Resurrection of European Jewry*. New York: Ballantine Books.

Kuypers, J. and Cooper, S. (2005) 'A comparative framing analysis of embedded and behind-the-lines reporting of the 2003 Iraq War', *Qualitative Research Reports in Communication*, 6(1): 1–10.

Kydd, A. and Walter, B. (2006) 'The strategies of terrorism', *International Security*, 31(1): 49–80.

Lachover, E. (2005) 'The gendered and sexualized relationship between Israeli women journalists and their male news sources'. *Journalism*, 6(3): 291–311.

Lamm, M. (1969) *The Jewish Way in Death and Mourning*. New York: J. David.

Lanoszka, A. (2016) 'Russian hybrid warfare and extended deterrence in eastern Europe', *International Affairs*, 92(1): 175–195.

Lanson, J. (2003) 'War isn't pretty, nor is news of it', *Christian Science Monitor*, 25 March. https://www.csmonitor.com/2003/0325/p09s02-coop.html

Lash, S. (2000) 'Risk culture', in Adam, B., Beck, U. and Van Loon, J. (eds), *The Risk Society and Beyond: Critical Issues for Social Theory*, pp. 47–62. London: Sage.

Lawson, A., O'Carroll, L., Tryhorn, C. and Deans, J. (2003) 'Claims and counter claims made during the media war over Iraq', *The Guardian*, 11 April.

Leahy, P. (2011) *Hungry Beast*, ABC Television, 23 March.

Lederer, E. (2001) 'From telex to satellite', *Media Studies Journal*, Summer, 16–19.

Lee, D. (2015) 'The daunting challenge of reporting on cyberwar', *BBC News*, 19 January. www.bbc.co.uk/news/technology-30813585

Leigh, K. (2013) 'One on one: Janine Di Giovanni', *Syria Deeply*, 23 March. www.syriadeeply.org/articles/2013/03/2300/one-janine-di-giovanni/

Lenhart, A. and Fox, S. (2006) *Bloggers: A Portrait of the Internet's New Storytellers*, 19 July. Washington, DC: Pew Internet & American Life Project. www.pewinternet.org/pdfs/PIP%20Bloggers%20Report%20July%2019%202006.pdf

Leonard, T. (2003) 'Kate Adie: A hard act to follow into the war zone', *The Telegraph*, 31 January.

Lewis, J. (2003) '"Daddy wouldn't buy me a Mau Mau": The British popular press and the demoralisation of empire', in Odhiambo, E. and Lonsdale, J. (eds), *Mau Mau and Nationhood*, pp. 227–250. Oxford: James Currey.

Lewis, S. (2012) 'The tension between professional control and open participation', *Information, Communication & Society*, 15(6): 836–866.

Lewis, J., Cushion, S. and Thomas, J. (2005) 'Immediacy, convenience or engagement? An analysis of 24-hour news channels in the UK', *Journalism Studies*, 6(4): 461–478.

Lewis, J., Brookes, R., Mosdell, N. and Threadgold, T. (2006) *Shoot First and Ask Questions Later: Media Coverage of the 2003 Iraq War*. New York: Peter Lang.

Liasi, T. (2013) *Baptism of Fire: A Freelance Photographer's Tale of War Reporting by Award Winning Photographer* [e-book].

Licon, A. G. (2012) 'Adriana Gomez Licon', in Storm, H. and Williams, H. (eds), *No Woman's Land: On the Frontlines with Female Reporters*. London: International News Safety Institute.

Liebes, T. and Kampf, Z. (2009) 'Performance journalism: The case of the media's coverage of war and terror', *The Communication Review*, 12(3): 239–249.

Livingston, S. (1997) *Clarifying the CNN Effect: An Examination of Media Effects According to Type of Military Intervention*, Research Paper R-18. Cambridge, MA: Joan Shorenstein Center for Press, Politics and Public Policy.

Livingston, S. and Van Belle, D. (2005) 'The effects of satellite technology on newsgathering from remote locations', *Political Communication*, 22(1): 45–62.

Lloyd, J. (2004) 'Martin Bell', *Prospect*, 20 February. https://www.prospectmagazine.co.uk/magazine/martinbell

Loo, E. (2006) 'Keeping emotions intact in war reporting: Shahanaaz Habib', *Asia PacificMedia Educator*, 17, 102–107.

Loyd, A. (2015) *My War Gone By, I Miss It So*, 2nd edition. London: September Publishing.

Loyn, D. (2013) 'Duty of care', in *Newsgathering Safety and the Welfare of Freelancers: A White Paper by the Frontline Club*, pp. 4–6. London: Frontline Club.

Luostarinen, H. (1992) 'Source strategies and the Gulf War', *Nordicom Review*, 2: 91–99.

Lupton, D. (1999) *Risk*. London: Routledge.

Lupton, D. and Tulloch, J. (2002) '"Life would be pretty dull without risk": Voluntary risk-taking and its pleasures', *Health, Risk & Society*, 4(2): 113–124.

Lynch, M., Freelon, D. and Aday, S. (2014) *Syria's socially mediated civil war*. Peaceworks, Number 91. Washington, DC: United States Institute of Peace.

Lyng, S. (1990) 'Edgework: A social psychological analysis of voluntary risk taking', *American Journal of Sociology*, 95(4): 851–886.

Lyng, S. (2005) *Edgework: The Sociology of Risk Taking*. London: Routledge.

Macintyre, D. (2003) 'UK forces discover macabre mortuary', *Independent on Sunday*, 6 April.

Mackey, R. (2010) 'Video from embed with the Taliban', *The New York Times*, 10 August.

Maenpaa, J. (2014) 'Rethinking photojournalism: The changing work practices and professionalism of photojournalists in the digital age', *Nordicom Review*, 35(2): 91–104.

Magee, H. (2014) *The Aid Industry – What Journalists Really Think*. London: International Broadcasting Trust.

Maltby, S. (2013) *Military Media Management: Negotiating the 'Front' Line in Mediatized War*. London: Routledge.

Maniati, M. (2013) 'Safety training for war reporters: Hope for the best, prepare for the worst', *Safety Management*, 18 December.

Manrique, P., Cao, Z., Gabriel, A., Horgan, J., Gill, P., Qi, H., Restrepo, E., Johnson, D., Wuchty, S., Song, C. and Johnson, N. (2016) 'Women's connectivity in extreme networks', *Science Advances*, 2(6): e1501742.

Mari, W. (2017) 'Technology in the newsroom', *Journalism Studies*, 19(9): 1366–1389.

Markham, T. (2012) 'The uses and functions of ageing celebrity war reporters', *Celebrity Studies*, 3(2): 127–137.

Marsh, K. (2010) 'Afghanistan: Truth and the unexamined war', in Keeble, R. and Mair, J. (eds), *Afghanistan, War and the Media: Deadlines and Frontlines*, pp. 67–84. Bury St Edmunds: Arima.

Marthoz, J. P. (2016) 'Giving up on the graft and the grind', *Index on Censorship*, 45(2): 23–28.

Martinson, J. (2015) 'Charlie Hebdo: A week of horror when social media came into its own'. *The Guardian*, 11 January.

Massey, B. and Elmore, C. (2011) 'Happier working for themselves?', *Journalism Practice*, 5 (6): 672–686.

Matheson, D. and Allan, S. (2009) *Digital War Reporting*. Cambridge: Polity.

Mathews, J. (1957) *Reporting the Wars*. Minnesota: Minnesota University Press.

Mathisen, B. R. (2017) 'Entrepreneurs and idealists', *Journalism Practice*, 11(7): 909–924.

Matloff, J. (2007) 'Foreign correspondents and sexual abuse', *Columbia Journalism Review*. http://judithmatloff.com/correspondentsandsexualabuse.pdf

Matusitz, J. and Breen, G. (2007) 'Unethical consequences of pack journalism', *Global Media Journal*, 6(11), 54–67.

McAfee, A. (2011) 'Women on the front line', *The Guardian*, 16 April.

McCamish, T. (2016) *Our Man Elsewhere: In Search of Alan Moorehead*. Carlton, Australia: Black Inc.

McCollough, K., Crowell, J. K. and Napoli, P. M. (2017) 'Portrait of the online local news audience', *Digital Journalism*, 5(1), 100–118.

McFate, S. (2016) 'America's addiction to mercenaries', *The Atlantic*, 12 August. https://www.theatlantic.com/international/archive/2016/08/iraq-afghanistan-contractor-pentagon-obama/495731/

McLaughlin, G. (2002) *The War Correspondent*. London: Pluto Press.

McLaughlin, G. (2016) *The War Correspondent*, 2nd edition. London: Pluto Press.

McLoughlin, K. (2007) *Martha Gellhorn: The War Writer in the Field and in the Text*. Manchester: Manchester University Press.

McMaster, H. R. (2014) 'Photography at war', *Survival: Global Politics and Strategy*, 56(2): 187–198.

McNair, B. (2006) *Cultural Chaos: Journalism News and Power in a Globalised World*. London: Routledge.

Mejias, U. and Vokuev, N. (2017) 'Disinformation and the media: The case of Russia and Ukraine', *Media, Culture & Society*, 39(7): 1027–1042.

Melki, J. (2009) 'Journalism and media studies in Lebanon', *Journalism Studies*, 10(5): 672–690.

Melki, J. and Mallat, S. (2016) 'Block her entry, keep her down and push her out', *Journalism Studies*, 17(1): 57–79.

Mellor, N. (2012a) '"My eyes were there": A comparative analysis of war reporters' testimonies', *Journal of War and Culture Studies*, 5(2): 157–171.

Mellor, N. (2012b) 'The culture of witnessing: War correspondents rewriting the history of the Iraq War', *Language and Intercultural Communication*, 12(2): 103–117.

Mercer, D., Mungham, G. and Williams, K. (1987) *The Fog of War: Media, Military Relations on the Battlefield*. London: Heinneman.

Meyer, C., Sangar, E. and Michaels, E. (2018) 'How do non-governmental organizations influence media coverage of conflict? The case of the Syrian conflict, 2011–2014', *Media, War & Conflict*, 11(1): 149–171.

Miles, H. (2006) 'Arab women journalists take their place in front line of war reporting', *The Telegraph*, 12 August.

Miller, D. (2003) 'Embed with the military', *Scoop Independent News*, 12 April. www.scoop.co.nz/stories/HL0304/S00126.htm

Miller, D. (2004a) 'Information dominance: The philosophy of total propaganda control', in Kamalipour, Y. and Snow, N. (eds), *War, Media and Propaganda: A Global Perspective*, pp. 7–16. Lanham: Rowman and Littlefield. [Also see www.coldtype.net/Assets.04/Essays.04/Miller.pdf]

Miller, D. (2004b) *Tell Me Lies: Propaganda and Media Distortion in the Attack on Iraq*. London: Pluto Press.

Miller, D. and Dinan, W. (2008) *A Century of Spin: How Public Relations Became the Cutting Edge of Corporate Power*. London: Pluto Press.

Milmo, D. (2004) 'Reuters expansion sees 100 jobs cut', *The Guardian*, 10 December.

Milton, D. (2016) *Communication Breakdown: Unraveling the Islamic State's Media Efforts*. West Point, NY: Combatting Terrorism Center.

Ministry of Defence (2013) *The Green Book*, Version 8. London: Ministry of Defence.

Mitchell, G. (2004) 'Shoot the messenger', *Editor and Publisher*, 22 November. www.editorandpublisher.com/news/shoot-the-messenger/

Moorcraft, P. (2016) *Dying for the Truth: A Concise History of Frontline War Reporting*. Barnsley, UK: Pen and Sword.

Moorehead, A. (2000) *African Trilogy*. London: Cassell.

Moorehead, C. (2004) *Martha Gellhorn: A Life*. London: Vintage.

Morgan, P. (2005) *The Insider: The Private Diaries of a Scandalous Decade*. London: Ebury Press.

Morris, E. (2004) 'Not every picture tells a story', *The New York Times*, 20 November.

Morrison, D. and Tumber, H. (1988) *Journalists at War: The Dynamics of News Reporting During the Falklands Conflict*. London: Sage.

Morse, T. (2013) 'Shooting the dead: Images of death, inclusion and exclusion in the Israeli press', in Aaron, M. (ed.), *Envisaging Death: Visual Culture and Dying*, pp. 140–156. Newcastle upon Tyne: Cambridge Scholars Publishing.

Morse, T. (2014) 'Covering the dead', *Journalism Studies*, 15(1): 98–113.

Morse, T. (2018) 'Mediatized war and the moralizing function of news about disruptive events', *Journalism*, 19(3): 384–401.

Mortensen, M. (2014) *Journalism and Eyewitness Images: Digital Media, Participation, and Conflict*. London: Routledge.

Moseley, R. (2017) *Reporting War: How Foreign Correspondents Risked Capture, Torture and Death to Cover World War II*. New Haven, CT: Yale University Press.

Motlagh, J. (2009) 'Did the Pentagon blacklist journalists in Afghanistan?', *Time*, 1 Sept.

Mueller, J. (1973) *Wars, President and Public Opinion*. New York: John Wiley & Sons.

Muller, B. and Measor, J. (2011) 'Theatres of war: Visual technologies and identities in the Iraq Wars', *Geopolitics*, 16(2): 389–409.

Murdock, G., Petts, J. and Horlick-Jones, T. (2003) 'After amplification: Rethinking the role of the media in risk communication', in Pidgeon, N., Kasperson, R. and Slovic, P. (eds), *The Social Amplification of Risk*, pp. 156–178. Cambridge: Cambridge University Press.

Murray, W. and Mansoor, P. R. (eds) (2012) *Hybrid Warfare: Fighting Complex Opponents from the Ancient World to the Present*. Cambridge: Cambridge University Press.

Murrell, C. (2010) 'Baghdad bureaux: An exploration of the interconnected world of fixers and correspondents at the BBC and CNN', *Media, War & Conflict*, 3(2): 125–137.

Murrell, C. (2014) *Foreign Correspondents and International Newsgathering: The Role of Fixers*. London: Routledge.

Mythen, G. (2010) 'Reframing risk? Citizen journalism and the transformation of news', *Journal of Risk Research*, 13(1): 45–58.

Mythen, G. and Walklate, S. (2006) 'Communicating the terrorist risk: Harnessing a culture of fear?', *Crime Media Culture*, 2(2): 123–142.

Nacos, B. (2016) *Mass-mediated Terrorism: Mainstream and Digital Media in Terrorism and Counter Terrorism*. Lanham, MD: Rowman and Littlefield.

National Public Radio (2016) 'Reporting on the war in Syria, despite the obstacles to being there', 2 June. https://www.npr.org/2016/06/02/480435504/reporting-on-the-war-in-syria-even-though-it-s-too-dangerous-to-go-there

STRATCOM COE (NATO Strategic Communications Centre of Excellence) (2014) *Analysis of Russia's Information Campaign against Ukraine*, Report No. 3. Riga, Latvia: STRATCOM COE.

Neilan, C. (2012) 'Women in war zones', *Broadcast*, 8 March. www.broadcastnow.co.uk/techfacils/production-feature/women-in-war-zones/5038972.article

Nelkin, D. and Brown, M. (1984) *Workers at Risk: Voices from the Workplace*. Chicago: Chicago University Press.

Neuman, J. (1995) *Lights, Camera, War: Is Media Technology Driving International Politics*. New York: St Martin's Press.

Newman, C., Simpson, R. and Handschuh, D. (2003) 'Trauma exposure and post-traumatic stress disorder among photojournalists', *Visual Communication Quarterly*, 10(1): 4–13.

Nguyen, A. and Lugo-Ocando, J. (2016) 'The state of data and statistics in journalism education: Issues and debates', *Journalism*, 17(1): 3–17.

Nicholas, S. (1996) *The Echo of War: Home Front Propaganda and the Wartime BBC, 1939–45*. London: Palgrave Macmillan.

Nicholson, M. (1992) *A Measure of Danger: Memoirs of a British War Correspondent*. London: Fontana.

Nicholson, M. (2011) 'Dispatches from the home front', *The Guardian*, 18 June.

Nicholson, M. (2012) *A State of War Exists: Reporters in the Line of Fire*. London:Biteback.

Noble, R. (1955) *Shoot First!*London: George Harrap & Co.

Nohrstedt, S. (2001) 'US dominance in Gulf War news? Propaganda relations between news discourses in US and European media', in Nohrstedt, S. A. and Ottosen, R. (eds), *Journalism and the New World Order*, Volume 1, pp. 175–215. Gothenburg: Nordicom.

Nohrstedt, S. and Ottosen, R. (2008) 'War journalism in the threat society: Peace journalism as a strategy for challenging a mediated culture of fear', *Conflict and Culture Online*, 7 (2): 1–17.

Nohrstedt, S. A. and Ottosen, R. (2014) *New Wars, New Media and New War Journalism: Professional and Legal Challenges in Conflict Reporting*. Gothenburg: Nordicom.

Nord, L. (2007) 'Investigative journalism in Sweden', *Journalism*, 8(5): 517–521.

Norton-Taylor, R. (2015) 'Secret and unaccountable: The double-edged sword of SAS mythology', *The Guardian*, 14 July.

Ojala, M., Panatti, M. and Kargas, J. (2016) 'Professional role enactment amid information warfare: War correspondents tweeting on the Ukraine conflict', *Journalism*, 19(3): 296–313.

O'Kane, M. (2005) 'Reporting on women during armed conflict: A war journalist's perspective', in Durham, H. and Gurd, T. (eds), *Listening to the Silences: Women and War*, pp. 89–93. Leiden, The Netherlands: Martinus Nijhoff Publishers.

Olds, I. (2009) *Fixer: The Taking of Ajmal Naqshbandi*, HBO.

Oliver, K. (2004) 'Witnessing and testimony', *Parallax*, 10(1): 78–87.

O'Loughlin, J., Witmer, F., Linke, A. and Thorwardson, N. (2010) 'Peering into the fog of war: The geography of the WikiLeaks Afghanistan war logs, 2004–2009', *Eurasian Geography and Economics*, 51(4): 472–495.

Olsen, G., Carstensen, N. and Hoyen, K. (2003) 'Humanitarian crises: Testing the "CNN Effect"', *Forced Migration Review*, 16: 39–41.

Olsson, C. and Malešević, S. (2016) 'War', in Outhwaite, W. and Turner, S. P. (eds), *The SAGE Handbook of Political Sociology: Volume 1*, pp. 715–733. Los Angeles: Sage.

O'Neill, B. (2012) 'Dangers of the "journalism of attachment"', *ABC*, 24 February. www. abc.net.au/news/2012-02-24/oneill-dangers-of-the-journalism-of-attachment/3850566

Orgeret, K. (2016a) 'Women in war: Challenges and possibilities for female journalists covering wars and conflicts', in Carlsson, U. (ed.), *Freedom of Expression and Media in Transition: Studies and Reflections in the Digital Age*, pp. 165–174. Gothenburg: Nordicom.

Orgeret, K. (2016b) 'Women making news: Conflict and post-conflict in the field', in Orgeret, K. and Tayeebwa, W. (eds), *Journalism in Conflict and Post Conflict: Worldwide Perspectives*, pp. 99–114. Oslo: Nordicom.

OSCE (2016) *New Challenges to Freedom of Expression: Countering Online Abuse of Female Journalists*. Vienna, Austria: Office of the Representative on Freedom of the Media Organization for Security and Co-operation in Europe.

Osinga, F. P. B. and Roorda, M. P. (2016) 'From Douhet to drones, air warfare, and the evolution of targeting', in Ducheine, P., Schmitt, M. and Osinga, F. (eds), *Targeting: The Challenges of Modern Warfare*, pp. 27–76. Berlin: Springer-Verlag.

Ottosen, R. (2007) 'Targeting the audience: Video games as war propaganda in entertainment and news'. Paper presented at The Philosophy of Computer Games conference, Reggio Emilio, Italy, 25–27 January.

Ottosen, R. (2010) 'The war in Afghanistan and peace journalism in practice', *Media War and Conflict*, 3(3): 61–78.

O'Tuathail, G. (1996) 'An anti-geopolitical eye: Maggie O'Kane in Bosnia, 1992–1993', *Journal of Gender, Place & Culture*, 3(2): 171–186.

Pakenham, T. (1979) *The Boer War*. London: Abacus.

Palmer, L. (2015) 'Outsourcing authority in the digital age: Television news networks and freelance war correspondents', *Critical Studies in Media Communication*, 32(4): 225–239.

Palmer, L. (2016) 'Being the bridge: News fixers' perspectives on cultural differences in reporting the "war on terror"', *Journalism*, 19(3): 314–332.

Palmer, L. (2018) *Becoming the Story: War Correspondents Since 9/11*. Urbana IL: University of Illinois Press.

Palmer, J. and Fontan, V. (2007) '"Our Ears and our eyes": Journalists and fixers in Iraq', *Journalism*, 8(1): 5–24.

Palmer, L. and Melki, J. (2018) 'Shape shifting in the conflict zone', *Journalism Studies*, 19(1): 126–142.

Patel, S. (2012) 'I went to Syria to learn how to be a journalist', *Vice*, 13 November. https://www.vice.com/en_uk/article/3b5yxy/i-went-to-syria-to-learn-how-to-be-a-journalist

Paterson, C. (2014) *War Reporters Under Threat*. London: Pluto Press.

Patrikarakos, D. (2017) *War in 140 Characters: How Social Media is Reshaping Conflict in the Twenty-first Century*. New York: Basic Books.

Patterson, T. (2013) *Informing the News: The Need for Knowledge-based Journalism*. New York: Random House.

Paul, C. and Kim, J. (2004) *Reporters on the Battlefield: The Embedded Press System in Historical Context*. Santa Monica, CA: Rand.

Peachey, P. (2001) 'Kate Adie: BBC employs women for their looks not skill', *Independent*, 23 October.

Pedelty, M. (1995) *War Stories: The Culture of Foreign Correspondence*. London: Routledge.

Pedelty, M. (1997) 'The marginal majority: Women war correspondents in the Salvadorian Press Corps Association (SPCA)', *Critical Studies in Mass Communication*, 14(1): 49–76.

Pedelty, M. (2002) 'Don your flak jackets', *Index on Censorship*, 31(1): 166–170.

Pendry, R. (2013) 'In Syria, freelancer demand amidst increasing restrictions: New outlets are happy to reap the rewards of dangerous reporting, so long as freelancers shoulder all responsibility', *Columbia Journalism Review*, 9 September. https://archives.cjr.org/behind_the_news/in_syria_a_freelance_demand_am.php

Pendry, R. (2014) 'The changing nature of the war reporter', *Centre for Journalism at the University of Kent*, 16 December. www.centreforjournalism.co.uk/content/changing-identity-war-reporter

Perlmutter, D. (1999) *Visions of War: Picturing Warfare from the Stone Age to the Cyber Age*. New York: St Martin's Press.

Peters, J. (2001) 'Witnessing', *Media Culture Society*, 23(6): 709–723.

Petley, J. (2004) '"Let the atrocious images haunt us"', in Miller, D. (ed.), *Tell Me Lies: Propaganda and Media Distortion in the Attack on Iraq*, pp. 164–175. London: Pluto Press.

Pfau, M., Haigh, M., Fifiick, A., Holl, D., Tedesco, A., Cope, J., Nunnally, D., Schiess, A., Preston, D., Roszkowski, P. and Martin, M. (2006) 'The effects of print news photographs of the casualties of war', *JMC Quarterly*, 83(1): 150–168.

Picard, R. G. (2014) 'Twilight or new dawn of journalism', *Journalism Studies*, 15(5): 500–510.

Picard, R. G. and Storm, H. (2016) *The Kidnapping of Journalists: Reporting from High-Risk Conflict Zones*. London: I. B. Tauris.

Pirmasari, D. A. (2016) 'Being a female journalist at the frontline: An autoethnography', in von der Lippe, B. and Ottosen, R. (eds), *Gendering War and Peace Reporting*, pp. 129–141. Gothenburg: Nordicom.

Poell, T. and van Dijck, J. (2015) 'Social media and activist communication', in Atton, C. (ed.), *The Routledge Companion to Alternative and Community Media*, pp. 527–537. London: Routledge.

Poggiolo, S. (1998) 'A strategy of rape in Bosnia', in Woodhull, M. and Snyder, R. (eds), *Defining Moments in Journalism*, pp. 93–98. New Brunswick, NJ: Transaction Publishers.

Pollard, N. (2009) 'Staying alive in the killing fields', *British Journalism Review*, 20(1): 27–32.

Pollard, R. (2012) 'Deadly risk for those who bear witness', *The Sydney Morning Herald*, 25 February.

Ponsford, D. (2014) 'Rusbridger on how no journalist's sources are safe, joining IPSO and why he would have kept the News of the World open', *Press Gazette*, 28 March. www.pressgazette.co.uk/rusbridger-how-no-journalists-sources-are-now-safe-joining-ipso-a nd-why-he-would-have-kept-news/

Powers, M. (2016) 'The new boots on the ground: NGOs in the changing landscape of international news', *Journalism*, 17(4): 401–416.

Prentoulis, V., Tumber, H. and Webster, F. (2005) 'Finding space: Women reporters at war', *Feminist Media Studies*, 5(3): 374–377.

Preston, P. (2008) *We Saw Spain Die: Foreign Correspondents in the Spanish Civil War*. London: Constable.

Prieto, J. (2007) 'Partisanship in balance: The New York Times coverage of the Spanish Civil War, 1936–1939', *Abraham Lincoln Brigade Archives*. www.alba-valb.org/resources/document-library/partisanship-in- balance- the-new-york-times-of-the-spanish- civil-wa r-1936-39

Quataert, J. (2014) 'International laws and the laws of war', in Daniel, U., Gatrell, P., Janz, O., Jones, H., Keene, J., Kramer, A. and Nasson, B. (eds), *1914–1918 Online: International Encyclopedia of the First World War: Introduction*. Berlin: Freie Universitat. https://encyclopedia.1914-1918-online.net/pdf/1914-1918-Online international_law_and_the_laws_of_war-2014-10-08.pdf

Radsch, C. (2012) *Unveiling the revolutionaries: Cyberactivism and the role of women in the Arab Uprisings*. Rice University James A. Baker III Institute for Public Policy Research Paper. https://ssrn.com/abstract=2252556

Ramsay, S. (2010) 'The case for the honest embed', in Keeble, R. and Mair, J. (eds), *Afghanistan, War and the Media: Deadlines and Frontlines*, pp. 23–32. Bury St Edmunds: Arima.

Rasmussen, M. (2006) *The Risk Society at War: Terror, Technology and Strategy in the Twenty-First Century*. Cambridge: Cambridge University Press.

Ray, V. (2003) *The Television News Handbook: An Insider's Guide to be a Great Broadcast Journalist*. London: Macmillan.

Rayner, G. and Spencer, R. (2012) 'Syria: *Sunday Times* journalist Marie Colvin killed in "targeted attack" by Syrian forces', *The Telegraph*, 22 February.

Read, D. (1992) *The Power of News: The History of Reuters*. Cambridge: Cambridge University Press.

Redden, G. (2003) 'Read the whole thing: Journalism, weblogs and the re-mediation of the War in Iraq', *Media International Australia*, 109(1): 153–165.

Reich, Z. and Boudana, S. (2014) 'The fickle forerunner: The rise of bylines and authorship in the French Press', *Journalism*, 15(4): 407–426.

Reid, C. (2004) 'Recalling life as an embedded reporter', *NBC News*, 15 March. www. nbcnews.com/id/4400708/ns/world_news-mideast_n_africa/t/recalling-life-embed ded-reporter/#.WavLAciGNPY

Ricchiardi, S. (1994) 'Women on war', *American Journalism Review*, March. http://ajrarchive. org/Article.asp?id=1513

Rid, T. (2007) *War and Media Operations: The US Military and the Press from Vietnam to Iraq*. Abingdon: Routledge.

Ridland, A. (2015) *Seizing the Digital High Ground: Military Operations and Politics in the Social Media Era*. Master's thesis, Joint Forces Staff College, Joint Advanced Warfighting School.

Risley, F. (2012) *Civil War Journalism*. Oxford: Prager.

Robbins, C. (1991) 'Sexism by colleagues', *Nieman Reports*, XLV(2), 38–39.

Roberts, A. (2010) 'Lives and statistics: Are 90% of war victims casualties', *Survival*, 52(3): 115–136.

Roberts, P. (2012) 'Syrian government using targeted Skype attacks, malware to spy on dissidents', *Threat Post*, 3 May. https://threatpost.com/report-syrian-government-using-ta rgeted-skype-attacks-malware-spy-dissidents-050312/76519/

Robertson, L. (2004) 'Images of war: This year the American news media have displayed pictures of burned bodies in Fallujah, flag-draped coffins coming home from Iraq and the abuse of Iraqi prisoners at Abu Ghraib. But were they too squeamish when it came to showing the carnage of war during the invasion last year?', *American Journalism Review*, 26 (5). http://ajrarchive.org/article.asp?id=3759

Robinson, N. and Schulzke, M. (2016) 'Visualising war? Towards a visual analysis of videogames and social media', *Perspectives on Politics*, 14(4): 995–1010.

Robinson, P. (2005) *The CNN Effect: The Myth of News, Foreign Policy and Intervention*. London: Routledge.

Robinson, P., Goddard, P., Parry, K. and Murray, C. (2010) *Pockets of Resistance: British News Media, War and Theory in the 2003 Invasion of Iraq*. Manchester: Manchester University Press.

Rodgers, J. (2012) *Reporting Conflict*. London: Palgrave Macmillan.

Roger, N. (2013) *Image Warfare in the War on Terror*. London: Palgrave Macmillan.

Rogers, P. (2006) *A War Too Far: Iraq, Iran and the New American Century*. London: Pluto Press.

Rogers, P. (2017) 'Remote war and public air', *Open Democracy*, 9 November. https:// www.opendemocracy.net/paul-rogers/remote-war-and-public-air

Rohde, D. and Mulvihill, K. (2010) *A Rope and a Prayer*. New York: Viking.

Royle, T. (1989) *War Report: The War Correspondent's View of Battle From the Crimea to the Falklands*. London: Grafton Books.

Reporters Without Borders (2017) 'Internet giants that tolerate or actively cooperate with censorship', 10 March. https://rsf.org/en/reports/internet-giants-tolerate-or-actively-cooperate-censorship

Ruigrok, N. (2008) 'Journalism of attachment and objectivity: Dutch journalists and the Bosnian War', *Media, War & Conflict*, 1(3): 293–313.

Rusch, T., Hofmarcher, P., Hatzinger, R. and Hornik, K. (2013) 'Model trees with topic model preprocessing: An approach for data journalism illustrated with the Wikileaks' Afghanistan war logs', *The Annals of Applied Statistics*, 7(2): 613–639.

Russell, A. (2011) *Networked: A Contemporary History of News in Transition*. Cambridge: Polity Press.

Russell, W. H. (1863) *My Diary North and South*, Volume 1. Boston: T.O.H.P. Burham.

Ryan, K. (2009) 'The performative journalist: Job satisfaction, temporary workers and American television news', *Journalism*, 10(5): 647–664.

Sa'adoun, M. (2017) 'Looking for a suicidal job? Try Iraqi War reporter', *Global Investigative Journalism Network*, 13 February. https://gijn.org/2017/02/13/looking-for-a-suicidal-job-try-iraqi-war-reporter/

Sacco, V. and Bossio, D. (2015) 'Using social media in the news reportage of war & conflict: Opportunities and challenges', *The Journal of Media Innovations*, 2(1): 59–76.

Sambrook, R. (2005) 'Citizen journalism and the BBC', *Nieman Reports*, 59(4): 13–16.

Sambrook, R. (2010) *Are Foreign Correspondents Redundant? The Changing Face of International News*. Oxford: Reuters Institute for the Study of Journalism.

Schechter, D. (2003) *Embedded: Weapons of Mass Deception*. New York: Prometheus Books.

Schneider, C. and Schneider, D. (2003) *Eyewitness History: World War II*. New York: Infobase Publishing.

Schudson, M. (1978) *Discovering the News: A Social History of American Newspapers*. New York: Basic Books.

Schudson, M. (2001) 'The objectivity norm in American journalism', *Journalism*, 2(2): 149–170.

Seaton, J. (2005) *Carnage and the Media: The Making and Breaking of News about Violence*. London: Allen Lane.

Sebba, A. (1994) *Battling for News: The Rise of the Woman Reporter*. London: Hodder & Stoughton.

Seib, P. (2002) *The Global Journalist: News and Conscience in a World of Conflict*. New York: Rowman and Littlefield.

Seib, P. (2004) *Beyond the Front Lines: How the News Media Cover a World Shaped by War*. London: Palgrave Macmillan.

Seo, S. (2016) 'Marginal majority at the postcolonial news agency', *Journalism Studies*, 17(1): 39–56.

Shachtman, N. (2008) 'Does embedding with the Taliban make you a traitor?', *Wired*, 30 October. https://www.wired.com/2008/10/does-embedding/

Shane, S. and Hubbard, B. (2014) 'ISIS displaying a deft command of varied media', *The New York Times*, 30 August.

Shaw, D. (1992) 'News often has to be seen before it is heard', *Los Angeles Times*, 26 October: A16.

Shaw, M. (2005) *The New Western Way of War*. Cambridge: Polity.

Shear, M. (2013) '"Obama calls for "moral courage" at Naval Academy Graduation', *The New York Times*, 25 May.

Sherwood, H. (2011) 'Egypt protests: Plea to keep women reporters out of Cairo withdrawn', *The Guardian*, 25 November.

Shoemaker, P. and Reese, S. (1991) *Mediating the Message: Theories of Influences on Mass Media Content*. White Plains, NY: Longman.

Sidorova, G. (2012) 'Safety: Do journalists need special treatment?', *BBC Blogs*, 18 October. www.bbc.co.uk/blogs/collegeofjournalism/authors/32232827-09f7-35e1-ba65-367913b985f9

Sigal, L. (1973) *Reporters and Officials: The Organization and Politics of Newsmaking*. Lexington, MA: D. C. Heath.

Silcock, B. W., Schwalbe, C. and Keith, S. (2008) '"Secret" casualties: Images of injury and death in the Iraq War across media platforms', *Journal of Mass Media Ethics*, 23(1): 36–50.

Silvestri, L. (2016) 'Mortars and memes: Participating in pop culture from a war zone', *Media, War & Conflict*, 9(1), 27–42.

Simpson (2017)

Singer, J. (2007) Contested Autonomy. *Journalism Studies*, 8:1, 79–95.

Sites, K. (2007) *In the Hot Zone: One Man, One Year, Twenty Wars*. New York: HarperCollins.

Skovsgaard, M. (2014) 'A tabloid mind? Professional values and organisational pressures as explanations of tabloid journalism', *Media, Culture & Society*, 36(2): 200–218.

Sloyan, P. (2003) 'What I saw was a bunch of filled-in trenches with people's arms and legs sticking out of them. For all I know, we could have killed thousands', *The Guardian*, 14 February.

Smith, A. (1977) 'The long road to objectivity and back again — the kinds of truth we get in journalism', in Boyce, G., Curran, J., and Wingate, P. (eds), *Newspaper History: Studies in the Evolution of the British Press*, pp. 153–171. London: Constable.

Smith, A. and Higgins, M. (2012) 'Introduction: Reporting war – history, professionalism and technology', *Journal of War & Culture Studies*, 5(2): 131–136.

Smith, V. (2010) 'The "brittle" compact between the military and the media', in Keeble, R. and Mair, J. (eds), *Afghanistan, War and the Media: Deadlines and Frontlines*, pp. 42–48. Bury St Edmunds, UK: Arima.

Snow, J. (2005) *Shooting History*. London: Harper Perennial.

Sobchack, V. (2004) *Carnal Thoughts: Embodiment and Moving Image Culture*. Berkeley, CA: University of California Press.

Sontag, S. (1979) *On Photography*. London: Penguin.

Sontag, S. (2001) 'War and photography', in Owen, N. (ed.), *Human Rights, Human Wrongs: The Oxford Amnesty Lectures, 2001*, pp. 251–273. Oxford: Oxford University Press.

Sontag, S. (2003) *Regarding the Pain of Others*. London: Penguin.

Sparrow, B. (1999) *Uncertain Guardians: The News Media as a Political Institution*. Baltimore, MD: Johns Hopkins University Press.

Spellman, R. (2005) 'Journalist or witness? Reporters and war crimes tribunals', *Gazette: The International Journal for Communication Studies*, 67(2): 123–139.

Spinner, J. (2015) '100 Meters: War Reporting and Objectivity', TEDx Talk, Columbia College Chicago, *YouTube*. https://www.youtube.com/watch?v=ctuS0HA4pbg

Standard Techniques (1987) *Diverse Reports*, Channel 4.

Stearn, R. (1992) 'War correspondents and colonial war, c. 1870–1900', in MacKenzie, J. (ed.), *Popular Imperialism and the Military, 1850–1950*, pp. 139–161. Manchester: Manchester University Press.

Steigrad, A. (2016) 'CNN war correspondent Clarissa Ward talks reporting in the Middle East as a woman', *WWD*, 7 April. http://wwd.com/business-news/media/cnn-war-cor respondent-clarissa-ward-reporting-middle-east-syria-10404622/

Steiner, J. (2016) 'Bodies at war: The dangers facing women war reporters', in von der Lippe, B. and Ottosen, R. (eds), *Gendering War and Peace Reporting: Some Insights – Some Missing Links*, pp. 33–48. Gothemburg: Nordicom.

Steiner, L. (2017) 'Gender and journalism', in *Oxford Research Encyclopaedia of Communication* [online]. Oxford: Oxford University Press. doi:10.1093/acrefore/9780190228613.013.91

Stewart, A. (2009). 'Evidence of Major General Andrew Stewart, Sir Hilary Synnott and Lieutenant General Sir Graeme Lamb. The Iraq Inquiry', 9 December. http://weba rchive.nationalarchives.gov.uk/20171123123448/http://www.iraqinquiry.org.uk/the-evi dence/witnesses/s/maj-gen-andrew-stewart/

Stratfor (2011) 'Social media as a tool for protest', 3 February. https://www.stratfor.com/ weekly/20110202-social-media-tool-protest

Styan, D. (1999) 'Misrepresenting Ethiopia and the Horn of Africa? Constraints and dilemmas of current reporting', in Allen, T. and Seaton, J. (eds), *The Media of*

Conflict: War Reporting and Representations of Ethnic Violence, pp. 287–304. London: Zed Books.

Sullivan, G. (2006) *Journalists at Risk: Reporting America's Wars*. Minneapolis, MN: Twentieth Century Books.

Sunday Show (2003) RTE Radio 1, 9 March.

Susman, T. (2012) 'Tina Susman', in Storm, H. and Williams, H. (eds), *No Woman's Land: On the Frontlines with Female Reporters*, pp. 25–27. London: International News Safety Institute.

Sweeney, M. (2006) *The Military and the Press*. Evanston, IL: Noerthwestern University Press.

Szoldra, P. (2017) 'Navy SEAL's book on the bin Laden killing shows the real reason photos of the body were never released', *Business Insider*, 10 April. http://uk.businessinsider.com/oneill-bin-laden-killing-2017-4

Tait, S. (2009) 'Visualising technologies and the ethics and aesthetics of screening death', *Science as Culture*, 18(3): 333–353.

Tait, S. (2011) 'Bearing witness, journalism and moral responsibility', *Media, Culture & Society*, 33(8): 1220–1235.

Tandoc, E.Jr, Hellmueller, L. and Vos, T. (2013) 'Mind the gap', *Journalism Practice*, 7(5): 539–554.

Taylor, J. (1998) *Body Horror: Photojournalism, Catastrophe and War*. Manchester: Manchester University Press.

Taylor, P. (2000) 'Introduction', *European Journal of Communication*, 15(3): 293–297.

Taylor, P. (2003) *Munitions of the Mind: A History of Propaganda from the Ancient World to the Present*, 3rd edition. Manchester andNew York: Manchester University Press.

Thayer, N. (2001) 'Freelancers' vital role in international reporting', *Nieman Reports*, 55(4): 28–30.

The Guardian (2015) '*The Guardian* view on Russian propaganda: The truth is out there', 2 March.

The New Arab (2015) 'On the frontline: Arab women in journalism', 8 March. https://www.alaraby.co.uk/english/blog/2015/3/8/on-the-front-line-arab-women-in-journalism

The New York Times (1862) 'Brady's photographs: Pictures of the dead at Antietam', 20 October.

The New York Times (2012) 'Secret "kill list" proves a test of Obama's principles and will', 29 May.

The Times (1854) 'The operations of the siege: The war in the Crimea', from our own special correspondent, Heights before Sebastopol, 19 October.

The World is Watching (1988) Director: Peter Raymont.

Thomas, T. (2016) *Thinking Like a Russian Officer: Basic Factors and Contemporary Thinking on the Nature of War*. Fort Leavenworth, KS: Foreign Military Studies Office.

Thomson, A. (2010) 'The rough guide to roughness', in Keeble, R. and Mair, J. (eds), *Afghanistan, War and the Media: Deadlines and Frontlines*, pp. 13–22. Bury St Edmunds, UK: Arima.

Thornton, R. (2015) 'The changing nature of modern warfare', *The RUSI Journal*, 160(4): 40–48.

Thurman, N., Cornia, N. and Kunert, J. (2016) *Journalists in the UK*. Oxford: Reuters Institute for the Study of Journalism.

Thussu, D. (2009) *News as Entertainment: The Rise of Global Infotainment*. London: Sage.

Thussu, D. and Freedman, D. (eds) (2003) *War and the Media*. London: Sage.

Tobin, J. (1997) *Ernie Pyle's War: America's Eyewitness to World War II*. New York: The Free Press.

Torregrosa, L. (2015) 'The rise of the female TV correspondent as global celebrity', *The New York Times*, 21 August.

Traub, J. (2014) 'The disappeared', *Foreign Policy*, 22 January. foreignpolicy.com/2014/01/22/the-disappeared/

TUC and Everyday Sexism Project (2016) *Still Just a Bit of Banter? Sexual harassment in the workplace in 2016.* https://www.tuc.org.uk/sites/default/files/SexualHarassmentreport2016.pdf

Tufekci, Z. (2011) 'Journalism, social media and packs and cascades: Lessons from an error', *Technosociology.* http://technosociology.org/?p=638 (accessed 23 June, 2016).

Tulloch, J. and Lupton, D. (2003) *Risk and Everyday Life.* London: Sage.

Tumber, H. (2006) 'The fear of living dangerously: Journalists who report on conflict', *International Relations*, 20(4): 439–451.

Tumber, H. (2008) 'Journalists, war crimes and international justice', *Media, War and Conflict*, 1(3): 261–269.

Tumber, H. and Prentoulis, V. (2003) 'Journalists under fire: Subcultures, Objectivity and Emotional Literacy', in Thussu, D. and Freedman, D. (eds), *War and the Media*, pp. 215–230. London: Sage.

Tumber, H. and Palmer, J. (2004) *Media at War: the Iraq Crisis.* London: Sage.

Tuotso, K. (2008) 'The "grunt truth" of embedded journalism: The new military/media relationship', *Stanford Journal of International Relations*, X(1): 21–31.

UNESCO (2015) *World Trends in Freedom of Expression and Media Development: Special Digital Focus.* Paris: UNESCO.

Urban, M. (2010) *Task Force Black: The Explosive True Story of the SAS and the Secret War in Iraq.* London: Little, Brown.

US Army Special Command (2014) *Counter-Unconventional Warfare: White Paper.* CreateSpace Independent Publishing Platform.

US Department of State (2012) '2012 International Women of Courage Award winners', 5 March. www.state.gov/s/gwi/programs/iwoc/2012/bio/index.htm

Usher, N. (2014) *Making News at The New York Times.* Ann Arbor, MI: University of Michigan Press.

Vaina, D. (2006) 'The vanishing embedded reporter in Iraq', *Pew Research Center*, 26 October. www.journalism.org/2006/10/26/the-vanishing-embedded-reporter-in-iraq/

Van Atta, D. (1998) 'Carbombs and cameras: The need for responsible media coverage', *Harvard International Review*, 20(4): 66–70.

Vandervoordt, R. (2016) 'Covering the Syrian conflict: How Middle East reporters deal with challenging situations', *Media, War & Conflict*, 9(3): 309–324.

Vandiver, J. (2014) 'SACEUR: Allies must prepare for "hybrid war"', *Stars and Stripes*, 4 September. www.stripes.com/news/saceuralliesmust-

Van Puyvelde, D. (2015) 'Hybrid war – does it even exist', *NATO Review Magazine.* https://www.nato.int/docu/review/2015/also-in-2015/hybrid-modern-future-warfare-russia-ukraine/EN/index.htm

Variety (1991) 'NBC's unaired Iraq tapes not a black and white case', 3 March. https://variety.com/1991/tv/features/nbc-s-unaired-iraq-tapes-not-a-black-amp-white-case-99126155/

Vasterman, P. (2005) 'Media-hype: Self-reinforcing news waves, journalistic standards and the construction of social problems', *European Journal of Communication*, 20(4): 508–530.

Vasterman, P., Yzermans, C. and Dirkzwager, A. (2005) 'The role of the media and media hypes in the aftermath of disasters', *Epidemiologic Reviews*, 27(1): 107–114.

Virilio, P. (1989) *War and Cinema. The Logistics of Perception*, trans. Camiller, P.London and New York: Verso.

Virilio, P. (1997) 'Cybernetics and society', in *Any*, pp. 1–13. New York: Architecture.

Von Oppen, K. (2009) 'Reporting from Bosnia: Reconceptualising the notion of a "journalism of attachment"', *Journal of Contemporary European Studies*, 17(1): 21–33.

Vulliamy, E. (1999) '"Neutrality" and the absence of reckoning: A journalist's account', *Journal of International Affairs*, 52(2): 603–620.

Waisbord, S. (2011) 'Journalism, risk and patriotism', in Zelizer, B. and Allan, S. (eds), *Journalism After September 11*, 2nd edition, pp. 273–291. London: Routledge.

Wardle, C. (2017) 'Fake news. It's complicated', *First Draft*, 16 February. https://medium.com/1st-draft/fake-news-its-complicated-d0f773766c79

Watson, A. (2017) 'The US continues to 'Trump' the UK on Special Forces transparency', *Small Wars Journal*, 17 February. http://smallwarsjournal.com/jrnl/art/the-us-continues-to-%E2%80%9Ctrump%E2%80%9D-the-uk-on-special-forces-transparency

Weaver, D., Beam, R., Brownlee, B., Voakes, P. and Wilhoit, C. (2007) *The American Journalist in the 21st Century: US News People at the Dawn of a New Millennium*. London: Lawrence Erlbaum Associates.

Webb, C. (2003) 'Blogging the war: A guide', *The Washington Post*, 28 March.

Webb, S. (2005) 'An American journalist in the role of partisan – Dickey Chapelle's coverage of the Algerian War', *American Journalism*, 22(2): 111–134.

Weinberger, D. (2009) 'Transparency: The new objectivity', *KM World*, 28 August. www.kmwoprld.com/Articles/Column/David-Weinberger/Transparency-the-new-objectivity-55785.aspx

Weiner, J. (2011) *The Americanization of the British Press 1830s–1914: Speed in the Age of Transatlantic Journalism*. London: Palgrave Macmillan.

Welch, D. (2007) 'Introduction: "Wining hearts and minds": The changing context of reportage and propaganda, 1900–2003', in Connelly, M. and Welch, D. (eds), *War and the Media: Reportage and Propaganda*, pp. ix–xx. London: I. B. Tauris.

Wessels, J. (2016) 'YouTube and evidencing war crimes; The role of digital video for transitional justice in Syria', *Tidskriftet POLITIK*, 19(4): 30–52.

Wicker, T. (1979) *On Press*. New York: Viking.

Wiesslitz, C. and Ashuri, T. (2011) '"Moral journalists": The emergence of new intermediaries of news in an age of digital media', *Journalism*, 12(8): 1035–1051.

Wilesmith, G. (2011) *Reporting Afghanistan and Iraq: Media, Military and Governments and How They Influence Each Other*. Oxford: Reuters Institute for the Study of Journalism.

Wilkinson-Latham, R. J. (1979) *From Our Special Correspondent: Victorian War Correspondents and their Campaigns*. London: Hodder & Stoughton.

Williams, K. (1992) 'Something more important than truth: Ethical issues in war reporting', in Belsay, A. and Chadwick, R. (eds), *Ethical Issues in Journalism and the Media*, pp. 154–170. London: Routledge.

Wilson, B. (2016) 'The corporate creation of the photojournalist: *Life* magazine and Margaret Bourke-White in World War II', *Journal of War and Culture Studies*, 9(2): 133–150.

Wolfe, B. (1965) *Strange Communists I have Known*. New York: Stein and Day.

Wolfe, L. (2011) *The Silencing Crime: Sexual Violence and Journalists*. New York: Committee to Protect Journalists.

Wolff, M. (2003) 'You know less than when you arrived', *The Guardian*, 31 March.

Wood, T. (2002) *War Torn: Stories of War from the Women Reporters Who Covered Vietnam*. New York: Random House.

Wright, K. (2015) '"These grey areas": How and why freelance work blurs INGOs and news organizations', *Journalism Studies*, 17(8): 1–21.

Wright, K. (2016) 'Moral economies: Interrogating the interactions of NGOs, journalists and freelancers', *International Journal of Communication*, 10: 1510–1529.

Wyatt, C. (2012) 'Caroline Wyatt', in Storm, H. and Peters, H. (eds), *No Woman's Land: On the Frontlines with Female Reporters*. London: International News Safety Institute.

Wyatt, C. (2013) 'Embedded in Iraq: "A tool in the military tool box, willingly or not"', *BBC Blogs*, 19 March. www.bbc.co.uk/blogs/collegeofjournalism/entries/6d495b61-c8f3-302f-857c-8e95d6838327

Yarchi, M. (2014) '"Badtime" stories: The frames of terror promoted by political actors', *Democracy and Security*, 10(1): 22–51.

Zelizer, B. (2000) *Remembering to Forget: Holocaust Memory through the Camera's Eye*. Chicago: University of Chicago Press.

Zelizer, B. (2004) 'When war is reduced to a photograph', in Allen, S. and Zelizer, B. (eds), *Reporting War: Journalism in Wartime*, pp. 115–135. London: Routledge.

Zelizer, B. (2005) 'Death in wartime: Photographs and the "other war" in Afghanistan', *Harvard International Journal of Press/Politics*, 10(3): 26–55.

Zelizer, B. (2007) 'On "having been there": Eyewitnessing as a journalistic key word', *Critical Studies in Media Communication*, 24(5): 408–428.

Zelizer, B. (2010) *About to Die: How News Images Move the Public*. Oxford: Oxford University Press.

Zelizer, B. and Allan, S. (2002) 'Introduction: When trauma shapes the news', in Zelizer, B. and Allan, S. (eds), *Journalism after September 11*, pp. 1–24. London: Routledge.

Zimmermann, P. (2000) *States of Emergency: Documentaries, Wars, Democracies*. Minneapolis, MN: University of Minnesota Press.

Zinn, J. O. (2004) *Literature Review: Sociology and Risk*. ESRC Social Contexts and Responses to Risk Network (SCARR), Working Paper 2004/1. Canterbury: SCARR.

INDEX